Coming Out, **Coming In**

Coming Out, **Coming In**

Nurturing the Well-Being and
Inclusion of Gay Youth in Mainstream Society

Linda Goldman

Foreword by Jody M. Huckaby

Routledge
Taylor & Francis Group
New York   London

Names and incidents have been modified in anecdotes appearing throughout the book to maintain privacy. People in the photographs are not related to the material on the page they appear unless specified by the individual.

Although every effort has been made to ensure that all owners of copyright material have been acknowledged in this publication, we would be glad to acknowledge in subsequent reprints or editions any omissions brought to our attention.

Routledge
Taylor & Francis Group
270 Madison Avenue
New York, NY 10016

Routledge
Taylor & Francis Group
2 Park Square
Milton Park, Abingdon
Oxon OX14 4RN

© 2008 by Taylor & Francis Group, LLC
Routledge is an imprint of Taylor & Francis Group, an Informa business

Printed in the United States of America on acid-free paper
10 9 8 7 6 5 4 3 2 1

International Standard Book Number-13: 978-0-415-95824-0 (Softcover)

Library of Congress Cataloging-in-Publication Data

Goldman, Linda, 1946-
    Coming out, coming in : nurturing the well-being and inclusion of gay youth in mainstream society
/ By Linda Goldman.
        p. cm.
    ISBN 978-0-415-95824-0 (softcover)
    1. Gay youth. 2. Gay teenagers. 3. Sexual minorities. 4. Coming out (Sexual orientation) 5.
Homophobia. 6. Gay youth--Services for. 7. Gay youth--Services for--United States. I. Title.

HQ76.27.Y68G65 2007
306.76'60835--dc22   2007018414

Visit the Taylor & Francis Web site at
http://www.taylorandfrancis.com

and the Routledge Web site at
http://www.routledge.com

We hold these truths to be self-evident,

that all men are created equal,

that they are endowed by their Creator

with certain unalienable Rights,

that among these are

Life, Liberty, and the pursuit of Happiness.

The Declaration of Independence, July 4, 1776

❧ Contents

PART I
Understanding Gay Youth: Society's Mirror

CHAPTER 1

CHAPTER 2

CHAPTER 3

PART II

Interventions With LGBT Young People:
Supporting a Healthy Outlook

C H A P T E R   4

Counseling Youth on LGBT Issues: Toward Self-Acceptance. 89

CHAPTER 5

CHAPTER 6

PART III
Possibilities for LGBT Participation in Daily Life: Evolving Relationships and Communities

C H A P T E R 7

CHAPTER 8

CHAPTER 9

CHAPTER 10

PART IV
Creating Equality in Society: Resources and Supports

CHAPTER 11

CHAPTER 12

∽ Foreword

For my family in small-town, conservative southwestern Louisiana, finding support and information as four of eight siblings came out as gay was an enormous challenge. Unlike in big cities, resources were scarce and my parents and straight siblings, nieces and nephews faced many obstacles. Getting accurate and accessible information wasn't easy—until my mother came across a Dear Abby column that referred a parent to PFLAG—Parents, Families and Friends of Lesbians and Gays.

PFLAG was a source for support, education, and advocacy for my parents and millions of others like them. More than a decade later, I find myself at the helm of PFLAG, which now has chapters in every state in the United States and more than 200,000 members and supporters. Much progress has been made thanks to the efforts of these people, but there is still a tremendously long way to go in reaching true equality for gay, lesbian, bisexual, and transgender people.

That is why this book is critically important. We continue to encounter misinformation about the lives of GLBT youth that negatively influences the way they are perceived, treated, and cared for.

The fact is that all GLBT youth encounter many steep challenges in their lives. From the rejection of friends and family, to being deemed unwelcome by their faith community, to the efforts of so-called medical figures to "change" them, to bullying and harassment at school, to political leaders who minimize their very existence to a mere campaign issue, the risk for harm is enormous. It also takes a steep toll on their loved ones and families.

In *Coming Out, Coming In,* Linda Goldman provides us with a comprehensive primer for psychologists, clinicians, educators, and families to help understand these forces in concrete, meaningful ways, and to take action. Her writing takes the issues from being merely statistics to being about real youth through their words and images. Most importantly, Linda calls on us to change the way we see these youth and offer real support.

As I read this book, I kept trying to imagine how the lives of my siblings and my parents might have been better if the book had been in the hands of teachers, school administrators, youth counselors, and others in our small town 20-plus years ago. And I think about all those young people who have suffered as a result of confusion, misunderstanding, and a complete lack of information about these issues. Today, I hope that this book will help us dispel myths, combat misinformation, and teach us how to provide the care, respect, and unconditional love that all youth deserve, regardless of differences.

May *Coming Out, Coming In* be the first step in helping you do this and in helping us all continue to keep moving equality forward. Many lives depend on it.

Jody M. Huckaby
Executive Director
PFLAG National (Parents, Families and Friends of Lesbians and Gays)

⋙ Preface

There is a light within every soul. It only needs the clouds that overshadow it to be broken for it to beam forth.

Hazrat Inayat Khan, (Bowl of Saki)

As a teacher, school counselor, private therapist, educator, and parent of a gay young person, my perspective of working with today's youth is a broad one. A deep understanding of lesbian, gay, bisexual, and transgender (LGBT) students and clients and their friends and family members has been enriched by the blending of professional and personal experience.

Throughout my career, I have strived to open new vistas of understanding for the grieving and traumatized child, adolescent, and young adult. I have presented many seminars throughout the United States and other countries, and this teaching experience has included serving as an adjunct professor at Johns Hopkins University Graduate School and the University Of Maryland's School of Social Work. I have authored many books for children and adults as well as a great many articles on children's grief, trauma, resilience, and working with LGBT youth. As an educator in the public school system for 18 years, as both a teacher and school counselor, I explored the school environment in terms of safety and civil liberties.

Participation on the PBS show *Keeping Kids Healthy: Children and Grief* and serving on the board of ADEC (The Association for Death Education and Counseling), the Advisory Board of TAPS (The Tragedy Assistance Program for [Military] Survivors), SPEAK (Suicide Prevention Education Awareness for Kids) and RAINBOWS for Our Children broadened my work for the public. This volunteerism within nonprofit agencies has enabled me to explore the concerns of youth within the community. I have had a private grief therapy practice since the mid-1980s, which has created the opportunity to work with LGBT and heterosexual young people in a clinical setting.

Teaching and counseling on grief and loss issues grounded my conceptualization of the many losses faced by gay and lesbian youth in today's society. All too often, these losses are based on misinformation and bigotry, which can result in violence, bullying, and other forms of victimization. Facing challenges as a mother and friend of many LGBT youth and witnessing those challenges with these teens has emphasized the need to enlarge the vision of character education and fairness at home, in the school, and throughout the community.

My desire to create this book was not simply the result of having some expertise in a particular field, but was driven by the hope of holding the space to stimulate a nonjudgmental forum for dialogue and heightened awareness on this very delicate, yet sometimes volatile, topic. Personally and professionally experiencing the suffering that girls and boys endure from the damaging projections of outdated thinking and cultural indoctrination became a motivation for creating change. Presenting updated and relevant information and an expansive vision of the potential of these children and youth became of paramount concern to me.

Issues and language centering on homosexuality seem to shift at lightning speed, with modifications, words, and outlooks being deemed acceptable or unacceptable as fast as they can be written and shared. Therefore, by the time the reader absorbs this material, new language may have evolved that did not exist at the time this book was written, or the meaning and use of existing terms may have changed. Although defining terminology for the purpose of clear discussion is crucial, the primary goal and challenge has been to focus on the broader concepts of *equality, respect, harmony, truth, and acceptance without judgment* to help pave the way for an emerging consciousness. *Coming Out, Coming In* presents a heartfelt and sincere attempt to paint a picture of the world and journey of LGBT young people in this new millennium.

The adage "it takes a village to raise a child" has never been more apparent than in our work with anchoring the positive trends regarding gay and lesbian youth. Sequential chapters bridging together young people, friends, parents, educators, health professionals, clergy, politicians, and community resources are presented to form the basic structure of *Coming Out, Coming In*.

This book is divided into four parts. The first is an exploration of understanding LGBT youth in present society. It begins with chapter 1, *The World of Gay Youth: From Exclusion to Inclusion,* and sets the stage for viewing LGBT youth in today's world. This chapter provides a background into the exclusiveness, marginalization and alienation these young people face. It then creates a foundation for objective language on LGBT issues to allow open discussion and aid in creating inclusion. Chapter 2, *Dispelling Old Myths: Creating New Insights,* states myths about homosexuality, and sets the framework to eradicate outdated bias by exploring current trends that examine new perspectives emerging in the LGBT world. Chapter 3, *Coming Out: Finding Freedom to Be,* examines the process of *coming out* and shares the voices and journeys of LGBT youth with helpful information to facilitate their coming out and being out.

Part II includes interventions with LGBT young people. Chapter 4, *Counseling Youth on LGBT Issues: Toward Self-Acceptance,* shares a comprehensive view of counseling LGBT teens and young adults including goals and interventions useful for effective therapeutic work. Chapter 5, *Speak Up and Share: Self-Expression and the Creative Arts,* demonstrates the effectiveness of the arts for self-expression by relaying thoughts and feelings, providing examples of poems, drawings, journaling, and so on that allow the reader to enter the world of the LGBT adolescent and young adult. Chapter 6, *The School Environment: Creating an Oasis of Safety,* takes a broad look at our schools and the degree of safety present in terms of persecution and stereotyping for the LGBT student. It provides positive interventions for these students, resulting in greater awareness and tolerance for the entire student body. This chapter includes present sexual harassment law on this subject and useful techniques.

The third part of the book presents possibilities for LGBT participation in daily life. Chapter 7, *Parenting LGBT Children: A Foundation for Love and Support,* reveals the nature of parental reaction to a child disclosing he or she is gay and practical ways parents can provide love and acceptance. Chapter 8, *"Coming In": LGBT Family Life,* explores life issues facing LGBT youth by including topics such as LGBT unions, marriage equality, places to live, raising a family, legalities, and issues of children of LGBT parents. Chapter 9, *Community Counts: A Place for Friends and Family,* presents an overview of community agencies supportive to the needs of the LGBT community. PFLAG (Parents, Families, and Friends of Lesbians and Gays) is used as a prototype showing the good work an organization can accomplish in many arenas. Other organizations include GLSEN (Gay, Lesbian & Straight Education Network), COLAGE (Children of Lesbians and Gays Everywhere), Family Pride Coalition, and the Human Rights Campaign. Chapter 10, *Conclusion: A Last Look at a New Beginning,* concludes with the goal of *Coming Out, Coming In* as the emergence of a new paradigm of inclusion and nurturing for LGBT youth.

Part IV includes resources and supports. Chapter 11, *Resources on LGBT Issues for Youth and Adults,* provides a list of organizations helpful to the LGBT community, and chapter 12, *Lesbian, Gay, Bisexual, and Transgender Organizations: Support for All,* includes an extensive annotated bibliography for adults and children covering major topics on LGBT issues.

Finally, I would like to add a comment about the use of photographs in this book. Although each image may or may not be specifically related to the corresponding issues discussed, their inclusion is designed to stimulate the heart as well as the intellect. It is my hope that the photos, artwork, and illustrations will help the reader stay mindful that *Coming Out: Coming In* is not only about a social subject but about real people.

Our charge is to become advocates as a cohesive community moving forward with a new energy and a strong conviction to instill useful paradigms and needed social actions. Teachers, principals, mental and physical health providers, religious and political leaders, media and entertainment professionals, and parents and children must all join together to aid the LGBT community. *Safety* for LGBT youth is paramount in the home, school, and community. Each caring adult must do their part to *eliminate bullying and harassment* of these students and create safe places to be. Taking a stand *against prejudice and stereotyping* by being informed on the facts and issues concerning LGBT youth is one of the many essential steps toward acceptance.

We can join together to eliminate false structures producing conflict and pain, help advance inclusion and nurturance for all, and recognize *"the light within every soul,"* whether they be straight, gay, lesbian, bisexual or transgender youth, when prejudice and rejection of spirit have been extinguished.

Linda Goldman

⨂ Acknowledgments

To Michael and Jonathan for their total love, support, and patience.

To Carol Conner for her inspiration, kindness, and beauty.

To Kyna Shilling for her extraordinary photography, including the cover photograph.

To Marge Dimond, Ursula Ferro, Joan Etherton Cochran, Charles Haynes, Dot Cooper, Joan Collings, Ron Wilder, and Andrew Merling for their generous feedback.

To Dana Bliss for encouraging this project. To Patricia Connolly for her meticulous editing, and to Robert Sims, the book's production project editor, for his thorough work.

To Jean Marie Navetta (PFLAG), Elizabeth Gill (The City at Peace), Meredith Fenton (COLAGE), and Jennifer Chrisler at FAMILY PRIDE for their value to the community.

To Daniel Chavkin and David Sternfeld for sharing their photographs.

To Ron and Mac, Doug and James, and Andrew and Douglas for their experiential contributions.

To Marguerite Kelly for her mentorship.

To all of the young people and their families and friends who volunteered their photos and stories to support all LGBT youth.

❦ Introduction

Here is a riddle that has been very popular during the past few decades.

> A boy was in a terrible car accident. His dad was driving and immediately killed. The boy was rushed to the hospital and wheeled into the emergency room. The doctor took a first look at the victim and exclaimed, "This can't be true. This is my son!"

As one ponders the riddle, the question can be puzzling. Many automatically assume the doctor was male, until one eventually discovers that the emergency room physician may be female, the boy's mom. Others may assume the doctor is a part of a two-dad family. This innocent riddle underscores a dramatic point. In today's world, gender identity, sexual orientation, and male/female role stereotyping exists on a broad continuum. Past and automatic assumptions of present prescribed norms are gradually being stretched to encompass a wider range of possible characteristics seen as male and female. These new roles are beginning to be creatively infused *into* society, not *outside* of it.

Compulsory Heterosexuality

Our culture has begun to assimilate the idea of a vast majority of human beings living within a wide continuum and interpretation of gender identity, sexual orientation, and culturally dictated male/female norms, in the gay, lesbian, bisexual, and transgender worlds and heterosexual worlds. Society can no longer continue to maintain the burden of *compulsory heterosexuality* in our homes, schools, communities, or media.

Mandatory false structuring and prejudicial stereotyping of our LGBT (lesbian, gay, bisexual, transgender) children by family, friends, and society at large can create their internalization of homophobia. Youth may feel dehumanized through hurtful projections on them and their world. Self-esteem and healthy identity plummet as they realize the realities of living as displaced teens. All too often they are forced outside the borders of the "acceptable mainstream."

Mark was 17 when he came out to his parents. He told them he was gay. His dad shoved him, fled the room, and refused to speak to him again. Five years later, there had been no dialogue between father and son.

Mark lived alone; he never finished high school, and he survived by working at occasional odd jobs.

Alienation from his father created a life of isolation and estrangement Mark had never imagined.

Research indicates that homosexuality is not a psychological disorder. But anxiety, depression, suicide ideation, and death by suicide can be by-products of

Photograph by Kyna Shilling

consistently being targeted and unconscionably slurred in a hostile environment. Current information *emphasizes* that core adjustment issues for LGBT youth stem from dealing with society's stereotyping and not the individual's attributes as the following quote explains. "Findings are consistent with the proposition that adjustment problems for gay [LGBT] youth emerge from the interpersonal stressors associated with coping with sexual orientation in society, rather than being a characteristic of gay, lesbian, and bisexual identities per se" (Floyd, Stein, Harter, Allison, and Nye, 1999, p. 738).

 # "Coming Out, Coming In"

When a young person first *comes out* as LGBT, his or her experience can be traumatic. Distress may result not only for the youth involved, but for their family, friends, educators, and other members of society as well. Once *out* there is a strong tendency for these young people to feel alienated and marginalized. One of the greatest dangers is that LGBT kids will become isolated and experience themselves as separate from (mainstream) society.

"Coming in" suggests a healthy process of reentry and reintegration into mainstream life. Sexual orientation and gender identity issues can be normalized as the result of a paradigm shift within both the LGBT population and straight "mainstream" population. This new paradigm results in a shift from apparently separate positions. Seemingly opposing groups can begin to merge as unified parts of a natural continuum of sexual norms.

Creating a "Home" For LGBT Youth

We must create a home for our LGBT youth. This home is an *inner and outer* dwelling where life is understood and respected in a safe place within mainstream culture. *Coming Out, Coming In: Nurturing the Well-Being and Inclusion of Gay Youth in Mainstream Society* lays the foundation for such a home, brick by brick, chapter by chapter. Creating unbiased constructs on a continuum of sexual identification brings freedom to the "straight" as well as the gay and lesbian world. Shedding the layers of misinformation and destructive bigotry can free the stay-at-home dad, the corporate female executive, the male nurse, the female doctor, the gay male airplane pilot, and the lesbian schoolteacher. Each has his or her role; each deserves to live without the intolerable burden of being the focus of negative judgments.

"Queering the Mainstream"

"Queering the mainstream" is an idea that pinpoints the essence of the gay movement. Rather than forcing a majority to "accept" the LGBT community, this popular inner-circle concept creates such vivid reeducation and imagery that the mainstream no longer recognizes *any* exclusive differences, according to one gay young man. He feared society might find this term too difficult to hold and take offense by its presence and its wording. I disagree.

The goal of this book is to encourage us all to join together in "queering the mainstream" by including lesbian, gay, bisexual, and transgender young people within a widening range of contemporary ways of being. We must anchor a new template of understanding that broadens the spectrum of lives on planet Earth to be all-encompassing. This is the hope for the future generation of gay, as well as straight, youth.

PART I

Understanding Gay Youth:
Society's Mirror

CHAPTER I
The World of Gay Youth: From Exclusion to Inclusion

Photograph by Kyna Shilling

FINDING MEANING • NATURAL STATE
SEXUAL PREJUDICE • HOMOPHOBIA
LANGUAGE FOR DIALOGUE • GENDER BINARY
QUEER • SEXUAL ORIENTATION
GENDER IDENTITY
TRANSGENDER IDENTITY • VOCABULARY
THE SEXUAL IDENTITY CONTINUUM
QUEERING THE MAINSTREAM • INCLUSION

"The time has come for us to think on a deeper level, on a human level and appreciate and respect our sameness as human beings."

The Dalai Lama

A Picture of LGBT Young People

Statistics provide an insight into the large number of lesbian, gay male, bisexual, and transgender (LGBT) youth, but these numbers cannot dictate human rights or eradicate prejudice. Too many of our LGBT young people are reporting an isolated experience in terms of their sexuality. They are bombarded with gay male and lesbian slurs, hatred and fear, stereotypical degradations throughout the media, and a feeling of inability to express affection for one another or openly display their sexuality in public.

LGBT adolescents and young adults face the possibilities of being excluded by friends and family, ostracized by society, and ridiculed for being unacceptable merely by *acknowledging* their sexual orientation or gender identity. These limitations to their lives and their "freedom to be" can manifest in secrecy, depression, isolation, suicide ideation (contemplating suicide), and actual suicide.

Some statistics indicate a significantly higher rate of both attempts and thoughts of suicide. Patrick Healy (2001) has studied teen suicide. He concluded that LGBT teens are "five times more likely to attempt suicide than their heterosexual peers." These statistics may vary but do emphasize the need for equal treatment for all.

Gender identity and sexual orientation have risen to the forefront of public scrutiny and opinion. Much debate on the "right and wrong" outlook is observable in social, emotional, educational, political, and spiritual arenas. Young people are searching for new meaning in reframing sexual issues to expand existing concepts. Often society has restrained, hidden, and disconnected from a gay and lesbian subculture viewed by some as a very "shadowy" side of life.

Photograph by Kyna Shilling

In the earlier years of the United States, many people chose not to marry, to live as bachelor men or spinster women as they were then known, or they lived within extended families in a natural way without creating partnerships or having an independent family life. Expressing sexual orientation or gender identity openly did not appear to be an accepted part of that world and there may have been a comfort in its nondisclosure, or a lack of awareness or choice about disclosure. In the 18th and 19th centuries, most Americans lived in rural communities. In today's world, all of our young people are far more visible. Many search to express themselves by addressing and dispelling gender barriers in order to enlarge their canvas of life to include LGBT adolescents in viable relationships of intimacy and meaning.

Our gay youth seek what every human being seeks: a chance to live, love, and grow within a relationship that nurtures and supports their true essence. All those who care about these teens must commit to anchoring this fact into present culture to create freedom for homosexual adolescents to live open, full, and productive lives.

We must look at the difficulties young LGBT people can encounter, once they have presented their gender issues to public view, and the stress and conflict created by exposure to ridicule. Many still face challenges after disclosing their sexual orientation and gender identity. Prejudice, verbal insults, and physical hate crimes, depression, and suicide ideation are a few forms that manifest from judgments about homosexuality.

We need to create a common language that allows the inclusion of our LGBT youth into a broader perspective of mainstream life. By extending the barriers of simplistic male and female stereotyping, we can help extinguish obsolete societal values.

All young people can live how they are rather than how others think they should be.

How Many Young People Are Exclusively LGBT?

In a 2002 Gallup survey, the average American indicated 21% of men are gay and 22% of women are lesbians. The popular press assumes a homosexuality rate of 10%.

Exploring Psychology
Myers, 2005, (p. 396)

As many as 7.2 million Americans under age 20 are lesbian or gay.

(PFLAG Upstate SC, 1994,
http://www.pflagupstatesc.org/statistics.htm)

Although these statistics show a sample of what has been found, the number varies widely from survey to survey. There seems to be a lot of information that is unknown at the present time. Regardless of the numbers—whether 10% of the population or 1% of the population—discrimination and mistreatment are never justified.

Homosexuality Is a Natural State: Not a Disorder

Homosexuality itself is not considered to be a psychological disorder, although depression and suicide ideation may be by-products. Research supports it as a natural state. Many gay/lesbian and straight adolescents accept their sexual orientation by electing celibacy, engaging in promiscuous sex, or becoming a part of a committed love relationship. The American Psychiatric Association (APA) dropped homosexuality from its list of mental illnesses in 1973. The World Health Organization (WHO) followed the same protocol in 1993, and Japanese and Chinese psychiatric associations followed suit in 1995 and 2001, respectively. According to the APA, "Homosexuality is not an illness. It does not require treatment and is not changeable" (PFLAG, Answers to Youths' Questions, 2005a).

Sexual Prejudice: Exposure to Bigotry, Prejudice, and Antigay Slurs

- Two million U.S. teenagers were reported in 2001 as having serious problems in school because they were taunted with antigay slurs. (Stepp, 2001, A1)

- 84.3% of Lesbian, Gay, Bisexual, Transgender, and Queer (LGBTQ) students reported hearing homophobic remarks using words such as *faggot* or *dyke*.

- 90% reported frequently hearing the expression "that's so gay" or "you're so gay."

- 83.2% of LGBTQ student's report being verbally harassed (name-calling, threats, etc.) because of both their sexual orientation and their race/ethnicity.

- 68.6% of LGBTQ students reported feeling unsafe in school because of their sexual orientation.

- 80.6% of students reported there were no positive portrayals of LGBTQ people, history, or events in classes.

(GLSEN 2003, p. 21)

In a university study of gay male and lesbian students in 1992, it was found that 99% surveyed had overheard antigay remarks on campus (Burn, 2000). This antigay harassment might seem innocuous in comparison to direct verbal or physical attacks, but it is quite detrimental to gay rights and can prevent an LGBTQ young person from developing a self-accepting gender identity and sexual orientation.

Telling 12-year-old Tommy "you're so gay" may not appear harmful to his psyche. Yet, it is an instant feedback system for acceptance of gay slurs.

Mental health professionals are now realizing the implications of homophobia because it jeopardizes the physical and psychological welfare of an individual and violates the human rights and civil liberties of this minority. These mostly psychological attacks instill in LGBT people the notion that the dominant heterosexual community sees them as abnormal and undesirable.

The Stigma of Antigay Slurs

Our society teaches our children to take a condescending view of homosexuality from a very early age. The result of gay and lesbian harassment, through slurs, bashing, and ostracizing, has severe consequences for the mental and physical health of LGBT adolescents. Sixteen-year-old Ryan was continually persecuted.

"You homo! You queer!
Go back and play with the girls."

These were familiar chants to Ryan.

It is important to note that these slurs not only impact LGBT youth but also are directed toward heterosexual children and teens. One teenage boy may tell a classmate "you're so gay," which to both gay and straight peers

Photograph by Kyna Shilling

can mean something like "you're stupid" or "you're being a pansy." If the classmate *was* gay, these remarks further add to the stigma and stress of being homosexual and may create deeper feelings of alienation from the community. If the classmate was *not* gay, the derogatory use of the word gay perpetuates prejudice.

Gay Bashing

Jimmy was a 14-year-old who came out as gay in his high school. He was taunted, bullied, urinated on, punched, and defamed on the Internet. His parents pleaded with the school to protect their son, but their cries fell on deaf ears.

Jimmy's mom and dad were told by the counselor that because he was openly gay, these incidents should have been expected. Sharing an incident of harassment with his coach, he relayed how a group of boys had tied him to a tree and repeatedly punched him in the stomach until he vomited.

Jimmy's coach only responded:

"Stop being such a faggot."

Photograph by Kyna Shilling

The level and constancy of this persecution led Jimmy to have a psychological breakdown.

All too often, this abuse is a common scenario in our schools and community, leading to depression, suicide ideation, self-hatred, and isolation because our young people are left unprotected, without firm and enforceable boundaries regarding harassment. The direct link between violence toward LGBT youth and a myriad of difficult life issues for them is impossible to ignore. A clear message must be sent, beginning with early childhood education, that it is unacceptable to persecute others verbally or physically.

 # Hate Crimes

Antigay hate crime can range from high-profile murder cases such as Matthew Shepard, a gay college student who in 1998 was brutally beaten, lashed to a fence, and left to die on a remote prairie in Wyoming, to local, everyday occurrences such as antigay insults, threats, gay bashing, and sexual violence. It also can include incidents of hate mail, offensive phone calls, e-mails, graffiti, theft, or damage to property that send a strong message of violence and fear into the world surrounding homosexual youth.

The 1999 film *Boys Don't Cry* is an example of media imitating life. This is the story of Brandon Teena, actually Teena Brandon, who hid her biological gender in order to live as a woman. The result was a homophobic hate crime murder by two men when the deception was uncovered.

 # Homophobia Hurts: Inclusion Heals

Our goal is inclusion of all youth, safety in homes, schools, and communities, and elimination of prejudice.

Homophobia may be internalized by young people, which inhibits their own ability to accept themselves. This internalized homophobia is generated by outside messages of homosexual social inferiority and undesirability, and is only abated by the individual's acceptance of his or her sexual identity. Heterosexual society's continued use of antigay derogatory words and actions threatens the homosexual's coming out and self-acceptance process, and psychological stability. Antigay derogatory language promotes a system of social interaction in which gay male and lesbian youth are made to feel inferior. Many heterosexuals have internalized this homophobia in such a way as to create constructs that marginalize LGBT teens from the dominant heterosexual society. One example of this marginalization is a school system's ban of same-sex couples at prom. Many people are forced to survive in a socially supported environment of judgment and restriction.

Internalizing Homophobia: Three Case Studies

Internalized homophobia is the outcome of gay, lesbian, bisexual, and transgender youth internalizing society's negative ideology about sexual minorities. *Sexual prejudice* is the outcome when heterosexuals internalize these harmful beliefs about LGBT individuals.

Thomas was 5 when he knew he was different. By 8, he knew he liked boys and thought about them a lot. By 15, he realized he was gay and came out to his parents. His dad's only words were "You are living in sin." Thomas internalized his dad's homophobia and began thinking God hated him. His self-hatred grew; he dropped out of school, and he no longer connected with old friends. The question plaguing Thomas throughout his adolescence was:

"What will God think?"

Tish was a young African-American woman with a top-level corporate position. She had been actively involved in an intimate lesbian relationship for 5 years. Tish told very few people about this relationship, being especially careful about her colleagues and superiors at work. She didn't want to be harassed or lose her job. However, her perceived homophobia was internalized at a physical level, with continuous and painful migraine headaches, often to the point of debilitation. The question plaguing Tish throughout her professional life was:

Photograph by Kyna Shilling

"What will my boss think if he finds out I am a lesbian?"

Jerry and Ramona were married for 30 years. On their anniversary, Jerry disclosed that he was gay and having a relationship with another man. Ramona was devastated, as this simple disclosure swept away her assumptive world of a past, present, and future marriage. Ashamed about her husband's sexual orientation, and hurt by the rejection, she internalized her perception of society's homophobia by limiting social contact and she began to withdraw. She decided not to call friends.

As a senior citizen, the question plaguing Ramona was:

"What will my friends think?"

These scenarios illustrate the impact of homophobia from childhood to maturity. It presents itself not only through prejudicial verbal or physical harassment from the outside world but also as an internalized component of reducing self-esteem.

Internalized homophobia manifests itself emotionally through self-hatred, physically through illness, and socially through isolation.

Photograph by Kyna Shilling

The Language of Prejudice and Exclusion

Words carry impact and power. The development of nonprejudicial dialogue is essential.

The language used to explain society's prejudice against LGBT youth evolved throughout the 20th century. George Weinberg first defined the term *homophobia* in the late 1960s. Its creation advanced new consciousness about the recognition of antigay marginalization and oppression. The 21st century is witnessing new language that seeks to explain hostility toward homosexuals through personal and cultural expression.

Today, in the early 21st century, the terms *sexual stigma, heterosexism,* and *sexual prejudice* are a few of the many terms used to expand the understanding of homophobia. "What is important is that the words for our new scholarship enable us to understand hostility and oppression based on sexual orientation and, ultimately, eradicates it" (Herek, 2004, p. 20).

Homophobia is a phobia or fear about homosexuals and it is now used more loosely to refer to LGBT. "It was a fear of homosexuals which seemed to be associated with a fear of contagion, a fear of reducing the things one fought for home and family. It was a religious fear and it had led to great brutality as fear always does" (Herek, citing Weinberg, 2004, p. 7).

Sexual stigma is "society's shared belief system through which homosexuality is denigrated, discredited, and constructed as invalid relative to heterosexuality" (Herek, Chopp, & Strohl, 2007, p. 1).

Heterosexism is "the discrimination or prejudice by heterosexuals against homosexuals" (Merriam-Webster Online Dictionary, 2006). It is a belief system that male–female sexuality is the only natural, normal, or moral mode of sexual behavior and this idea results in a reinforcement of stigma and power differentials associated with this belief.

Sexual prejudice is "the internalization of sexual stigma by heterosexuals resulting in hostility and negative attitudes toward sexual minorities. This leads many adults to view homosexuality as immoral." (Herek, Chopp, & Strohl, 2007, p. 14).

Core stressors for LGBT youth begin to surface as they experience the stereotyping of being a member of a sexual minority. This stereotyping usually manifests in the form of ideology derogatory toward and ridiculing LGBT. Herek, Chopp, & Strohl (2007) presents three major stressors that result from the stigmatized status. They include sexual stigma, stigma awareness and felt stigma, and internalized homophobia.

Brenda came out as a lesbian at 16. Homophobia was overt in her school. Both peers and teachers distanced themselves from her. Slurs such as *dyke* and *lesbo* were common. Brenda hated school and stayed home a lot. Her parents barely spoke to her, and no one ever called. She began taking drugs and having promiscuous sex.

"I hate myself and everyone around me hates me, too.
What's the use of living? Nothing will ever get better.
What's the use of trying?"

She had nowhere to turn and no one to turn to. The stress of sexual stigma, sexual prejudice, and internalized homophobia had created a hopeless situation for Brenda. She felt very alone. The biggest danger for LGBT youth is *isolation* from friends, relatives, parents, and community.

Photograph by Kyna Shilling

In order for some young people to come to terms with their homosexuality, they must first come to terms with the idea that a segment of society dislikes them. These feelings can only be exacerbated by homophobic or culturally biased and derogatory language.

It should be clearly understood that if being hateful and bigoted are seen to be symptoms of pathology, then all of us must stand up against homophobic slurs in order to promote the mental health of our mainstream heterosexual population. It is the same principle of prejudice at work when witnessing a white person, for example, degrading himself or herself and demonstrating pathology when using insulting slurs or actions against people of other races or cultures. In degrading others, the bigot degrades himself or herself.

Alicia was a sophomore in high school and also an African-American lesbian. She had lived with racial profiling throughout childhood. Alicia felt marginalized when she and other friends were targeted by community agencies as perceived juvenile offenders and at school as a group outside of the system. A white police officer pulled Alicia's car over with Alicia and her friends inside. He immedi-

Photograph by Kyna Shilling

ately warned them, "I know you people are only up to trouble." At 17, she came out as a lesbian to friends and family. Her aunt could not contain her anger.

"You are a black girl. You can't be a lesbian too! What is wrong with you?"

Alicia was overwhelmed with racial and homophobic prejudice, both of which were equally hurtful and equally difficult to endure.

The evolution of words used to describe LGBT youth often carries hateful and bigoted connotations. Saying these words, even in passing, is to continue promoting ideas of inferiority and marginalization regarding sexual orientation and gender identity. Sometimes instances of antigay harassment may not be hate-motivated. Yet, it is the responsibility of both the LGBT and heterosexual communities to stand up against homophobia and other cultural bias in order to promote the mental health of our young people.

 # The Language of Acceptance and Inclusion

The development of objective language allows for the development of understanding.

We as a society can generate new concepts by envisioning and evaluating broad understandings through appropriate language. Just as language can hurt, it also can heal. Creating discerning and insightful vocabulary is a present challenge for the LGBT movement, but it can be done. We can break sensitive topics down into meaningful pieces as we form a unique dialogue that carries deeper and more thoughtful insights to bring fresh ideas into humanity. New ideas result in new language to describe them. New language allows us to think about and process new ideas. We really cannot easily consider innovative ways of thinking without fresh ways of expressing these thoughts through appropriate language. Imagine trying to describe a flower without a general understanding of the word flower.

As we begin to clarify concepts and they become more defined, we often find a word or expression is too generalized or vague. In its place, a new expression or a set of subcategories often arise, making the former one archaic. Previously, the word "gay" was used to include what is now properly expressed by several words: gay, lesbian, bisexual, and transgender. The mainstream heterosexual ways of life are constantly being refined. It is reasonable to anticipate further refinement and changes in what is to be considered appropriate language.

Until recently, there were very few words available to create a reasonable dialogue on the subject of gender identity and sexual orientation. There was no shared language to explain and present gender bias, orientation, or social constraints. In order to expand understanding, we need an inclusive language. Too many LGBT youth are forced into a confined pigeonhole by the restriction of words necessary for communication.

The outcome has been a fractioning off from mainstream society to form exclusive homosexual social structures. Limited language had created a pressure to conform to the preconceived role models prescribed. Perceived available choices are too often false images filled with "should" and "must" instead of *is*. Withdrawal, isolation, or existence in a parallel LGBT subculture is often the result. Even using *lifestyle* has been debated, as it implies there is a choice. Many promote its replacement with *life, lives,* or *sexual orientation.*

GENDER BINARY

Gender binary is a very contemporary term for the distinction between male and female expectations as defined by preexisting roles in their society or culture. Every culture dictates how men and women should act based on cultural norms, expectations, and male or female roles, creating a societal construct of male and female. Examples of existing stereotypical roles are moms being the homemaker and dads being the breadwinner.

BABY BLUES KIRKMAN & SCOTT

© *Baby Blues Partnership: King Features Syndicate. Reprinted with permission.*

This cartoon is a simple illustration of gender binary. This social construct of sexual characteristics is based on *perceived attributes of gender* that often ignore or diminish the true nature of human beings who exist along the full continuum from hypersexualized heterosexuals to members of the LGBTQ community.

Gender binary can be defined as the cultural construction of male and female roles based on perceived gender. These constructs are assumed to speak to the ability of everyone to function within perceived boundaries. Yet, it highlights precisely what marginalized gay adolescents feel that they are not a part of. It sets up a dichotomy of a majority identity versus a marginalized minority identity.

Too many young people cannot or do not want to conform to the preconceived notions of this gender binary.

How they are perceived by others is not how they perceive themselves.

Society must hold a spotlight on heterosexual culture's constructs as false structures and bring this artificial marginal-

Photograph by Kyna Shilling

ization of our LGBT youths into the light of day. This begins with creating awareness of sexual stereotyping with young children. With this in mind, heightened awareness of most men and women being subjected to false cultural constructs is apparent. These ideas not only impact adults but children as well. They can limit everyone's full participation in life and highlight the fact that *both straight and LGBT* communities are falsely limited. Examples of restrictive thinking can easily be understood in the following statements children may make by the age of 3 or 4.

"Girls can't be doctors."
"Boys can't be dancers."
"Girls can't have blue rooms."
"Boys can't wear pink shirts."

This cartoon illustrates how gender stereotyping easily can begin with toddlers.

Although heterosexual people are usually less aware of limitations imposed by the gender binary than LGBT individuals, they are still

THE FAMILY CIRCUS BIL KEANE

"Go away, Billy. This is girl talk."

©*BIL KEANE, INC. King Features Syndicate. Reprinted with permission.*

impacted. The oppressive nature of cultural gender bias has existed throughout time. Societal projections have impacted present and past generations, influencing restrictive gender norms for grandparents, parents, teens, children, and toddlers in every cultural, social, religious, and sexual context. Until this is recognized, there cannot be equality.

QUEER

The word *queer* is a broad-based concept referring to one's self-identification. Although "queers" can be LGBTQ, LGBTQ are not necessarily "queer"—*only* if they identify as part of a group larger than their gender identity or sexual orientation. Straight people can be queer, too. A heterosexual who enjoys cross-dressing is an example. They may feel the gender binary doesn't define them, as they don't conform to the standard, allegedly perceived gender roles.

Queer identity is an individual decision. One chooses whether or not to identify oneself as queer, and an acknowledgment of a nonbinary reality and identifying outside that. The queer community bridges all sexual and gender issues to form a group of supportive people who understand our culture doesn't always provide for everyone to feel normal.

The queer community is those people that don't support our culture's standard ideas of sexuality and gender role as true human nature for everyone. It allows people the option of expressing themselves if what they feel is not standard and creating an environment where they do not have to live with the assumption that the dominant culture ideology works for everyone.

SEXUAL ORIENTATION

Sexual orientation is a self-identified enduring attraction toward another person. It can be felt and expressed by attraction to members of one's own gender (homosexual, gay or lesbian), the other gender (heterosexual or straight), or toward both genders (bisexual).

- "Research suggests sexual orientation is likely determined during early childhood."
- "Prospective studies indicate many gay and lesbian youth self-identify at about age 16, and that their first awareness of homosexual attraction occurred at about age nine for males and 10 for females."
- "In a representative sample of 1,067 teens, only one youth self-identified as gay although 5% engaged in same-sex sexual behavior."

Earls, Advocates for Youth Fact Sheet, 2005

This research may vary greatly. Although the percentages may range considerably as to the age of awareness of sexual orientation, any child of any age needs to be treated with dignity and equality.

Some experts in child development feel awareness of the biological differences between boys and girls begin as early as age 3. It is common for 2-year-olds to notice, comment on, and confirm that "boys have a penis" or "girls have a vagina." Children may wonder about their sexual orientation at an early age but have no age-appropriate way to speak of their feelings. "Zach knew he was different by kindergarten, but he had no name for it, so he would stay to himself" (Winerip, 2007, p. 1). He came out as gay in 7th grade.

A well-respected preschool educator relayed the following story. Mrs. Andrews had worked as the head of early childhood for a well-established private school. Hearing that one of her former students, Tim, was now 18 and openly gay, she remembered the following scenario. Tim was brought to her at age 5; distraught that he was being teased. Following standard procedures, she spoke to all of the kindergarteners involved. Yet when she heard of Tim's homosexuality, she immediately became sad.

"I wonder if I protected him enough. I worry I didn't. I had a momentary inner glimpse of Tim being gay and dismissed it. I thought he was much too young to be able to tell. He was so kind, so sensitive, and different in a way that made him very special." As she told the story she lamented,

"I hope I didn't let him down."
A tear rolled down her cheek.

Soon after Mrs. Andrews heard of Tim's *coming out,* she unexpectedly ran into him. He openly discussed his sexual orientation and she, too, was open in her recounting of the teasing scenario. Tim said, "You were right then. At five I didn't feel like other kids. By ten I knew I thought a lot about other boys. When my friends would pretend or dream about being the prince and finding a princess, I would pretend and dream about being with the prince."

This well-established educator of young children realized her instincts were correct and she now regretted not acting on them. Very young children may be self-aware of their sexual orientation or gender identity, and professionals and family may well be advised to look for early signs. By holding the possibility of a child being gay or lesbian at an early age, one can deepen one's commitment to advocacy and elimination of discrimination for the youngest of girls and boys.

Although few children can define themselves as lesbian or gay, many LGBT adolescents who have come out explain they have always known, but couldn't find the right words to express their feelings. Others were fearful of rejection and discrimination or uncertain about their sexual orientation.

GENDER IDENTITY

Gender identity refers to whether an individual identifies as a male or female. It is his or her internal sense of being male or female.

Controversy exists as to whether the feelings of gender identity begin at birth or at very early stages of development. Nine-year-old twin boys appeared on a segment of *60 Minutes* in March 2005. One loved sports, cars, trucks, and all of the "so-called normal boy things." His twin had a pink bed and bright nail polish on his fingers.

This boy explained his own theory. "I was supposed to be a girl in my mom's stomach. But my mom wished for all boys. So, I turned into a boy." When he was asked if he wished that he was a girl, he nodded yes. One doesn't know if he will grow up with a sexual orientation toward other men or women, or if he will later realize that he is transgender and perhaps decide to have hormones or surgery to outwardly match an inner identity. At this early age, he clearly expresses identification with being female in a male body.

His mother was very accepting. She created an environment in which both sons were comfortable expressing similar sentiments of "being happy the way they are." Yet, the story-line left the viewer wondering how the school accepted these gender identity differences and if the larger community's stereotypical standards had any impact.

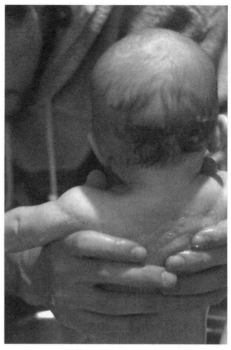

Photograph by Kyna Shilling

> *Our gender identity is something we feel in our soul. But it is also a continuum, and it evolves.*

> Dr. Robin Dea, Mental Health Director/Kaiser Permanente, CA
> (Brown, 2006, p. 2)

In a *New York Times* article, "Supporting Boys or Girls When the Line Isn't Clear" (2006), Patricia Brown reports that there is growing advocacy for children who do not conform to gender norms in clothing and behavior. This advocacy for gender-identity rights is exemplified by New York City's ruling to allow the sex listed on a birth certificate to be altered. Gender-identity rights issues are being supporting more and more by parents, educators, and mental health professionals. Physicians are beginning to advise parents to let these children be "who they are" to reduce depression and suicidal ideation.

One director of a school in California explained the shift in trends. "First we became sensitive to two mommies and two daddies, now it's kids who come to school who aren't gender typical" (Brown, 2006, p. 1). One teacher explained that her colleagues were unnerved by a young boy coming to school in a dress. Another educator reacted by blaming the parents and stating it just wasn't normal. A 7-year-old elementary school boy was thrown into a large trash bin by a group of boys who relentlessly teased him for his effeminate traits. The principal told his parents that it was their fault for not teaching him to be tough enough.

Some school systems are implementing a gender-neutral vocabulary and guidelines. One approach involves students lining up by sneaker color rather than gender, hoping to promote nonconfinement to cultural norms. Another measure required each student be addressed with *a name* and *pronoun* corresponding to the gender identity. For example, if a boy named Jake wanted to be called Jane and identified as a girl, *she* would be called Jane. Still another provided a changing room that corresponded to a child's chosen gender.

Still another public school in New Hampshire created an unusual and heartfelt memorial for a fifth-grade boy. Joe died suddenly in a tragic fire. He was a beloved student and classmate, admired for his sports skills, his sense of humor, and his academic abilities. Joe was everyone's friend and truly popular. There was a special thing Joe liked to do—dress up and wear nail polish. It was okay with everyone at school. After Joe's death, his school deeply mourned the loss.

A year later, Joe's class had moved on to sixth grade. As the date of his death approached, the class began to brainstorm ways to remember him. Some wanted to plant trees, others send off a balloon, but one suggestion won all of their hearts.

"Let's do what Joe loved best to do."

On the anniversary of Joe's death, the children participated in a fingernail painting activity. The class felt he would have chosen this and it was a happy reminder of him. They thought of Joe all day. Many smiled at the sense of fun he would have had if he would have been with them.

One mom realized she had a gender-variant child when he was age 5. He began wrapping his head in a towel and pretending it was long flowing hair and was becoming stressed when he had to wear boy clothes. His mom finally realized he wanted to wear a dress. He admitted that was true. This kindergartner strongly identifies as a girl, wants to be called "she," and wears ponytails and pink jumpers to school.

Photo by Courtney Cioffredi

Parents are searching for advice on how to make life acceptable for children who want to cross-dress in public and totally identify with the gender other than their biological one. Dr. Herbert Schreier, a psychiatrist with Children's Hospital Research Center in Oakland, is one of many professionals who see gender variance as a naturally occurring phenomenon rather than a disorder. He explains, "These kids are become more aware of how it is to be themselves" (Brown, 2006, p. 2).

Dr. Edgardo Menvielle, a child-adolescent psychiatrist at the Children's National Medical Center in Washington, DC, agrees. He founded a national outreach program in 1998 for parents of gender-variant children with a 200-parent membership. Dr. Menvielle's outlook is simple. Although many children role-play involving gender, in some it creates extreme distress. "We know that sexually marginalized children have a higher rate of depression and suicidal thinking. The goal is for the child to be well adjusted, healthy and have good self-esteem. What's not important is molding their gender. The key question is how intense and persistent the behavior is" (Brown, 2006, p. 2).

When a child expressed his deepest feelings at age 6 that "it feels like a nightmare to be a boy," there were no clear-cut guidelines for adults to follow. His parents worry about his safety and self-esteem as they balanced their love for their son with society's marginalization of him. One mother's response to friends and relatives was only, "It's who your kid is."

TRANSGENDER IDENTITY

Most people don't know the difference between a transsexual and a transvestite. And that's very sad, because I could tell you the difference between the American and the National League of baseball, even though it doesn't interest me.

RuPaul, *New York Daily News,* 2005

Transgender is a broad term used for individuals whose gender identity or gender expression is different from their biological sex or physical anatomy; they may not conform to conventional societal norms. Transsexuals and transvestites fall under this umbrella, as can straight, gay, lesbian, or bisexual individuals.

A transsexual is a transgender person who internally identifies biologically and psychologically with the opposite gender and sometimes desires a physical alteration of the body (gender-reassignment surgery) or hormones to become more aligned with that gender with which they identify. Some express that they feel "trapped in the wrong body." Transsexuals do not always present themselves as a single gender and may display highly fluid gender expressions.

A *transvestite* is a man or woman who adopts the identity of dress and behavior of the opposite gender. They may not necessarily be gay. They may gain enjoyment, sexual pleasure, or emotional comfort from assuming this identity. An example of this identity is cross-dressing, or wearing clothes of the opposite sex.

The understanding of the transgender male or female relates to the concept of how the person truly feels they are inside, regardless of society's perception of his or her identified role. A transmale in a woman's body feels like a male inside. A transfemale in a man's body feels like a woman inside. One transgender male explained, "It's not about whom you are attracted to, or elective surgery, but a feeling that a man or woman has, about who they really are inside their skin that seems to involve their spirit or self-image more than their genitals."

Dr. Michelle Angelo (interviewed on Larry King Live in 2006) said that transgender issues are a media concern and bravely commended those who have openly allowed their stories to be told. She offered two categories of understanding. The first is sexual orientation, or "Who am I attracted to?" and the second is gender identity or "Who am I in my heart and soul?" Dr. Angelo examines the dissatisfaction with one's body, the incongruity between the brain and body, and the awareness that although sexual surgery is not essential, identifying as a transperson is. She underscores the essential need for transsexuals to "be perceived by the outside world as the gender they feel they are [inside]," and that there are varied ways to do this. Many transgender people don't feel the need to have sex changes and are content to be a "fluid" amalgam of both genders.

The movie *Transamerica* has created a depth of understanding and pathos for the plight of the transgender population and the need to broaden the paradigm of what is normal throughout our world. Dolly Parton wrote the film's award-winning song, "Travelin' Thru." She adeptly summarizes the thoughts and feelings of a transgender person in the quest for inner peace in the following lyric:

I'm just a weary pilgrim trying to find what feels like home
Where that is no one can tell me, am I doomed to ever roam?

 # Helpful Terminology

Bisexual or "*bi*" refers to an enduring attraction toward both sexes.

Gay male is a male with an enduring homosexual attraction toward another
   male.

Gender binary is the distinction between male and female expectations as defined by preexisting roles in their society or culture.

Gender fluid refers to stepping out of preconceived roles into what feels right to the person or switching "fluidly" from one gender role to another as that individual feels necessary at any given moment.

Gender identity refers to whether an individual identifies as a male or female. It is his or her internal sense of being male or female.

GLBT stands for gay, lesbian, bisexual, and transgender.

GLBTQ stands for gay, lesbian, bisexual, transgender, and queer (or questioning).

Heterosexual or *"straight"* refers to people whose sexual and romantic feelings are mostly for the opposite sex: Men who are attracted to women, and women who are attracted to men (PFLAG, 2002).

Homosexual or *"gay"* refers to people whose sexual and romantic feeling are mostly for the same gender: Men who are attracted to men, and women who are attracted to women (PFLAG, 2002).

Queer defines a community of those people that feel the gender binary doesn't define them. They may not conform to standard alleged perceived gender roles and don't want to be limited by the gender binary.

Lesbian is a woman with an enduring homosexual attraction to another woman.

LGBT stands for lesbian, gay, bisexual, and transgender.

LGBTQ stands for lesbian, gay, bisexual, transgender, and queer (or questioning).

Metrosexuality refers to the characteristics of a metropolitan male of any sexual orientation (usually heterosexual) who carries a strong aesthetic presence and exerts a large amount of time and expense on appearance and living.

Photograph by Kyna Shilling

Sexual orientation refers to which gender an individual feels sexually, emotionally, and romantically attracted.

Transgender is a person who dresses as, desires to be, or has undergone surgery to become or identify as someone of the opposite sex (transsexuals and transvestites).

Transman is a female who feels *he* is a male inside. This person feels like a man and is a biologically female person who identifies as a male. Transmen feel they should be correctly be referred to as male.

Transwoman is a male who feels *she* is a female inside. This person feels like a female and is a biologically male person who identifies as a female. Transwomen feel they should correctly referred to as female.

Transsexual is a person who identifies with the opposite of their biological gender and sometimes desires a physical alteration of their body or hormones to become more aligned with their gender of identification. Transsexuals do not always present themselves as a single gender and may display highly fluid gender self-expressions.

Transvestite is a man or woman who adopts the identity of dress and behavior of the gender with which they identify, and gains sexual pleasure from assuming this identity.

Transition is the inner and outer state of passage from one sex to another.

 # The Emerging Sexual Identity Continuum

A little boy was walking down the street in
  New York.
He yelled to his mom.
"Look, that lady on the horse is a policeman!"

In the real day-to-day world, people have biologies and psychologies that prevent simple labeling or pigeonholing. They are not just this or just that. Rather, on closer examination, we see a continuous range from one extreme to the other with regard to sexual orientation, gender identification, and society's constantly evolving masculine and feminine roles.

There is a sexual identity continuum of men and women that extends the borders of simplistic male and female stereotyping. Some men fall into roles of being macho, tough, and supersexed, while others enjoy flowers, beauty, nature, and perhaps cooking. Women's roles can range from CEOs of corporations to police officers and ballerinas. Men and women exist as LGBTQ and heterosexual in varied ways with differing attributes. Many are comfortable in the role of gay men, lesbian women, and straight individuals. The film *Bend It Like Beckham* is an example of limiting gender norms. An Indian girl in England shocks her family's cultural mores by aspiring to play professional soccer.

Some people find their comfort zone as transgender. One of two identical twin girls decided to become a transmale, appearing quite macho, with a beard, tattoos, and broad shoulders, with no further desire to complete genital reassignment surgery. He seemed perfectly content to have externalized partial male characteristics without a complete medical sex change. Yet others on this continuum expressed the need for genital surgery for their expression of what they feel they are inside.

People in our culture may use language such as mailman instead of postal clerk and fireman instead of firefighter. Gender identification related to occupation is common, yet changing. There is now a continuum whereby male nurses and female police are acceptable in society. Being a gay male, lesbian, bisexual, or transgender youth *is part of this continuum*. It needs to be included in the spectrum of life possibilities that exist beyond the assumption of a heterosexual and gender normative world.

If each of us would or could examine our own natures we might make a surprising discovery.

Few of us would fit neatly into the media's cultural representation of what a man or woman should be.

How many of us look in the mirror and see a runway model or a James Bond image?

Photograph by Kyna Shilling

Would such an image resonate with our true nature? Yet, in today's world, most of us are greatly influenced by TV and film to become the represented stereotype. Many spend endless time, energy, and money chasing this illusion through weight control, plastic surgery, possessions, cosmetics, and social positioning.

Humanity can create a place for all people to fit in. We need to develop social spaces or safe zones for each and every individual to be able to externalize characteristics of his or her gender identity or sexual orientation without stigma. Rather than having to choose between feelings of normality and a queer identity, a person should be seen as having the right to "mix and match" internal and external characteristics congruent with his or her own sense of self.

A black-and-white dichotomy or dualism forces many youth to make extreme choices, often traumatically exacerbating the artificial sense of differences that exist. In contrast, we can promote the true existence of a single continuum that goes from black *to gray* to white, where any place on it can be seen as okay. No longer would gay young people be locked into a gender binary. They would freely become a natural part of this continuum, no matter where they place themselves on it.

The goal of this continuum is for any person to find a place on it that works *for who they feel they are inside their own skin*. It precludes deferring to some phantom, arbitrary group dictating a narrow and limiting illusion of roles that change in character and appearance from place to place, culture to culture, and time to time. Societal limitations need to *expand* to include all people without the imposition of restrictive, artificial cultural norms.

Forcing conformity *to* these narrow and limiting cultural norms is harmful.

It is the goal of the LGBT and heterosexual community to expand these norms to be as broad and inclusive as possible.

Photograph by Kyna Shilling

Queering the Mainstream

Why are there no gays in Hollywood when there are so many gays in Hollywood?

Anonymous LGBT teen

The term we discussed earlier, *queering the mainstream,* is helpful in understanding the essence of the gay rights movement's drive to get conventional society to mainstream "queer" identity so that it becomes a part of the mainstream. The implementation of this concept is central. It frees people too often viewed as *less than* in society to be *part of* society.

Today's society is beginning to transform itself from a "straight" alliance that allows no room for LGBTQ individuals into a mainstream community that views racial, sexual, and cultural issues as a merging of all people. By accepting diversification, we can meld these issues into one multifaceted mainstream. This movement is the ultimate ideology to promote the well-being of our gay and straight youth.

We need to open up windows of opportunity to live more expansive lives, existing outside the old, outdated cultural norms. Like old clothes that no longer fit, these

Photograph by Kyna Shilling

norms can be taken off and discarded. In this way, a fresh comfort zone arises for an idea whose time has come, the replacement of "innocent ignorance" and subliminal prejudice with freedom of expression and being. As Anne Stockwell, editor of the *Advocate,* explained (CNN NEWS, 2006), "It's not shameful to be gay, it's shameful to behave shamefully."

This transformation frees the gay and straight population alike. Society as a whole and the internal satisfaction of the individual are both enriched. The goal is to see the continuum as all-inclusive. This view tremendously reduces the pressure of succumbing to false conformity, not just for LGBT youth, but for everyone.

Open a new window, open a new door.

Jerry Herman

Photograph by Kyna Shilling

CHAPTER 2

Dispelling Old Myths: Creating New Insights

Photograph by Kyna Shilling

RAISING AWARENESS • INVISIBLE ASSUMPTIONS

SHARED PREJUDICE • DISPELLING THE MYTHS

A BIOLOGICAL BASE • IS IT A CHOICE?

RELIGION • ACCEPTANCE TRENDS

FIRST AMENDMENT GUIDELINES • POLITICS

THE MILITARY

POWER OF WORDS AND IMAGERY

THE MEDIA: A CATALYST FOR CHANGE

"We do not see things as they are.
We see them as we are."

The Talmud

Gender issues lack a home in people's minds and hearts. Our culture is uncomfortable with open discussion of this subject and there has been difficulty in creating language that meets the needs of the subject. Too often gestures, energies, and innuendoes bombard our youth *below the radar* of conscious integration. Yet, nuances such as a disapproving stare, a negative thought, or a judgmental inference are felt. Mainstream myths about homosexuality drift into everyday conversation with the ease and comfort of acceptability. The filtering and dispelling of false stereotyping and illusory constraints have not yet become a common reality. Our young people are faced with a continual barrage of prejudicial ideology they hear too often at home, in school, in the community, and through the media.

Raising Awareness: Invisible Assumptions of Shared Prejudice

In a restaurant, diners at one table were overheard discussing the film *Brokeback Mountain* and making derogatory remarks about it. As one woman loudly proclaimed, "I am not interested in any movies like that!" There was no self-consciousness about the bigoted remarks being overheard. There seemed to be little awareness that anyone in the room might possibly be offended. But inappropriate and degrading conversation became apparent to three teens, Sara, Barbara, and Joan. The girls could not help but overhear. Had this been a discussion about racial issues in America, these otherwise seemingly intelligent people would have been much more cautious, self-aware, and restrained about disparaging statements. They would have lowered their voices and controlled impulses to make negative slurs with the automatic awareness that others in the room could be offended.

The first step in expanding new cultural norms regarding the gay community is the awareness that everyone in the universe does not share outdated stereotypical thought forms, ranging from the ultramasculine Marlboro Man to the extremely feminine Lipstick Lesbian. The targets of bigoted slurs are human beings who hear and feel these critical words and are hurt by them.

In the previous restaurant scenario, Sara was disturbed by the conversation she overheard containing disparaging comments. Her brother, Dillon, whom she loved very dearly, was gay. Her friend Joan was a lesbian.

She was frustrated and felt a need to do something to inform these people she had overheard. On her way out of the room, walking by their table, she clearly and purposefully commented to Barbara and Joan, "Wasn't *Brokeback Mountain* a wonderful film!" She hoped to create awareness that antigay rhetoric is heard and does hurt.

In most of the United States today, derogatory and narrow comments about LGBT issues are often made with the automatic assumption that any listener would automatically be like-minded. There is almost an unspoken agreement that these concealed (and less concealed) misconceptions are shared by all. LGBT individuals, their families, and their friends are constantly flooded with these unconsciously expressed thoughts and ideas throughout the day, which hurt their self-image and foster prejudice.

Photograph by Kyna Shilling

 # "It's Not What You Say, but the Way That You Say It"

Alice was a 20-year-old who had come out as a lesbian. While she was at her workplace, a seemingly benign dialogue unfolded into quite a meaningful life commentary. Alice heard a mental health professional, Dr. Gaines, begin to discuss with colleagues a new synagogue "with a very different congregation" adding this caveat with a slight smirk: "The rabbi was a gay male, but there weren't many others as congregants."

Alice felt that he was subtly conveying that this synagogue was acceptable *because* the majority of the congregation was *still* heterosexual. The underlying energy of his words left her inwardly shaken, as his invisible negativity became increasingly physically palpable. Alice casually responded, "I am interested in that temple." She didn't share a past experience of being shunned as a sinner by her own religious group and that now she was desperately seeking spiritual acceptance.

That evening, Alice had difficulty sleeping as this short interchange floated through her mind. She awoke needing to continue the dialogue with Dr. Gaines. Catching his eye right before lunch, she approached him with the following words.

"I wanted to let you know that not only am I interested in that synagogue because it appears liberal and I respect diversity but because I am gay just like the rabbi."
She slept much better that night.

Photograph by Kyna Shilling

Dispelling the Myths of Homosexuality

Each of the following seven myths has been dispelled as untrue. By dispelling the myths of homosexuality with factual and well-grounded information, we can best serve our young teens in both the gay and straight world in creating better understanding and eliminating prejudice.

- Homosexuality is linked with problems in a child's relationship with parents, such as a domineering or possessive mother and an ineffectual or hostile father.
- Homosexuality involves a fear or hatred of people of the other sex, leading individuals to direct their sexual desires toward members of their own sex.
- Homosexuality is a choice.
- Homosexuality is caused when children were victimized, seduced, molested, or sexually assaulted by an adult homosexual. There is no biological basis for homosexuality.
- Homosexuality is a mental disorder.
- Homosexual men are pedophiles.
- LGBT parents raise their children to be homosexual.

Myth 1: Homosexuality Is Linked with Problems in a Child's Relationship with Parents, Such as a Domineering or Possessive Mother and an Ineffectual or Hostile Father.

Researchers conclude that LGBT individuals were no more likely to be smothered by maternal love than heterosexuals, nor were they more neglected by fathers or sexually abused (Myers, 2005). If "distant fathering" was a catalyst to becoming gay, we would assuredly find more gay sons in families with absentee fathers, especially with the rise in the number of families with absentee fathers. This is not the case.

Alex was 16 when he came out as gay. His greatest fear was his parent's reaction. He was an only child and had always had a close relationship with his mom and dad.

He and his father had worked on projects together, talked about social issues, and shared a great love for Mom. Alex didn't want them to be disappointed in him. His dreaded reaction was rejection.

Photograph by Kyna Shilling

He was astonished when Mom's first reaction was asking "What did I do wrong?" She began to cry. Too often, she had heard the myth it was the parent's fault if a child was gay. Dad wondered the same thing inwardly and later confided this to Alex. He reassured them they had been the most loving parents, and his *gayness* had always been a part of him. Now he could recognize and share it. Together this family spent many hours extinguishing the myth of parental responsibility for homosexuality.

Myth 2: Homosexuality Involves a Fear or Hatred of People of the Other Sex, Leading Individuals to Direct Their Sexual Desires toward Members of Their Own Sex.

Even the most casual observations will reveal that heterosexuals and homosexuals share an increased ease in forming friendships with members of the sex they are not sexually attracted to. With that in mind, homosexuals often find their closest friends are members of the opposite sex, as portrayed by the TV sitcom, *Will and Grace*.

Andrew was a gay young man and his best friend was Lizzie. He did everything with her, confiding and sharing life in a deep way. He had many female and male friends, and he enjoyed their company tremendously.

But Lizzie was his favorite. He would tell her, "If I wasn't gay, I would marry you." She felt the same way.

LGBT youth are very capable of warm friendships and loving ties with both the opposite and same sex and appear to have positive feelings toward both.

Photograph by Kyna Shilling

Myth 3: Homosexuality Is a Choice.

Reframing the assumption that "there is *a choice* to sexual orientation" and transforming this assumption to "there is *no choice* for the homosexual adolescent" begins the evolutionary trend leading to acceptance of homosexuality as being a state one is born with.

The tide is turning in acceptance of a biological explanation for homosexuality with steadily increasing genetic, prenatal, and brain findings. Many mental health professionals accept the premise that *nature more than nurture* predisposes sexual orientation and explain a deeper understanding of why these biological influences are so difficult to change. "Evidence suggesting that biology plays an important role in the development of male and female sexual orientation is rapidly increasing" (Myers citing Hershberger, 2005, p. 400). Mustanski et al., 2002, (cited by Myers, 2005, p. 399) assert "Genetic research using family and twin methodologies has produced consistent evidence that genes influence sexual orientation."

Photograph by Kyna Shilling

Tommy and Adam had been best friends from fourth grade through high school. When Tommy told Adam he was gay at the senior dance, Adam was shocked.

"I don't believe it. You can change your mind. Why don't you just try a vagina? That will cure you."

Tommy spent a long time with Adam, dispelling the myth that his sexual orientation was a choice. Adam seemed convinced he could change his mind if he just kept trying to have sex with women. His Uncle Frank convinced his mom that if he went to therapy he could be talked out of his *gayness*. Luckily for Tommy, he chose a therapist that dispelled this myth that he had a choice.

This therapist supported his understanding and inner knowledge that being gay was a natural part of who he was.

Tommy could choose to accept himself and decide who he wanted to tell and when.

Photograph by Kyna Shilling

Myth 4: Homosexuality Is Caused When Children Are Victimized, Seduced, Molested, or Sexually Assaulted by an Adult Homosexual. There Is No Biological Basis for Homosexuality.

New research indicates that sexual orientation is at least partly biological, as the brain differs with sexual orientation. This research affirms the possibility of homosexuality not being linked to sexual abuse as a child. Simon LeVay (1993) explains his findings in the following way: "Gay men simply don't have the brain cells to be attracted to women" (Myers citing LeVay, 2005, p. 398). His study indicates a cell cluster in the brain that was noticeably larger in woman and gay men.

Some researchers feel investigative data is still controversial, causing some skepticism in the scientific community. Other researchers indicate evidence of a genetic component to homosexuality as well as the influence of prenatal hormones. Ellis and Ames, 1987, assert "Were it not for delicately balanced combinations of genetic, neurological, hormonal, and environmental factors, largely occurring prior to birth, each and every one of us would be homosexual" (cited by Myers, 2005, p. 399).

Sandra was talking to her math teacher, Mr. Nelson, one of the sponsors of the LGBT club at her school. She liked him very much and appreciated his support for the gay students. As they were planning the club's next event, the LGBT Information Assembly, they began to list discussion points about homosexuality to be shared with fellow students at the assembly.

Mr. Nelson commented, "You need to remind them most gay and lesbian teens have been sexually abused." Sandra argued this simply wasn't true. She had never been victimized, abused, or sexually assaulted, and neither had her LGBT friends.

He refused to believe her and answered abruptly, "Well, the gay and lesbian kids I know have."

He ended the discussion and changed the subject. She felt disappointed that one of her favorite teachers was so steeped in the myth of the *causality of being gay by childhood abuse* that he would not change his mind. She still chose to present this as a myth at the LGBT Information Assembly and inform the students of the biological basis for homosexuality.

Photograph by Kyna Shilling

Myth 5: Homosexuality Is a Mental Disorder.

In 1973, the American Psychiatric Association removed the term homosexuality from the list of mental and emotional disorders stating sexual orientation is not a disorder. Therefore, it does not need to be cured. So often, our LGBT youth are bombarded with ideological assumptions of sexual identity stemming from mental illness. It is compounded if these thought forms are steeped in cultural mores as well. Sophie was 17 when she came out to her family from Malaysia.

Her mother became terrified, screaming, "This can't be true. There is something wrong with you. You are sick in your brain. You need help."

Sophie felt helpless to battle the inherent bias her family system was so steeped in. They were sure that homosexuality was a mental disorder.

Myth 6: Homosexual Men Are Pedophiles.

"To call molestation of a boy by a man 'homosexual' is to misunderstand pedophilia. No true pedophile is attracted to adults, so neither the term *homosexuality* nor *heterosexuality* applies. Often pedophiles do not develop a sexual orientation towards adults. Rarely does a pedophile experience sexual desire for adults of either gender. The majority (of pedophiles) self-identify as heterosexual" (Kort, 2006, p. 1). The predominant view of researchers and professionals who work in the field of child sexual abuse does not see homosexual and bisexual men posing a threat to children. Holmes and Slap (1998) authored a study in the *Journal of the American Medical Association* reporting research findings that "98% of all male perpetrators who had sexually abused boys were identified in their families and communities as heterosexual."

Yet, recent antigay activists argued to exclude gay scouts and scoutmasters from the Boy Scouts of America. This perpetuates the myth that gay people are child molesters.

One must be careful, therefore, not to confuse homosexuality with pedophilia.

"The man who offends against prepubertal or immediately postpubertal boys is typically not sexually interested in older men or in women" (Herek, 2006a, citing McConaghy, pp. 5–6). Scandals such as the congressional page and Congressman Foley (2006) surround males who were at least 16 years old. In Washington, DC, this is the age of consent. Although he targeted very young people to whom he was in a dominate role, he wasn't a pedophile. Many scandals involving the Catholic Church also involved victims of sexual abuse being adolescent boys rather than small children. There is constant confusion over the use of the term *pedophilia,* which properly refers to offenses against or attraction to prepubescent children.

There is no inherent connection between an adult's sexual orientation and her or his propensity for transgressions against children. There is no factual basis for organizations to avoid hiring homosexual or bisexual people on the basis of their sexual orientation for positions that involve responsibility for or supervision of children, adolescents, or adults. "The empirical research on adult sexual orientation and molestation does not show that gay men are any more likely than heterosexual men to molest children" (Herek, 2006a, p. 5).

Seth loved children and always wanted to teach second grade. He was openly gay. He achieved a teaching degree and his evaluations were excellent in working with young children. Yet, over and over he was asked. "Why would a man want to be an elementary school teacher? There must be something wrong with you. You might hurt the children."

Seth was never hired. Try as he may, he couldn't convince school personnel that he was a safe adult to be around children. The idea that men don't teach elementary school was too pervasive. This myth was so strong in public education that he was forced to abandon his dream of helping children.

Yet, progress has been made in this stereotyping of gay men. In 1970, a national survey indicated that more than 70% of respondents agreed with assertions stating "homosexuals are dangerous as teachers or youth leaders because they try to get sexually involved with children. In contrast, a 1998 national poll expresses the belief that most gay men are unlikely to molest or abuse children, the idea (of homosexuals being dangerous) was endorsed by only 19% of heterosexual men and 10% of heterosexual women" (Herek, 2006a, p. 1).

Myth 7: LGBT Parents Raise Their Children to Be Homosexual.

The gender identity of preadolescent children raised by lesbian mothers has been found consistently to be in line with their biological gender.

9% of sons of gay fathers identified as bisexual or homosexual in orientation (about the same as sons of heterosexual fathers).

(Pawelski et al., 2006, p. 360)

The myth that LGBT parents will raise their children as homosexual has not been validated by experience or research. Herek (2006b) reported in *American Psychologist* that "the vast majority of children raised by lesbian and gay parents eventually grow up to be heterosexual" (p. 613). Yet, all too many homosexuals are confronted with uncomfortable questioning on this topic.

Mark and Adam were raising their 5-year-old Greg as same-sex parents. Mark's Uncle Henry stopped in for an unexpected visit. After playing with Greg and getting to know him, he said:

"Greg's a great kid. Are you going to raise him to be straight or gay?" Mark responded, *"My parents were straight—did they raise me to be a homosexual?"*

 # The Trend toward Acceptance

"Gay teenagers are 'coming out' earlier than ever, and many feel better about themselves than earlier generation of gays. The change is happening in the wake of opinion polls that show growing acceptance of gays, more supportive adults and positive gay role models in popular media" (Elias, 2007, p. 2).

- "In one recent poll, more than half of adults supported protecting the civil rights of GLBTQ people."

- "In another survey, 95 percent of youth supported expanding current hate crimes laws to cover gender and sexual orientation."

- "A recent study of GLBTQ youth who received gay-sensitive HIV prevention education in school showed they engaged in less risky sexual behavior than similar youth who did not receive such instruction."

(Earls, 2005)

The trend toward greater acceptance of the biological component of being born LGBT is growing. The 2002 Gallop Poll (Myers, 2005, p. 400) reports a rise from 13 to 40% of the American public shared recognition of this natural element of homosexuality. A new effort towards acceptance is *The Welcoming Schools Guide* (welcomingschools.org), a comprehensive resource for creating elementary school environments that support and affirm all children. Its uniqueness lies in that it provides LGBT inclusive resources and lessons on family diversity, gender stereo-typing, and name calling for the primary grades.

The following information illustrates a few of the changing trends towards acceptance of homosexuality by age, year, and region.

- Acceptance rose from 32% in 1982 to 60% in the year 2006.

- Acceptance within the generation of young adults ages 18–29 increased to 62% as compared to 35% acceptance among ages 80+.

- The most accepting regions in the United States include New England and the Pacific Northwest.

(Elias, 2007, p. 3)

Photograph by Kyna Shilling

The shift of attitudes and extinguishing of myths creates a further rationale for civil rights protection for our LGBT youth. It also creates hopefulness for the future of young people.

The *hope* is that this trend will continue until a critical mass occurs when the majority of the population accepts being gay as a natural part of a person's inherent makeup.

Photograph by Kyna Shilling

MOVING TOWARD GAY-STRAIGHT ALLIANCES (GSAs)

Gay–Straight Alliances (GSAs) are fully initiated and student-led alliances. They create an opportunity to build understanding between gay and straight youth, which includes issues such as bullying, slurs, and other forms of harassment.

- There are at least 3,000 Gay–Straight Alliances at U.S. schools.
- Nearly 1 in 10 high schools have one now, as do at least 290 middle schools.
- Six percent of 16-year-olds have same-sex attraction.
- Gays' mean age of first same-sex contact: 15. Girls 16, boys 14

(Cloud, 2005, p. 44).

Kevin Jennings, founder of GLSEN (Gay Lesbian Straight Education Network), believes a majority of heterosexuals find antigay rhetoric as offensive as racism. His organization registers and advises GSAs in the schools. In the academic year 2004–2005, GSAs were created in American schools at the rate of three per day. "We're gonna win," he says, as he explains his position on an expanding gay movement, "because of what's happening in schools right now. This is the generation that gets it" (Cloud, 2005, p. 45).

A leading example of how the gay movement has responded to the emergence in this decade of hundreds of thousands of openly gay and lesbian adolescents is an organization named the Point Foundation. Created in 2001, it generously provides extensive scholarships to gay and lesbian students, and it is one of the few national groups conceived solely to help LGBT youth. Cloud (2005, p. 44), reports, "Young Americans including many young conservatives are becoming thoroughly, even nonchalantly, gay positive. From young ages, straight kids are growing up with more openly bisexual, gay and sexually uncertain classmates." Cloud continues to explain, "Children who become aware of their homosexual attractions no longer need endure the baleful combination of loneliness and longing that characterized the childhood of so many gay adults."

THE BATTLE OVER LGBT TEENS

The *gay movement* and the Christian Right have both found strategies for engaging youth with gender issues. Although the gay activist movement creates Gay–Straight Alliances in schools, scholarships, and the promise of acceptance, the Christian Right bolsters LGBT participation in other ways. Often they present ideas offering inclusion, prayer, and the *promised* change of sexual orientation (although one cannot promise to change sexual orientation).

"Inqueery" is a new effort by the Christian Right to work with gay kids using words such as diversity and tolerance. Chad Thompson, founder of "Inqueery," maintains a Web site designed to appeal to LGBT youth with pink borders, stylish teens, and relevant issues in text. Thompson realized in fourth grade that he was attracted to boys and was hurt by antigay slurs. Yet he never accepted a *"gay"* identity, claiming, "Heterosexuality is God's design," and he feels that his homosexual feelings have greatly diminished. He feels a new bigotry has arisen against those who have not chosen to embrace this orientation.

The Christian Group *Focus on the Family* has warned that boys as early as the age of 5 may have "gender confusion" and need professional help. Yet Dr. Jack Drescher (Cloud, 2005) of the American Psychiatric Association studied programs that attempt to alter sexual orientation. According to his findings, "Trying to reject one's homosexual impulses will usually be fruitless and depressing and can lead to suicide" (p. 45).

Ritch Savin-Williams, author of the *New Gay Teenager,* explains that increasingly gay and lesbian kids are more like straight kids. "At many schools around the country it is now profoundly un-cool to be seen as anti-gay. Straight kids meet and gossip on websites like *Facebook.com,* where a routine question is whether they like guys or girls or both" (Cloud, 2005, p. 45).

Savin-Williams believes that some kids are moving toward a "postgay" identity, and that just because they are gay or lesbian they don't need to be openly political. Their attraction to others is personal and developmental. Many are tired of the homosexual stereotyping and promiscuity of the bar-scene life and choose to reject that for the larger world of partnership and community. Many do not want to be condemned only to a *"gay"* world, as their world is filled with heterosexual friends and family as well.

A SAFE PROM

A prom is a formal dance held for a school class toward the end of the academic year.

Its very definition infers inclusion for all.

Yet, this is not always the case. Every year, thousands of high school teens prepare for this annual prom celebration. Too many gay, lesbian, bisexual, and transgender students dread its approach. They wait

Photograph by Kyna Shilling

for it to pass, fearing ridicule and closed-mindedness will destroy any possibility of their attending or being accepted if they do.

Linda, a high school senior, explained that the prom did not work out the way that she had hoped. Her date was her girlfriend Mary, and it became more of a nightmare than the sweet, romantic evening she had fantasized about. Linda admitted she felt watched all evening, sensing everyone was waiting for something to blow up about their presence. Other teens have experienced alienation at proms, some to the degree of forming off-campus *queer* proms, an event that can be one without ridicule. Loitz attended a Youth Prom for LGBTQ teens and felt this prom "was the best experience I've had in the LGBTQ community. We weren't afraid, which is a wonderful feeling. I wish everyone would have a gay prom" (Kennedy, 2006, p. 24).

SCHOOL SAFETY POLICIES

More schools are creating prom policies, dress codes, activities, student pledges, and adult training that include LGBT students. GLSEN (2002) provides the following useful policies for safe proms.

1. Offer inclusion of same–sex/gender couples, allowing students to attend any way they wish.

2. Create dress codes allowing assurance that any young person can wear prom attire of their own choice, regardless of their sexual orientation or gender identity.

3. Present prom activities allowing flexibility to broaden the traditional king and queen of prom to those who may not fit the established heterosexual roles.

4. Implement ideas including self-nominated "kings" and "queens" with each category open to all regardless of gender expression or "couples."

Photograph by Kyna Shilling

5. Adapt a student pledge policy for prom attendees to sign acknowledgment of their support for creating a safe space for all students, regardless of sexual orientation or gender identity.

6. Supply school training for staff and chaperones on ways to ensure all students are treated equally.

GLSEN PITTSBURGH: A MODEL FOR SAFETY

GLSEN (2005) created their "First Annual Making Proms Safe for All Report." Sponsored by GLSEN Pittsburgh, this group approached prom season with a fresh point of view. The report reflects, "Prom season produces excitement for many and increased anxiety or alienation for others. It is a wonderful time for students to express themselves and feel adult and free. The tone you [the schools] set for your prom can make a significant difference in keeping self-expression positive, and ensuring the inclusion, enjoyment and safety of all students." GLSEN Pittsburgh created a safe, chaperoned, fun social environment for homosexual and heterosexual students with diverse religious, geographic, and cultural backgrounds.

The annual *Safe Prom for All* was held at the Pittsburgh Hilton.

Posters similar to this one were displayed to underscore the atmosphere of inclusion.

Permission by GLSEN Pittsburgh

The following are findings among student participants in "A Safe Prom for All Report" (GLSEN Pittsburgh, 2005, p. 49). They indicate the significant difference of GSAs in school as an indicator of creating more safe environments.

- "When asked how safe it would be at their home schools for someone to bring a same-sex date to the prom, 40% said it would not be safe. Only 14% said it would be very safe to do so, with the remainder indicating it would be somewhat safe."

- "The main way in which respondents said it would not be safe was 'verbal abuse'/'threats' (45% of responses) or 'not be allowed' (28%). High school students' responses also cited 'discomfort' (20%) and the fear of 'physical abuse' (15%)."

- "The presence of a GSA in schools made a statistically significant difference in students' sense of safety. 81% of total respondents from schools with a GSA said it would be somewhat or very safe to bring a same-sex date as compared with 49% of students from schools without a GSA."

The purpose of this report is to underscore the school's moral obligation to create safety for all students, and to recognize the legal obligation to allow all students to form GSAs while supporting diversity and minimizing fear of harassment. Milestones such as proms are then able to become a positive experience for any young person whose right it is to attend such a function freely. As one high school student explained about the prom,

"When I realized I was gay, it didn't change what was supposed to happen. It just changed who was in the picture with me" (Rachel, in Kennedy, 2006, p. 24).

Photograph by Kyna Shilling

GENDER NEUTRAL HOUSING IN COLLEGE DORMS

Gender Neutral Housing is a policy growing rapidly in schools throughout the country. Occidental College in Los Angeles, California, is an example of this policy in action. The college has established a nondiscrimination policy for sexual orientation and gender identity and implemented Gender Neutral Housing as an option for students. This "living and learning" community expands the already existing campus diversity, which includes multicultural dorms and a Women's Center.

The new housing provides an area where room assignments are not based on biological gender. Students can request a specific roommate. The area is gay-friendly.

The majority are gay, but not exclusively gay or gay-themed. Many young people feel more comfortable not being placed with random people of the same gender, or living in such an environment. As one freshman commented, "I'm excited about it. It's a nice opportunity to live with gay friends."

A First Amendment Framework

The Christian Educators Association International and GLSEN are two organizations usually with opposite views. They became part of a drafting committee (2006) to write guidelines and promote them to the huge constituencies they represent. The opposing debate of homosexuality being sinful and a choice is one side. The alternate view emphasizes safety from harassment and acceptance. Schools have begun to find language for guidelines that is a compromise between these two views.

The First Amendment Center, the organization convening this initiative, strove to dissolve controversy stemming from textbooks, proms, course studies, and clubs by asking both groups to engage in civil dialogue within First Amendment guidelines and principles. The guide is not prescriptive. No one was asked to compromise their convictions. A *process* was offered for addressing differences with civility and respect. These guidelines are intended to present all points of views. Yet the inclusion of curriculum content is the decision of the school districts after processing these viewpoints.

Conservative Christian groups and gay advocates joined in creating guidelines for developing ways educators, parents, and teachers can work with all aspects of school life involving sexual orientation. A First Amendment framework was unveiled by this unlikely partnership to dissipate the conflicts over homosexuality and find common ground.

This has become groundbreaking civil mediation, allowing opposing views the arena of honest exchange without bitter or slanderous debate. "Schools are encouraged to form a task force of people with divergent views, agree on ground rules for civil debate, understand the First Amendment and the law, and ensure kids don't go to school in fear" (Feller, 2006, p. B2). These "tips" are from *Public Schools and Sexual Orientation Guide.*

AGREED-UPON GUIDELINES: "TIPS" FOR EDUCATORS

- Take seriously complaints of harassment and discrimination regardless of the reason.
- Assure parents and students the school district will listen and be fair to both parties.
- Talk openly with parents.
- Do not discriminate against student clubs or expression simply because the political or religious message is unpopular or potentially offensive.

AGREED-UPON GUIDELINES: "TIPS" FOR PARENTS AND STUDENTS

- Find out what is happening in your district, ask questions, and seek information rather than make accusations.
- Share your concern with those closest to the problem, such as teachers, administrators, the school board, or a district staff.
- Understand the school has a responsibility to provide a safe environment for people with opposing views.

(The First Amendment Center, *Public Schools and Sexual Orientation,* 2006, p. 5)

The Christian association wanted to be certain their views were included and the advocacy groups for gay students wanted to be assured of the safety of their youth. "This is not about compromising convictions," said Charles Haynes, senior scholar at the First Amendment Center which helped formulate this alliance. "This is about finding ways to work and live together as American citizens" (Feller, 2006, B2). These viewpoints will be heard by school districts and may or may not be approved for curriculum development.

A New Look at Gays in the Military

The don't ask don't tell policy is so contradictory to what the armed forces stand for but they force you to lie in order to serve your country.

Reichen Lehmkuhl, Air Force captain and author
(Amazon.com Editorial Review, *Here's What We'll Say,* 2006)

Three quarters of more than 500 service members returning from Afghanistan and Iraq said they were comfortable interacting with gay people.

Twenty-four foreign nations let gays serve openly, with none reporting morale or recruitment problems (including Israel, England, and other allies fighting terrorism).

(Shalikashvili, Zogby Poll, 2007, p. 2)

In 1993, the media thoroughly debated the question of having openly gay men and lesbian women serve in the military. There were extreme opinions and feelings on both sides on their military ban. Many military personnel were opposed to letting openly gay men and lesbians serve. President Clinton supported lifting the ban but was overwhelmed by the huge dissent. The compromise policy of "Don't ask, don't tell" emerged, temporarily quieting the sea of controversy.

At that time, the chairman of the Joint Chiefs of Staff was General John M. Shalikashvili. On January 2, 2007, he wrote an op-ed article in the *New York Times,* "Second Thoughts on Gays in the Military." In this article, he explained that at the time of his service, "a change in the current policy of not allowing gays in the military would have been too burdensome for troops and commanders. The concern among many in the military was homosexuality was incompatible with service, [and] letting people who were openly gay serve would lower morale, harm recruitment and undermine unit cohesion."

In his op-ed article, Shalikashvili questioned if the time is right to take a fresh look at a military policy of nondiscrimination based on sexual orientation. He believes evidence suggests that it is. After meeting with openly gay and lesbian soldiers and marines, he felt that the military had changed and gays and lesbians could be accepted as peers. The general offered the following words of caution in addressing this issue and supporting a change of policy:

By taking a measured, prudent approach to change, political and military leaders can focus on solving the nation's most pressing problems while remaining genuinely open to the eventual and inevitable lifting of the ban. When that day comes, gay men and lesbians will no longer have to conceal who they are, and the military will no longer need to sacrifice those whose service it cannot afford to lose.

(Shalikashvili, 2007, pp. 2–3)

The Media: The Power of Words and Imagery

A TV show or film is more than a collection of words; it is imagery. And the imagery representing homosexuality in the media is a powerful tool in presenting stereotypes and prejudices transmitted with subliminal messages to innocent onlookers watching a seemingly innocuous program. Although *Will and Grace* and other TV sitcoms include a homosexual male as a friend or ally in a heterosexual world, the stereotyping of the gay male is still apparent. *Queer Eye for the Straight Guy* is another show that exposes the viewer to the stereotypical view of gay men as hairdressers, decorators, and advocates for the *uneducated* straight male in the world of women, appearing as a necessary tool for the heterosexual community.

One experienced, openly gay psychologist explained that many of his young gay clients struggled with gender issues. The depiction of homosexual people in the media was often a topic of their concern. This therapist discussed his interesting and forgiving perspective with LGBT youth. First, he recognized that homosexuals most often have been characterized in ways that overly stereotype and usually present excessive flamboyance compared to the "average" real gay personality. He noted, with optimism and obvious satisfaction, that depiction of gays in the media is becoming gradually more normal.

He pointed out that from about 1930 to 1953, America was not yet ready for serious confrontation about racial equality issues. *Amos 'n' Andy,* however, was a very popular radio and then early television show among both black and white audiences. There were many conscious and unconscious prejudices and inaccurate stereotypes in the minds of many if not most of the white audience, so the characters were intentionally innocuous and funny, more like clowns than real, normal people.

Similarly, some of the present-day gay characters in film and TV such as *Will and Grace* and *Queer Eye for the Straight Guy* are exaggerated and more likely light and humorous rather than serious and thoughtful. As the viewing public becomes more "comfortable" with gay issues, we will perhaps be less likely to tell, or even care, which characters are gay and which are straight. Until then, the *Amos 'n' Andy* comparison may be helpful for those of us that are impatient for the rest of society to catch up!

The ABC TV series *Brothers and Sisters* (2006) shares a very humane and inspiring representation of family life with parents and siblings accepting, enjoying, and engaging a gay son with great respect. It presents a heartwarming portrayal of a gay male romance, and the subsequent deepening of this relationship with the full acceptance of Mom and siblings. Mom even explained in one episode she was "a card-carrying PFLAG (Parents, Families and Friends of Lesbians and Gays) member." One segment ends with all of the brothers and sisters enjoying a dance with their mates at a country club together with one couple being the gay son and his date. It was presented in an exceedingly natural way whereby the viewer can feel the kindred love and equality for all in the family.

 # A Catalyst for Change

It is a heterosexual and homosexual world. This reality is gaining a deeper and broader spectrum of understanding by increased media portrayal of LGBT individuals. Dominick, a gay male teen, explained one day he was flipping through channels on the TV. He caught a fleeting segment of a comedy routine similar to the following:

"Every family has a cousin or somebody else that is gay. If you look around in your family and can't find them, then *probably* it's you."

Perhaps this scenario illustrated the huge influence a split second of humor can have

Photograph by Kyna Shilling

in impacting mainstream American culture. Dominick found the anecdote very amusing, and felt the subtle level of truth the levity portrayed.

The Super Bowl (2007) broadcast aired a commercial by Mars, Inc. featuring a brief, unintentional kiss between two men. Their reaction was to tear out their chest hair to prove they are really *"manly."* An alternative ending appeared on the Snickers Web site, showing one man grabbing a wrench to beat the other, who responded by slamming a car hood on his head. Mars withdrew this multimillion-dollar commercial from the air and Web site after being flooded with a wave of protest including condemnation from gay rights organizations. Neil Giuliano, president of Gay and Lesbian Alliance Against Defamation (GLAAD), explained, "I don't know what kind of mind-set it takes to think it's okay to slug another guy because of a mistaken kiss. It's just unacceptable" (Farhi, 2007, p. C7). Advocacy against stereotyping in the media was extremely *present and powerful* by many viewers who openly expressed displeasure for this ad.

The media's ability to become a catalyst for change extends to portraying value for LGBT entertainers. Richard Chamberlain revealed his homosexuality in his memoirs, *Shattered Love* (2003). Ellen DeGeneres bravely came out as TV's first openly lesbian lead in the ABC comedy *Ellen* in 1997. Her present success as a very high-profile TV host endears her to audiences as a likeable and wonderful person. She serves as a role model for many LGBT youth of an accomplished, successful lesbian woman to be admired and respected.

Queer as Folk, discussed previously, depicts the urban, sexual gay life. *The L-Word* is a show portraying lesbian life. Although many of these programs still illustrate a stereotypical gay or lesbian world, their value is in depicting real gay characters. By exploring *gay* life, however fictitious the storyline may be, fresh representations allow the LGBT youth to see images of their community that are positive compared to those in the past.

Through the presentation of real homosexual people, many gay male and lesbian youths can enjoy a TV show with which they are able to identify. Lisa and her friends Mary and Alice were lesbians. They loved watching *The L-Word*. Getting together to watch it was a social event, and each took turns bringing food and making it a party.

"It's like the 'Desperate Housewives' of the straight world for the lesbian community," Lisa explained. "It is so much fun."

Photograph by Kyna Shilling

The media is often a reflection of mainstream culture. The public is beginning to be allowed to see somewhat normalized representations of gay and lesbian life in terms of relationships and family living.

Using Creativity to Expand Consciousness

Recently, the film industry has taken dramatic steps in broadening public perceptions on these issues. Using creative imagery to expand acceptance, recent films reveal understandings in a normalizing, compassionate venue never before presented. The film *In and Out,* starring Kevin Kline, was a sweet portrayal of a teacher who realizes he is gay. Although loved and respected in his school system, he is asked to leave because he is a homosexual. The movie resolves the predicament by a community meeting, whereby a huge vote of affirmation is given to this teacher as his mother, father, friends, and coworkers all announce "I'm gay too!"

The Family Stone (2005) is another film that revolutionized the acceptance of a gay child and his partner in the most loving of ways within a family system. As Sarah Jessica Parker, a dinner guest, asks at the family dinner table, "Don't you want your child to be normal?" Diane Keaton, the mother of the gay son, said she wanted all of her children to be gay but wasn't that lucky. She had immediately addressed the ignorance of the question with humor and the sense of respect she held for her gay son and his partner. The film delivers an important message by the portrayal of the "ordinariness" of having a LGBT family member and the acceptance of this person without threat of a negative outcome.

And the movie acclaimed as the *Gone with the Wind* of the gay rights movement, *Brokeback Mountain,* did an extraordinary job of presenting the viewer with images that were not so earth-shatteringly terrifying of two men in a sexual encounter. Instead, it presented a love story surprisingly void of stereotypical gay overtones. Ang Lee, the film's director, explained that *Brokeback Mountain* as a story of love that was repressed. "Liberals ... see the film as a beacon of tolerance, a study of the cruel pathologies of intolerance, a plea for acceptance for the humane principle that love between consenting adults, no matter their gender or orientation, should be celebrated. ... It's a story of a love that dare not speak its name because nobody in it knows the word for its name.'" (Hunter, 2006, p. C1).

"The movie depicts a repressed America, whereby gay men are forced to bury their personalities and violent conformism is the rule of the day. The visceral imagery of Ang Lee gives the gift of speaking louder with images than most of his ideological opponents do in words" (Hunter, 2006, p. C5). An interesting parallel to consider is one between *Brokeback Mountain* and Shakespeare's *Romeo and Juliet* as tragic love stories. Each narrative is made tragic solely because of limitations imposed on the young lovers by the social structure existing at that place and time.

A syndicated cartoon, *Jane's World,* freely expresses through humor situations involving LGBT life. Portraying these issues in cartoon form in the media gives comic expression to daily scenarios. The following is an example of automatically assuming a relationship to be between a man and a woman instead of a woman and a woman.

Given with permission by Jane's World

This current trend of humanizing gay and lesbian life within the media is a great aid in the normalization process for homosexual adolescents and the creation of public acceptance for many of these sensitive issues. From *Brokeback Mountain* to *The Family Stone* to *Jane's World,* the portrayal of LGBT love relationships and family life has taken a quantum leap toward greater understanding. By actually seeing and relating to a love story about two men or two women, or a family loving a gay son and his partner, our culture can begin to experience new images of real people in real relationships.

Religious and Political Influence

Love, having no geography, knows no boundaries.

Truman Capote

There is a strong legacy of historically limiting views expounded by religion and politics continuing to mold the thinking of the general public and shape existing prejudices. Many take these opinions as fact and reteach them to the next generation. Others use them as political agendas. Children and adults are influenced by phrases such as "gays are sinners" and "all gays will go to hell, and so will their supporters."

This can create not only bigotry but also great terror of God's wrath, and make acceptance extremely difficult. These ideas can often *polarize* instead of *unify* different groups.

Photograph by Kyna Shilling

Although we may assume that these statements are well intentioned and human interpretations of old ideas whether right or wrong, we also can ask if the world might be ready for a more humanistic perspective.

Herek, Chopp, and Strohl (2007) maintain that individual congregations may contest homosexuality as against God's will but "most denominations define romantic love, committed relationships, and families solely in heterosexual terms and condemn homosexuality as sinful. Through these doctrines, religion simultaneously negates homosexuality in the realms of relationships and families while providing a rationale for marginalizing and attacking people who are gay, lesbian, or bisexual" (p. 6).

There are increasing people of faith who support the rights of LGBT citizens to live and work free from discrimination. Various mainstream churches have made political statements in support of civil rights protections for homosexuals (see chapter 11). Unitarian Universalism (the UUA's Office of BGLST Concerns) is a community determined to create an inclusive environment for all congregants. It serves as a model of *living* the welcoming congregation by advocating for the rights of LGBT citizens. Religious segments may differ in interpreting God's word. It is important to protect people from being *forced* to live someone else's interpretation of religious convictions and yet allow *all* to state their religious convictions.

Out in Scripture, http://www.hrc.org/scripture, is a free online resource for preaching by the Human Rights Campaign. It offers weekly preaching as a devotional resource written from an LGBT and straight-supportive perspective. Its motto states, "All people are welcome to be members here." PFLAG offers several free brochures on the topic of religion and homosexuality, an example being *Is Homosexuality a Sin?* 2nd ed. (2005b). This booklet shares goals of different religious leaders pertaining to LGBT people. It provides alternatives to people of faith who believe LGBT relationships are not a sin, and presents resources for those who want to learn more about various religions' approaches to LGBT issues.

LGBT REPRESENTATIONS AS ROLE MODELS

Fourteen-year-old Keith asked his friend, "Who are famous gay and lesbian people?" "I can't think of one." Keith had just come out. He was desperately seeking an adult LGBT role model.

Barney Frank is an openly gay member of Congress. Political leaders such as Dick Cheney and Richard Gephardt have LGBT kids. Elton John and Rosie O'Donnell are openly gay or lesbian celebrities. Billie Jean King is a well-respected lesbian sports figure. LGBT clergy are leading religious congregations throughout the country. Reverend Gene Robinson was the first openly gay bishop in the Episcopal Church. Gay role models need to be visible for our youth. Lance Bass of the vocal group N'SYNC openly disclosed being gay. This helps other teens to do the same. He told *People Magazine* "I'm more liberated and happy than I have ever been. I feel like myself. I'm not hiding anything. I've already gotten so much support . . . I'm so glad it is 2006" (Laudadio, 2006, pp. 86, 88).

In the book *Outstanding Lives* (1997), Brelin and Tyrkus profile lesbian and gay men who have made lasting contributions to the world. "If we consider the diverse talents of so many individuals in light of their mutual gayness we can expunge some of the empty stereotypes that limit our thinking, and postulate the infinite variety of ways that gayness is manifest in culture and society" (xv). These role models include Edward Albee, Roberta Achtenberg, Aaron Copland, Allen Ginsberg, Merle Woo, and Gore Vidal.

New role models in the military, religious, and sports arena have emerged to kindle hope and inspiration in LGBT youth. Reichen Lehmkuhl, in his book *Here's What We'll Say* (2006), reveals the difficult journey of being gay and also being a graduate of the U.S. Air Force Academy, an Air Force captain, the winner of CBS's *Amazing Race*, and a gay rights activist. In an editorial review of this book on amazon.com, 2007, Reichen says, "One of the hardest things for me to reconcile was the fact that with my family and friends [I was free to be myself] but faced the very real possibility of being court-martialed [in the Air Force for being gay]."

The Reverend Bradley Schmeling is the pastor of St. John's Lutheran Church. He openly shared his homosexuality with his bishop and congregation before he was chosen as pastor, and had served for seven years in that capacity. Then the Reverend bravely told his bishop he had found a lifelong partner. This disclosure spurred a ruling (2007) by the disciplinary committee of the Evangelical Lutheran Church of America (ELCA) that he be defrocked for participating in a relationship with another man—and the possibility of St. John's Church and its members being cut off from numerous resources. Many members of the church hope this will not happen. They prefer the denomination change its ruling about sexually active gay clergy. One church member explained in a *Washington Post* article, "Gay Pastor Loses Ruling, But Not His Flock—Yet" (Dell'Orto, 2007, p. B9), "We are not an activist church, even though we can stand for issues of justice. [Reverend Schmeling] exemplifies the kind of love and empathy I envision Christ to have had."

The congregation of almost 350 members finds itself in the middle of a campaign to allow sexually active gays to be pastors within their denomination. One dad with young children stated, "It hasn't been a problem to explain Brad or his relationship to our children as much as what the church wants to do" (p. B9). Dell'Orto (2007, p. B8) reports that "many Lutheran churches support ordaining partnered gays and performing same-sex blessing ceremonies despite the policy." The disciplinary hearing committee of ELCA felt they had no choice but to defrock Schmeling because of present church law. Yet they suggest that the ELCA remove its rule and reinstate gay clergy who were removed or resigned because they were in a same-sex *lifelong partnership*. Schmeling states, "The best thing I can do for this issue is to be the best pastor I can be" (Dell'Orto, 2007, p. B8). He confirmed his ability to be a role model to youth with his steadfastness for excellence in his work.

Esera Tuaolo became one of the first openly gay professional football players. Born a Samoan immigrant, Esera retells his youth and his life while playing in the NFL for 9 years and hiding his homosexuality. He explains his dread of discovery in his book, *Alone in the Trenches* (2006). Tuaolo recounts his terror during the 1999

Super Bowl, "Not one teammate, coach or sportswriter knew I was gay. What if one of those billion watching recognized *me* as the stranger he had picked up in a gay bar? All he had to do was out me to the press and the story would read 'Gay Man Makes Final Tackle in Super Bowl.' My football career would be finished" (p. 2). His book bravely establishes his identity to be much larger than his sexual orientation or professional career. He had to silently live with the fear of homophobia in the extremely *macho* world of national and international sports.

"You know, I hate gay people, so I let it be known. I don't like gay people and I don't like to be around gay people. I am homophobic. I don't like it. It shouldn't be in the world or the United States" (Kaufman, 2007, p. 1). This was the reaction by retired NBA guard Tim Hardaway on the coming out of the first gay professional basketball player, John Amaechi. In Amaechi's book, *Man in the Middle* (2007) he candidly explains his life in professional basketball and teammate and coach relationships.

John makes clear in an interview (Kaufman, 2007, p. 2) that he still believes that there is a lot of homophobia in society and in professional sports locker rooms. "We are much further behind than I'd like. People in America and England would like to think racism is over, sexism is over and homophobia is over, but it's not. My coming out will show that gay people don't all look like Jack from *Will and Grace*. Some of us are big, athletic men, and that should be OK."

Amaechi said he had not heard from any former teammates or NBA players, only from one of his coaches. He challenges "professional male athletes to be active supporters, and that doesn't mean putting a rainbow decal on their car. It means letting other guys in the locker room know that it's not OK to make gay jokes, that it's hurtful, and that it's not OK to be homophobic. But it's hard to get straight guys to step up. When men stood by women during the suffrage movement they were called progressive and bold. When whites stood by blacks, they were heroes. But a straight guy standing up for a gay guy faces discrimination, and that's a big part of the battle we're fighting" (Kaufman, 2007, p. 2).

Martina Navratilova, a very well-known, openly gay athlete, commended John Amaechi's decision to come out because of what she refers to as an epidemic of suicides among young lesbians and gays. She emphasizes the importance of young people having someone to look up to (Sheridan, 2007, p. 1). "It's hugely important for the kids so they don't feel alone in the world. We're role models. We're the adults, and we know we're not alone but kids don't know that . . . [Amaechi] will definitely help a lot of kids growing up to feel better about themselves."

U.S. MARINE, IRAQ WAR HERO, AND GAY ACTIVIST: SGT. ERIC ALVA

Marine Staff Sergeant Eric Alva had been sworn into the Marine Corps at age 19 and stationed in Japan and Somalia. He came from a family of servicemen; his dad was a Vietnam veteran and his grandfather a World War II and Korean War veteran. Alva had been in charge of 11 marines in a supply unit in Iraq when he lost his right leg after stepping on a land mine on March 21, 2003. This was the first day of Operation Iraqi Freedom. As the first soldier wounded in the Iraqi war, he gained immediate notoriety, appearing on the Oprah Winfrey show and being awarded the Purple Heart by President Bush. He was treated as a celebrity throughout his service in the military.

In the fall of 2006, 36-year-old retired Sgt. Alva contacted the Human Rights Campaign (HRC) and asked to become involved with the lobbying effort initiated by Representative Martin Meehan to repeal the military's *Don't ask, don't tell* policy on gay, lesbian, and bisexual military personnel. Revealing his sexual orientation, he became a national spokesperson in an effort to revoke the ban on gays serving openly in the military. "Who would have ever guessed the first American wounded was a gay Marine?" (Associated Press, 2007). Alva publicly announced he was gay during a Capitol Hill news conference to reintroduce the Military Readiness Enhancement Act, legislation to rescind the *Don't ask, don't tell* guidelines.

Eric expressed his appreciation of being recognized as a brave soldier. Yet, a proud moment in the military came when he confided to friends he was gay and was still treated with the same respect as before. Lying about his sexual orientation when applying to be a marine was what Sgt. Alva hated most." I had to keep on doing it and it took a toll on me."

In a question-and-answer section of *The Washington Post,* "Defending His Country, But Not Its 'Don't Ask, Don't Tell' Policy" (Vargas, 2007), Sgt. Alva explains (p. C1) that people might say, "He's that gay marine. I'm OK with that. The truth is something's wrong with this ban. You're asking men and women to lie about their orientation, to keep their personal lives private, so they can defend the rights and freedoms of others in this country, and be told, if you ever decide to really meet someone of the same sex and you want the same rights, sorry, buddy. You don't have the right. That's one factor. The other factor is, we're losing probably thousands of men and women that are skilled at certain types of jobs from air traffic controllers to linguists, because of this broken policy."

"When Eric Alva lost his leg in Iraq, it didn't matter whether he was gay or straight, only that he was a courageous American serving his country."

"Eric's voice represents the sacrifice of thousands of gay and lesbian service members fighting for the safety and freedom for all Americans."

"We salute Eric for his bravery on and off the battle-field. The courage and sacrifice of gay and lesbian service members, like Eric Alva, should be heralded, not silenced."

Human Rights Campaign (HRC)
President Joe Solmonese,
First Service Member Wounded in Iraq Comes Out,
02/28/07, http://www.edgeboston.com p. 1–2.

HRC Photo Permission

The faint recognition of LGBT citizens being a part of so many families and friendships is often hidden in the shadows without conscious acknowledgment of the fact that homosexuality is a part of many, if not most, family systems, in all segments of right- or left-wing politics and conservative or liberal religious affiliations. This is sometimes acknowledged and yet sometimes ignored when one segment of our government lobbies against gay rights and another lobbies for them.

Working side by side with a homosexual person doesn't result in either "catching" being homosexual yourself or being harmed in any way. In fact, just the opposite trends are occurring. It is most often by knowing, working with, living with, or loving an LGBT person and their family that we learn to finally see them as human beings. Then we discover our old, outdated, limiting stereotypes no longer fit our new paradigm of acceptance.

Photograph by Kyna Shilling

Coming Out:
Finding Freedom to Be

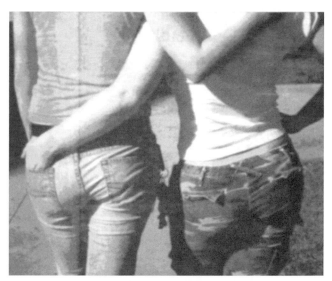

Photograph by Kyna Shilling

COMING OUT • CHANGING TIMES
COURAGE TO BE • STEREOTYPICAL SLURS
REJECTION • CONFUSED GENDER IDENTITY
RISKS • DANGERS AT SCHOOL
FAMILY REJECTION AND HOMELESSNESS
TEEN LGBT VOICES • CREATING FREEDOM
ACCEPTANCE • DISCLOSURE • STORIES
EMAIL • INTERNET • IT'S OK TO BE LGBT YOUTH

"You are a child of the universe no less than the trees and the stars; you have a right to be here."

Max Ehrmann

Many young people struggle with their sexual orientation and gender identity. Some may ignore or deny their desires, others attempt to change those desires through prayer, psychotherapy, or sheer will. Yet the feelings persist, and may remain hidden as the fear of coming out becomes greater than the burden of keeping the secret. Forced into living an underground life, self-hatred may evolve as this struggle between the inner and outer self rages. The language of coming out speaks for itself. Youths confined to a closet status by themselves and the society surrounding them must come out from the shadows of a hidden identity held throughout childhood. Often *when* they do come out, they realize they don't know *where* to go next.

Richard believed he had always been gay. Nevertheless, throughout elementary, middle, and high school, he lived the pretense of a heterosexual life, dating girls, and even having a girlfriend named Alison. Richard joked with others guys about "gays and fags" as if they were far removed from his world. His secret was kept way below the radar.

Yet his relationship with Alison wasn't working. He truly felt so much affection for her, but found he was disinterested in sex and often fantasizing about other teen boys. Alison began to doubt herself and her own sexuality. This compelled Richard to confide in her he was gay and also engaged in an intimate relationship with their good friend Thomas. Alison was devastated. She loved Richard, and was saddened over the loss of their existing relationship. Flooded with hurt feelings, her anger surfaced at not being told the truth about his sexual orientation and another ongoing gay male relationship. There was so much she didn't understand.

Richard was at a loss for words.

He had *come out* and begun to realize he didn't know where to go or what to do.

Photograph by Kyna Shilling

The Times Are Changing

Today's teens self-label on average several years before high school graduation.

Savin-Williams, 2005, p. 36.

Creating intelligent and factual discussion for young people is paramount as the wave of boys and girls revealing or questioning their sexual orientation or/gender identify is present at earlier and earlier ages. "The average age of first same-sex attractions has only recently been called the *magical* age of ten, and only for boys" (Savin-Williams, 2005, p. 118). One study cited by Professor Ritch C. Savin-Williams at Cornell University reports young boys begin coming out to themselves at age 13, and young girls by 15, with both coming out to others by age 16.

Don Woog is the founder of OutSpoken, a gay youth group begun in 1993. Woog explains in a *New York Times* article (Winerip, 2007, p. 2) that for the first 10 years of working with LGBT kids, the age of coming out ranged from 17 to 22 years old. "I'm gay. My life is over" would be a common initial comment. In recent years, he says, young people are coming out earlier, between the ages of 14 to 17, and appear more confident. A frequent first remark in 2007 might be, "Hi, I'm gay. How do I meet people?"

Confusion about Gender Issues

Gender stereotyping can begin at these young ages regardless of a young person's predisposition to be gay or lesbian, and it can be disturbing to any child. This disturbance is amplified for young LGBT children and teens who have self-identified but are still fearful of coming out to friends, family, and community. Young people constantly bombarded with the following stereotypical slurs can only become more terrified about disclosure and more confused about their sexual orientation and gender identity.

Stereotypical Gender Slurs

"Boys don't cry. Be a man. Be tough."
"Go play with the girls."
"You are a fag, faggot, queer."
"You're a dyke. She is a real butch."
"Girls like dresses. What is wrong with you?"
"You are so gay." "Don't be so gay."
"Butch."

 # The Risks of Coming Out

Open LGBT identity can mean family rejection and make school a dangerous place to be. Often LGBT youth keep their gender identity and sexual orientation a secret. Yet, releasing these hidden pieces can become a driving force within them. Too many adolescents are unprepared for repercussions. Some consequences may threaten their health and well-being. Young people often face grave risks after disclosure.

DANGER AT SCHOOL

In one nationwide survey, over 84 percent of GLBTQ students reported verbal harassment at school. Over 39 percent of all gay, lesbian, and bisexual youth reported being punched, kicked, or injured with a weapon at school because of their sexual orientation while 55 percent of transgender youth reported physical attacks because of their gender identity or gender expression.

The consequences of physical and verbal abuse directed at GLBTQ students include truancy, dropping out of school, poor grades, and having to repeat a grade. In one study, 28 percent of gay and bisexual youth dropped out of school due to peer harassment.

(Earls, 2005)

After disclosing themselves as LGBT youth, these teens may face tremendous difficulties. Earls (2005) explains, "In a society where heterosexuality often seems the only acceptable orientation, homosexuality is regarded as deviant, and variation from cultural concepts of normal gender often evokes hostility or violence."

Ueno (2005) presents findings to the effect that adolescents with homosexual and bisexual orientation have higher levels of psychological distress than their straight peers largely because of the interpersonal problems that they experience at home and school. Their research indicates LGBT youth experience more problems with peers at school and subsequent increase in stress levels when not connected closely with other peers. They found that friendships "reduced psychological distress and protected them from the psychological harm associated with interpersonal problems" (Ueno, 2005, p. 258). Ueno concludes that the presence or lack of social support by peers at school greatly impacts interpersonal stressors associated with sexual orientation.

 # Family Rejection and Homelessness

After coming out to their family or being discovered, many GLBTQ youth are thrown out of their home, mistreated, or made the focus of their family's dysfunction.

Service providers estimate that 25 to 40 percent of homeless youth may be GLBTQ. These rates may be conservative since many GLBTQ youth fear disclosing their orientation or gender identity.

(Earls, 2005)

George was kicked out of the house at 16 after coming
  out as gay to his parents.
His father threw him out bodily while screaming, "I never
  want to see you again."

Abandoned emotionally and physically, he lived on the
streets, many times harassed and victimized for his
homosexuality, as all too many LGBT youth experience. Without an income, he often sold his body for sex,
which exposed him to the danger of sexually transmitted diseases and violent crimes. The streets were a
dangerous place for George.

Van Leeuwen et al. (2006) report the results of their
study of homeless youth providers which measures and

Photograph by Kyna Shilling

compares the risk factors between lesbian, gay, and bisexual (LGB) homeless youth
and non-LGB specifically for homeless youth. This article strongly recommends that
the child welfare service provide services to homeless LGB youth to the child welfare
field. It presents existing gaps in services and areas where more training and technical support is needed, and the subsequent public health risks. Emphasis is placed on
greater risks for LGB homeless youth who have self-identified. This research informs
"child welfare providers and policy makers about the substantial vulnerability of
LGB youth beyond that of non-LGB homeless youth and the need to fund programming, training, technical assistance and further research to specifically respond to
the complex needs of this population" (p. 151).

Research by Whitbeck et al. (2004) compares participation in
deviant subsistent strategies, street victimization, and lifetime prevalence of five mental disorders including conduct
disorder, major depressive disorder, posttraumatic stress
disorder, alcohol abuse, and drug abuse among heterosexual
and LGBT homeless and runaway adolescents. The results
indicate LGBT youth were more likely than heterosexual
homeless to have been physically and sexually abused by
caretakers, to have engaged in risky survival strategies
when in their home, to be physically and sexually victimized when on the streets, and to meet criteria for mental
disorder.

Their recommendations concur with those of Van Leeuwen et al. (2006), stating
"sufficient evidence to warrant targeted interventions with these high-risk young
people (with) a critical need for special approaches aimed at protecting those run-
aways who are at great risk for sexual exploitation and accompanying physical and
psychological harm" (p. 241).

"To engage in serious discussion about issues of gender and sexual orientation in child welfare in the United States must begin not with the problems of LGBT persons but with the imperfection of the American society, rooted in historic inequalities and long-standing cultural stereotypes. As long as LGBT children, youth, and families are viewed as a 'them,' the burden falls on LGBT persons to do all the work necessary for sound gender and sexual orientation relations. The development of practice competence and policy development in this area hold promise for preserving and supporting families as well as establishing appropriate LGBT-affirming child welfare services for those whose lives are affected by the child welfare system" (Mallon & Woronoff, 2006, pp. 121–122).

Strong recommendations are made for *safe and welcoming "safe places"* as explicit shelters for LGBT youth.

 # Youths Speak on Coming Out

That is the thing about coming out. You make the conscious decision to release from heterosexual normative culture but the gay culture is not mainstreamed so you don't know where you fit in, like moving to another country.

Frank, age 20

I finally feel I am "out."
It feels great!

LeRoy, age 21

Photograph by Kyna Shilling

I was walking in the mall with a friend and a kid I knew yelled 'faggot.' How am I supposed to defend myself?

Tommy, age 13

Things you hear about words not hurting is a fairytale.

Angie, age 14

This was absolutely the most emotional thing I had ever done. I was relieved and happy and filled with joy.

Cantwell, age 15

Every aspect of your life is heterosexist, including bathrooms—single stalls— college roommate assignments, store layouts, colors, words, music and movies.

Rick, age 17

Everything pretty much can be viewed as heterocentrist and heterosexist. I'm moving to Canada. It's too hard here (in the US).

Marcus, age 21

It's like being a foreigner in your own land.

Sam, age 17

A heavy burden was lifted from my shoulders.

Alice, age 14

There is no way to show affection in public.

Mark, age 20

Photograph by Kyna Shilling

Lois's Coming Out: Ever Since Childhood

Seventeen-year-old Lois explained that she always knew she was a lesbian, ever since she could remember. "When my parents gave me a baby carriage and doll I immediately turned it into a go cart. That was more fun, I didn't want to play with dolls." When my dad saw what I had done he turned it back and with insistence corrected me. "This is what you do with it. You play with dolls." Lois was 4 years old.

When she was eight, she gave a friend a ring at school and asked her to get married. She didn't understand why she did that, it just felt right. By age 10, she realized that it might not be safe to express these deep parts of her to others. Lois saw kids being taunted at school and called names like "fag" and "dyke." Afraid of being teased, she kept more and more inside herself. At thirteen, she tried to kiss a boy. "It felt like cardboard," she admitted to herself. "I was bored." Lois wondered what was wrong for feeling that way. At age 14, she wanted to talk to someone about her inner feelings. She went to her mother and explained she *just liked girls better than boys* and didn't know what to do. Mom told her not to worry, girls always like their girlfriends a lot.

Again and again the message for Lois was clear. Disregard your inner feelings and conform.

She couldn't. She came out at 17. Many friends accepted her. A few did not. Lois told her mom that she was a lesbian. She explained, "I'm the same person, you just know one more thing about me." Her explanation fell on deaf ears. From that point on her mother refused to speak to her. With great anger and disgust, her mom *threw her out* of the house and ignored any calls or notes. Lois felt alone, isolated, and abandoned by her family.

Coming Out by E-mail: Marge's Struggle

Marge knew she was a lesbian by 17. She carried her secret for years, afraid of parental rejection and judgment. She never told anyone, feeling very alone even in a huge crowd.

Dating boys and keeping the outward facade of heterosexuality took a huge toll emotionally and physically. By age 21, Marge needed seven medications for colitis and eventually was hospitalized for depression.

Photograph by Kyna Shilling

Finally, Marge e-mailed her parents a note and awaited a response. "I'm a lesbian" was the very first sentence. After four days of silence, her dad wrote back. "We love you and it is unconditional." All the pain stuffed inside with her shadowy secret began to dissipate, and she began to feel relief physically and mentally.

Marge decided it was time to come out to her brother George as well. She explains, "That part was easy." They were riding in the car, talking and listening to music, on their way to a favorite restaurant.

Marge turned to George and muttered, "I think I'm a lesbian." He was silent for a minute and then responded, "Couldn't you be a socialist or communist or something easier?" "No, I'm serious," she emphasized. George looked in her eyes and asked "Aren't we still going to dinner?" That was the absolute end of the conversation.

The Internet: A Vehicle for Coming Out

With the important safety caution of Internet nondisclosure of identity, this vast arena of networking is often a lifeline to the LGBT teenager isolated from mainstream society.

Sometimes young people live in isolated communities where it is impossible to feel safe enough to disclose their sexual orientation. Parents, peers, teachers, and clergy openly oppose homosexuality, and no visible ally is available. Living under the shadows of secrecy, some teens find the internet the only link to others who can relate. They seek reliable information, supportive organizations, and connectedness with other LGBT youth.

Sean lived in an area where no one else he knew was gay. He was 17 and longed to be able to communicate his sexual identity with someone. His family had strong religious beliefs against homosexuality, and his minister preached against it at church. Even Sean's siblings taunted him for planting flowers and writing poetry. He dared not tell them he was gay. Peers in school were openly homophobic. Graffiti covered parts of the school with slurs painted boldly on walls. "I hate gays. Faggots should die. Kill homosexuals." The principal allowed it to remain. Sean feared for his life if his being gay was disclosed.

The Internet became his lifeline. He located an LGBT chat room and found for the first time other teens to share his deeply hidden secret with. Coming out online, Sean realized that many were hiding this same secret. The more those in the chat room shared, the more he began to see his anger, sadness, and frustration was a lot like others in his situation. Condemned to silence, his inner voice grew as he gained a support system in cyberspace.

"Out" at School: Life-Threatening or Life-Affirming

Just as the same tree can appear barren and stark in winter and alive and renewed in spring, so too can a young person know the extremes of bigotry or the joy of acknowledgment with the disclosure of being homosexual.

Two fifteen-year-old gay male teens had diametrically opposing experiences after coming out at school. Steve was tormented continually and manifested phobias and isolation. Cantwell was accepted and loved, experiencing freedom to be.

STEVE'S COMING OUT: LONELINESS AND FEAR

Homophobic Abuse

Steve had come out to friends and family in ninth grade. From that moment on, he was taunted daily, continuing until the last day of 12th grade. He was heckled, kicked, sneered at, spit on, and punched constantly for being gay. He was called faggot and queer and pussy. Steve hated school and stayed home as much as he could. Bright as he was, his grades plummeted and he had no friends.

Terrified for his safety, he sought out new routes to travel to and from school to avoid a confrontation with his tormentors. Any episode would be traumatic. Often he would arrive at his house crying, hide in the closet sobbing, and wish he was dead.

Depression and Suicide Ideation

Steve became more and more isolated, not socializing with peers. Signs of anxiety increased as he would experience panic attacks when he left his house. Simply walking out of the door created a wave of terror so great he was immobilized. His desire to escape increased, expressing his hopelessness by leaving notes around the house. The following one terrified his parents:

"I don't fit in this world. I can't live in this world. I want to leave."

School became repugnant, grades dropped from As to Fs, and more and more Steve internalized his homophobic experiences. He would say, "I'm a freak. I don't fit in." Steve barely graduated high school. He felt hopelessness about life, isolated, and alone.

Getting Help

Deeply concerned about Steve's emotional and physical well-being, his parents encouraged him to seek professional help with Dr. Russell. There was an immediate connection that deepened through time as Steve struggled to release his traumatic teen years and accept himself as gay. His therapist underscored the message: "You are safe here."

Through time, he realized his deep philosophical nature, sensitivity to others, and creative talents were important attributes. One day, Steve shared his feelings about other kids his age. "They worry about clothes or grades, when there are big things to worry about like wars and the terrible stuff that goes on in the world."

His therapist explained, "You are not a freak. You are a compassionate human being. Pick one thing to fix in the world and work on it." He motivated Steve to begin participating in life, and he eventually found a job as an advocate for gay rights. After working together quite some time, Steve's anxiety, low self-esteem, and depression diminished.

One day Dr. Russell handed Steve a colorful gay rainbow flag and asked, "What do you need to write on there?" His response was, "I belong here."

He went back to his high school and planted the flag in the school rose garden. He told Dr. Russell that he finally felt at peace.

CANTWELL'S COMING OUT: SELF-GROWTH AND REJUVENATION

Support and Encouragement

The following is Cantwell's coming out speech at a school assembly. The assembly was sponsored by the GLBTQ Club to inform the student body on gender issues. His membership and support from this club offered him a forum to disclose his homosexuality to peers and faculty.

"Hello, my name is Cantwell. I'm in tenth grade, my favorite colors are red and orange, and I'm gay. It is easy for me to say it now and it is easy for me to tell all of you, but this was not always the case. It used to be something that I kept hidden deep inside of me in a small box without a key. It was something that I thought would never find its way to the surface, but this special part of me somehow made its way out into the light and I am so happy that it did. I thought I would open my speech with this quote that gives a short description of what coming out is like:

> Every gay person must come out. As difficult as it is, you must tell your immediate family, you must tell your relatives, you must tell your friends if indeed they are your friends, you must tell your neighbors, you must tell the people you work with, you must tell the people at the stores you shop in. And once they realize that we are indeed their children, that we are indeed everywhere—every myth, every lie, every innuendo will be destroyed once and for all. And once you do, you will feel so much better.
>
> (Harvey Milk, San Franciscan city supervisor)

This quote explains perfectly what I went through this past year, and what every gay person must go through. Coming out is not an easy process and it is not a fun one, but when you can finally call yourself 'gay,' you *will* feel so much better.

The History

"I have known that I am gay since around the sixth grade. This was when I first began to realize that I was sexually attracted to people of the same sex. Before this time, I had just thought that I preferred the company of guys. However, between the ages of about 8 and 11, I was very popular with the ladies and some might have considered me a ladies' man. In the third grade I even received a love letter from a girl in my class. At that age however, I don't think I even knew what homosexuality was, I mean, at that time I had lots of crushes on lots of different girls and I'm sure many of them have had crushes on me, but it was never anything more than that. I had grown up thinking that that was normal, so I just went along with the flow."

Keeping the Secret

"However, it wasn't until sixth grade rolled around that I realized that I was different from all of my other friends. Or at least, most of them. This was not something that I could easily understand and it was not something that I particularly wanted to. I hated being different and instead of accepting what I had become, and what I had been from the beginning, I decided to try and suppress it. I hid these feelings deep inside of me and I pretended that they did not exist. I went through all of middle school lying to myself and the people around me.

I hated lying to my friends but I just wasn't ready to let them in on my BIG SECRET. I didn't think that they would understand. Also, hearing words like gay and faggot used with negative connotations helped to convince me and reinforce my feelings that coming out was a bad idea. I knew on the inside that I was gay, but I had never told anyone on the outside and for a while that was how I thought I would live my entire life. With this giant secret inside me but trying to live a normal life in the world around me.

Luckily, I finally realized that was not the right road to go down. I saw that it was a miserable one filled with lies and deception and one that my heart would not be able to handle. There would be no happiness for me in that future. I came to the conclusion that there was only one thing for me to do; I had to come out of the closet. Saying that I would do it and actually doing it, however, turned out to be much more difficult than I had expected."

Disclosure

"After a long struggle I finally decided to tell my sister. She was the best candidate; I love her a lot, she has always been there for me, and she is absolutely the most accepting and open person I have ever known. So, on Tuesday, May 13, of the year 2002, I pulled together all of the courage that I could muster. I picked up the phone, dialed the number and my sister answered the phone in the most peppy and happy voice I had ever heard with, 'What's cookin' good lookin.'

I told her that I had something important to tell her and she kind of quieted down and waited for me to speak. I took a deep breath, and in the most serious voice that I could, I said, 'Alie, I'm gay.' She was surprised but she was also grateful that I told her. She was glad that I felt that I could trust her enough with that very personal information."

Inner Chaos—I've Come Out

"My description of these events does not sound too eventful or difficult to an outside observer, but on the inside I was in utter chaos. This was absolutely the most emotional thing that I have ever done. And after I told her my big secret I cried. It was all that I could do. I just cried and cried. I was so relieved and happy and full of joy. The biggest burden had just been lifted from my shoulders and I felt as light as air. This was the first time I had ever said 'I'm gay' out loud. I had said it many times in my head, but never out into the world for everyone else to hear. Just forming the words with my lips and speaking them made the whole thing real.

Before it had been a thought that I kept to myself, but at this point, it had finally been made into a reality. At that point it finally hit me that, 'Yes, I am gay.' There are not words to describe what a wonderful experience it was. It was the greatest thing that I've ever done, it was the hardest thing that I've ever done, it was the most satisfying thing that I've ever done, and it was the most trying experience of my life. However, even though I felt so great after this accomplishment, I still had miles to go before I could really call myself 'out.'"

My Parents

"The next step was telling my family and friends. This also turned out to be much harder than I had expected. Even with the experience of telling my sister, it was almost just as difficult as it had been the first time. I stayed up at night, staring at the ceiling, telling myself that tomorrow would be the day. Tomorrow I will tell my parents that I'm gay, tomorrow I will tell my friends that I'm gay. I kept setting it off for another day, until finally the right day came.

This perfect day that I had been struggling so hard to find came a few days before the beginning of my sophomore year. I called my parents downstairs, and told them that I had something important to tell them. They seemed to know what was coming, and after I told them my big news, they were not as surprised as I thought.

One sign of great parents is when they know things about you that you sometimes don't even know about yourself. I seemed to be the one who came out of that conversation the most surprised. Many people have asked me why I even bothered to tell my parents at all, but I personally feel that they deserve to know the person that I have become. And once again, a heavy burden was lifted from my shoulder, but this time I was stronger and more able to contain my overwhelming joy."

Support at School

"However, there was still one more group of people who deserve to know that I am gay. These people are my friends. Lying to them was the hardest of all and I was getting extremely tired of trying to keep the 'real me' a secret. Literally and figuratively, I was staying up late trying to figure out what to do and my mind was in a constant battle with itself. I wanted to tell them, but at the same time I was completely terrified. I was afraid that things would be different after I told them and I didn't want things to be different. I thought that things would be strange and I thought that my friends would become uneasy around me. All I could think of was the worst-case scenario.

I decided to start at the Gay–Straight Alliance. I joined because I knew that it was full of the most accepting people this school had to offer. I even felt so comfortable around them that I was somehow able to tell everyone in the club in our very first meeting that I am gay. We were going around the circle and all saying something about ourselves and as it got closer and closer to me I began to shake and my mouth went dry. I was amazed that words were even able to come out of my mouth. However, words did form and I was able to tell all of them. Nothing changed except that I got a few hugs from some very attractive girls who I had never really talked to before. After that I looked forward to our weekly meetings because it was the only place in school where I could be honest about who I am. However, I wanted to be able to feel this way in every part of the school, and I knew that could only happen after I told the rest of my friends."

Telling Friends

"So that's what I started to do. The very first person that I told was Ariel. She has always been a great friend and she was just as accepting as I knew she would be. I told her on *National Coming Out Day*. I figured that was a very appropriate time.

The rest of my friends ended up being exactly the same way. Not one of them treated me differently, not one of them stopped liking me and not one of them made me feel uneasy. I somehow ended up with the most amazing group of friends that the world had to offer. They were all supportive and loving and they made this process of coming out that much easier. Even though I might have been able to do it without them, they made the road as smooth as they possibly could and I just wanted to say thank you to all of them."

Join Me

"I am now finally able to call myself 'out' and it feels great. I feel more open and honest and I don't think I've ever felt better. However, before I leave this stage, there is something very important that I need to say and it is directed towards the people who are not as lucky as I and who are not yet able to call themselves 'out.' Don't . . . be . . . afraid. This school is one of the most accepting environments in the entire world. Your friends will not desert you and your life will not end. You will be happier than you ever thought possible and you will no longer have to lie to the ones you love.

It feels great out here and I would love for you to join me."

Caldwell received a standing ovation from classmates, teachers, and staff. His experience optimizes the huge contribution an accepting and supportive school environment played in his coming out process.

 # Okay to Be Lesbian, Gay, Bisexual, and Transgender

The pain, suffering, myths, and labeling around our LGBT youth remain locked in the hands of today's society. Parents, teachers, doctors, therapists, educators, and politicians must speak out to the facts as they are now known to exist.

The lack of understanding gay youth grow up with coupled with many of society's messages of being weird, sick, or repulsive is a mirror few of us could look through and live with in a meaningful way. Creating an open and supportive environment for "coming out" can be a key issue for successful integration and a paramount intervention for nurturing mental health.

There is and will be a significant percentage of our youth that will be gay, lesbian, bisexual and transgender. This is an irrefutable fact. It is important to establish a new framework for life for LGBT individuals devoid of virulent homophobia but instead filled with normalcy and freedom to be.

What Can We Do?

By providing safe havens for expression and protection from harassment, we allow LGBT youth to process life issues. In this way, their learning and emotional, social, physical, intellectual, and spiritual growth can be enhanced.

We can facilitate the adolescents' *coming out* and support their *being out* by:

1. Seeing the teens in the "now" and seeing at-risk behaviors as a "cry for help."

2. Becoming their friend, support, or guide to walk them through coming out and being out.

3. Creating a safe environment to express feelings and thoughts without harassment.

4. Helping young people identify sexual orientation and gender identity, recognize their individual process, and disclose stored and secret perceptions.

This is the Human Rights Campaign Foundations Publication Resource Guide to COMING OUT for African Americans. *It is a helpful example of available material.*

Permission by the Human Rights Campaign

5. Protecting them through advocacy and education.

6. Providing resources for coming out, mentorship, and role modeling.

It is essential that we manifest into actuality a paradigm of *"coming in"* or being integrated into mainstream society after disclosure of being gay. Young people need to be understood for who they are and accepted without bias.

The more we reinforce acceptance of LGBT youth the more we establish ground-work for their *coming out* to encourage well-being, health, and self-acceptance. Our task is to reframe cultural attitudes and harmful judgments into a framework of majority agreement that "children can be both gay and OK" (Bernstein, 2003).

Photograph by Kyna Shilling

PART II

Interventions With LGBT Young People: Supporting a Healthy Outlook

C H A P T E R   4

Counseling Youth on LGBT Issues: Toward Self-Acceptance

Photograph by Kyna Shilling

ESTABLISHING COUNSELING GOALS • SELF-EMPOWERMENT
TEEN NATURE • AT-RISK YOUTH • GRIEF AND LOSS
SELF-IDENTITY • RELIGIOUS CONFLICTS • HOMOPHOBIA
SHAME AND STIGMA • ADVOCACY • PEER SUPPORT
THERAPY CHOICE • INTERNET
SEXUALLY TRANSMITTED DISEASE • RESILIENCE

"Love is letting go of fear."

Gerald Jampolsky

Health professionals are recognizing the special challenges for our gay youth in today's world. Statistics indicate a significant number of LGBT young people struggling to achieve acceptance and to understand, process, and embrace the difficulties of their sexual orientation. Straight children of LGBT parents also may find acceptance difficult. Counseling can provide beneficial support. It is critical that the counselor is knowledgeable regarding LGBT issues.

Awareness is essential by therapists, counselors, social workers, physicians, educators and clergy of this population's constant bombardment with prejudice, fear, undermining, and ridicule. Our greatest challenge is to instill self-love through support, encouragement, education, advocacy, mentorship, and nonjudgment.

Distinguishing and separating societal homophobic and stereotypical constraints from the young person's own self-worth and identity is an integral piece of the counseling process.

Goals of Working with LGBT Youth

GOAL 1

To recognize that this is a societal problem. It is imposed as a prison of bigotry on too many of our youth. This is manifested by the injustice of not seeing these young people or their families as human beings who must be respected for their ability to love in their own way.

GOAL 2

To help LGBT youth process their myriad of feelings with the recognition of their gender identity or sexual orientation. By creating methods that provide a safe passage for them to come out, they can share themselves in the most protected way.

GOAL 3

To create safe homes, schools, and communities. This offers the LGBT youth all the rights, privileges, and respect deemed worthy to any other young person their age.

Another goal for emotional well-being is to establish accurate representations of gay youth and their life. Helping young people understand and identify clear differences and similarities between themselves and their heterosexual peers will broaden their insight that these comparisons present challenges to be faced and integrated.

 # The Nature of Adolescence

Adolescence is life between childhood and adulthood. It starts with the physical beginnings of sexual maturity and ends with the social achievement of independent adult status.

(Myers, 2005, p. 124)

Adolescence is usually a time when peer group support and approval is imperative. Johnson and Johnson (2000, p. 620) defines *adolescence* as a period of time that includes puberty (ages 10–14), teen years (ages 13–19), and time of leaving parental home (usually 18–21). Life seems to be in a state of constant change and turmoil, and feelings of separation from parents may increase. Beginning with puberty, young teens experience physical signs of maturing, with a growth spurt and the appearance of primary and secondary sex characteristics as well as an increased awareness and interest in sexuality.

Promoting Self-Empowerment

An important goal in increasing self-advocacy for gay youth is the promotion of empowerment through the application of socially empowering strategies. Savage, Harley, and Nowak (2005) present the following six interlocking assumptions useful in developing the affirmation of LGBT young people:

1. Being a gay male or lesbian is not a pathological condition.
2. The origin of sexual orientation is not completely known.
3. Gay and lesbian individuals lead fulfilling and satisfying lives.
4. There are a variety of ways to live an LGBT life.
5. LGBT individuals come to counseling with no desire to change their sexual orientation and should not be coerced into doing so.
6. Counseling that is affirmative of lesbians and gay males should be available. (Savage et al., citing Schwartz & Harstein, 2005, p. 135)

Often, cognitive development is marked by a new level of social awareness and moral judgment, as adolescents think a lot about what others think of them, especially peers. The highs and lows of relationships become all important, and can cause great pleasure or stress. Impulsivity and egocentricity are common characteristics of this age.

Mary, age 15, became totally devastated after the breakup of a lesbian relationship, coupled with age-appropriate thinking of "no one can understand what I am going through." Teens internalize misunderstood feelings, thinking adults, mostly parents, can't ever imagine their experience. Teens can focus on an ideal and criticism of society, parents, and even themselves can emerge. Eric Erikson (1963) explains the adolescents' task socially as being to "synthesize past, present, and future possibilities into a clearer sense of self" (cited in Myers, 2005, p. 128). They may wonder:

"Who am I?"

"What will I be?"

"What are my values and beliefs?"

Photograph by Kyna Shilling

Forming this identity becomes the work of the adolescent. They experiment in social, school, and home settings to see which piece of them feels right and true at the time. This can change enormously from day to day, causing unexpected friction. Erikson further relays the adolescent's developing need for intimacy or formation of emotionally close relationships. These close relationships usually diminish on intensity with parents and become all important with peers. Larson (2001) explains that teens in the United States compared with other countries spend "more time watching TV and hanging out with friends and less time on school work" (cited by Myers, 2005, p. 131). Although the parental relationship may become less active or more subtle, teenagers need to know their parents are there for them.

For those excluded or ostracized, it can be extremely painful and isolating. "The social atmosphere in most high schools is poisonously clique driven and exclusionary," says social psychologist Elliot Aronson, 2001 (cited by Myers, 2005, p. 131). Many students suffer in silence. Often, silent rage is projected inwardly as depression or suicide ideation or outwardly as hostility and violence. Rejected adolescents can become withdrawn and vulnerable, developing low self-esteem and diminished hope for the future.

 # Adolescent Developmental Tasks

1. Accepting one's body as it is and creating more mature relationships with peers
2. Seeking to become responsible members of society and achieving their evolving values
3. Preparing for a future of economic success, marriage, and family life

These developmental tasks become more complex for the LGBT youth. They experience the challenges commonly associated with adolescence development. Additional complexities arise from exposure to stereotyping and rejection. Hidden agendas, gender orientation, and gender identity conflicts often create larger problematic concerns in counseling that must be recognized, overcome, and integrated into a healthy life outlook.

Additional Challenges Facing LGBT Youth

Understanding the basic nature of adolescence is inherent in understanding the challenges faced by our LGBT youth. Teenage years are a time when peer support is paramount. *Sexual harassment and homophobic slurs* may hinder evolving self-identity. Acceptance of one's body is an important developmental task for young people. This becomes increasingly difficult for the homosexual youth as he or she *struggles with sexual orientation* in the midst of societal constraints.

Alice told her lesbian daughter Lynn about a slur she overheard. "Dykes are so odd. There is something wrong with them." Alice was appalled. Her daughter Lynn responded,

"Mom, I live with that every
  day of my life."

Photograph by Kyna Shilling

Living with secrecy involving sexual orientation causes many young people to hide pieces of themselves, creating self-consciousness and lack of self-acceptance. Coming out sometimes leaves the LGBT teen more bewildered. He or she *struggles to fit into a new world* that appears so heterosexual with few guideposts to help create a homosexual community as well. Adolescents seek meaningful relationships in terms of friendships and romantic involvement. For the homosexual teen, these relationships become all important. Discomfort and stress can be associated with and surrounding these bonds.

Lisa Diamond, a Utah psychologist (Elias, 2007) explains that LGBT youth worry that they will never be able to find the kind of romantic partner they want, and she emphasizes that gay and lesbian teens *worry more* than their straight counterparts because best friends are often the same sex. They may *agonize about turning a friendship into a romance* because of the risk of losing a needed friendship.

Anxiety and depression can be linked to this huge focus on finding a partner.

Martin and Alexander had a long-term gay relationship, based mostly on friendship. They met on vacation abroad and, after a short and meaningful time together, college studies and locality separated their being together. A second meeting was arranged almost a year later. Martin flew across the country and again several days of enjoying each other prevailed. However, the decision of friendship or romance plagued both young men, with the ultimate decision expressed by Alexander.

"We decided to remain friends. That is the most important thing—that we be friends."

Photograph by Kyna Shilling

LGBT youth are more similar to heterosexual peers than people imagine. Many are conventional, seeking the same goals most young people seek, that is, long-term meaningful relationships, home, family, and children. Yet, barriers to achieving these aspirations remain apparent.

The adolescent task of preparing for a future of meaningful relationships, marriage and family may be more difficult for the homosexual youth as a result of *constraining gender roles and unstable legalities.* Acceptance of LGBT partnership, marriage equality, and a life without prejudice is limited. Although creative alternatives are being developed, the establishment of these patterns remains challenging and varies greatly. (See chapter 8.)

Are LGBT Young People
at Greater Risk?

While there is a lot of controversy regarding hard statistical data, the following give a sense of the magnitude of these issues.

- Gay, lesbian, and bisexual youth may comprise 1,500 of the 5,000 youth suicides each year. (McFarland, 1998, p. 26)
- Gay adolescents are nearly seven times more likely to have been threatened or injured with a weapon at school.
- LGBT teens are twice as likely to use alcohol, tobacco, marijuana, and inhalants.
- LGBT adolescents are 10 times more likely to have used cocaine.

(Vermont Youth Risk Behavior Survey 1995,
http://www.outproud.org/article_vyrbs.html)

A by-product of societal judgment, inability to visualize a comfortable future, and much more likelihood of rejection from family and peers can lead some LGBT youth into depression and suicide ideation. They also may exhibit a greater degree of dangerous behaviors than their straight peers, or be subjected to more harassment because of their sexual orientation or gender identity. Gay young people can become a part of a *high-risk subgroup*. It is therefore important to recognize the following signs of *any* at-risk young person when working with the LGBT population.

SIGNS OF AT-RISK YOUTH

- Wishing they were dead
- Use of drugs and alcohol
- Sudden drop in grades
- Risk-taking behaviors
- Truancy

- Hurting themselves or others
- Becoming socially isolated
- Promiscuity
- Giving possessions away
- Feeling life isn't worth living
- Expressing self-hatred
- Discussing their funeral

Photograph by Kyna Shilling

When working with LGBT teenagers and young adults, information needs to be presented on viable alternatives to future ways of life as well as existing support groups and resources. A keen understanding must develop of the importance of separating societal stereotyping from sexual orientation and gender identity. Focus must be placed on peer, school, and family support and, when possible, active advocacy and positive role models.

Suicide Ideation in LGBT Youth

"According to research conducted in the past two decades, sexual minority youth (gay, lesbian, and bisexual) exhibit more suicidal ideation than do their heterosexual peers."

(Rutter & Soucar, 2002, p. 290)

"Being a gay [LGBT] adolescent is a significant risk factor for suicidal thoughts and attempts. More than 15 different studies conducted within the last 20 years have shown consistently significantly higher rates of suicide attempts, in the range of 20–40% among gay [LGBT] adolescents. In a study involving over 6,000 adolescent girls and over 5,000 adolescent boys, they concluded adolescents with a same-sex orientation were more than twice as likely to attempt suicide" (Kitts, 2005, p. 624). Rutter and Soucar (2002) estimated rates of suicidal ideation for gay young people range from 50% to 70%.

Although research findings vary greatly, and studies are devised in a variety of ways, several reports indicate LGBT youth may be more at risk for depression and suicide ideation. A discussion of the special factors regarding these teens is essential. Therapists, educators, parents, physicians, clergy, and all other caring adults must take a discerning look at causes of this depression in nonheterosexual adolescents.

RISK FACTORS FOR LGBT YOUTH

Many young LGBT adolescents can be at risk for rejection and depression. They may seek mental health agencies and shelters with the purpose of finding counseling and community support as a means to counteract external negativity from peers, family, and society. Often, young girls and boys search for guidance in exploring low self-esteem and isolation that may arise from overt and covert variables impacting their life. Some feel that they have few places to turn. The following are risk factors for suicidal feelings and actions in nonheterosexual youth.

Psychological distress associated with being homosexual

Although *straight* teens may experience some of the following stressors, they become more apparent with homosexual adolescents.

- Gender nonconformity
- Lack of support
- School dropout
- Family problems
- Victimization
- Homelessness
- Substance abuse
- Suicide attempts

Photograph by Kyna Shilling

Understanding the depth of their psychosocial stress load and its impact on suicide risk can be paramount in helping to improve the LGBT adolescent's quality of life.

"Gay and lesbian youth often turn to unsafe activities such as alcohol and drug use or high-risk sexual behaviors to cope with their sexual orientation. These high-risk behaviors place these young individuals at greater risk for addiction, unintended pregnancy, sexually transmitted diseases, including HIV/AIDS" (Lindley & Reininger, 2001, p. 17). Kitts (2005) lists other significant issues faced by LGBT teens (p. 626):

1. Being a gay male has been recognized as a risk factor for eating disorders and body image disturbances.

2. At a time when heterosexual adolescents are dating and talking about boyfriends and girlfriends, a LGBT adolescent may not know a single homosexual individual or community center or have access to the Internet for communication.

3. Negative sexual experiences can result. Some adults use the Internet to take advantage of LGBT adolescents. Bars may be the only places that teenagers can interact with other LGBT people and this can be just as dangerous.

4. Cultural and religious intolerance toward homosexuality can compound stigmatization for an LGBT adolescent.

Keeping the secret of being homosexual

"One study involving 350 gay adolescents between the ages of 14 and 21 reported that 54% made their first suicide attempt before coming out to others, 27% made the attempt during the same year they came out, and 19% made the attempt after coming out" (citing by Kitts, 2005, D'Augelli et al., 2001, p. 624).

Kitts (2005) maintains that "Important issues such as suicide among gay [LGBT] adolescents remain invisible not only to mainstream psychology, but to mainstream healthcare" (p. 623). The medical profession needs to become aware that being an LGBT youth may be a factor for suicide ideation. Physicians raising this issue in case conferences and lectures can educate and deepen understanding of why it may be so unbearable for many to reveal their sexuality or live with being homosexual.

Lack of family support

LGBT youth have a much greater incidence of being thrown out or opting to leave their homes than their straight peers. Goldfried, 2001, reported that " 1 out of 3 was verbally abused by family members; 1 out of 10 was physically assaulted by a family member" (citing by Kitts, 2005, p. 625). The fear of potentially experiencing this rejection and abuse is a tremendous stressor. The following statistics from Lindley and Reininger (2001, p. 17) indicate the huge segment of LGBT adolescents impacted by family abuse and violence.

- 20% of gay and lesbian youth reported being verbally abused by their mothers due to their sexual orientation, 14% reported verbal abuse by their fathers.

- Among violent incidents reported against gay and lesbian youth, 46% involved family members.

- Another 26% of gay and lesbian youth are forced to leave home after disclosing their sexual orientation to their families.

- Gay and lesbian youth constitute between 20 and 40% of all homeless youth.

Because they can be rejected, humiliated, victimized, and abandoned by their own families, too many gay adolescents cannot help but feel marginalized. They have a much greater incidence of being thrown out or leaving their homes than their heterosexual counterparts. It is hard to imagine how an LGBT teen feels when parents vehemently reject *marriage equality*. "Only 10 to 14% of gay [LGBT] adolescents who had not come out to their parents predicted parental acceptance (Kitts citing D'Augelli, 2005, pp. 625–626) and gay [LGBT] adolescents who report a history of a suicide attempt score significantly lower on scales of family support, self-perception and self-esteem" (Kitts citing Nelson, 2005, p. 626).

Support structures can be strengthened by physicians, clergy, educators, and mental health professionals offering information on resources such as PFLAG (Parents, Family and Friends of Lesbians and Gays), Lesbian and Gay Child and Adolescent Psychiatric Association, Association of Gay and Lesbian Psychiatrists, and the Gay and Lesbian Medical Association.

Discrimination and victimization of homosexual youth

Ploderl and Fartacek (2005, p. 661) indicate a higher incidence for most suicide-related risk factors with increased psychosocial stress and vulnerability, and lack of family support. LGBT youth who decide to come out risk rejection and abuse from parents, friends, family members, and society at large. Goldfried (2001) states that "one out of four LGBT students had experienced physical abuse at school" (cited by Kitts, 2005, p. 625). "Research has demonstrated that adolescents struggling with issues surrounding their sexual orientation who do not receive appropriate health care services, accurate information, or support from family, school, and community, are in jeopardy of serious emotional, social, and physical difficulties" (Lindley and Reininger, 2001, p. 17).

Carlos came to school every day in terror. Sixteen years old and Latino, he knew his peers saw him as gay, although he was too petrified to openly disclose his sexual orientation. "Faggot, queer, and sinner" were his daily taunts. The lavatories, the halls, the path to school were dangerous zones. Anything could happen, and too many times it did. Carlos was punched, shoved, spit at, and thrown into a dumpster without consequence to his tormentors by the educators in charge. On his 17th birthday, Carlos died of suicide. He left a note for his mom and dad with just a few lines.

"I love you. I can't take it anymore."

Without an ally and appropriate measures for sexual harassment, he could find no safe place and no help.

Photograph by Kyna Shilling

Suggestions for eliminating this discrimination and victimization within the school are offered by the youth themselves. Lindley and Reininger (2001) explain when homosexual students were asked what could be done, they responded schools need to offer support groups for gay and lesbian students, boundaries to not allow homophobic "put downs," consequences for students who constantly harass LGBT peers, and teachers and other school personnel addressing and treating the topic of homosexuality with more respect. Lindley and Reininger (2001, p. 22) recommend from their research findings the following interventions in the schools to aid LGBT youth.

 # Research Recommendations: Interventions in Schools for LGBT Students

- Extensive efforts are made to educate the public school staff and legislators about the importance of providing instruction about homosexuality in the public schools.

- These populations must be educated about the health needs and concerns of LGBT youth.

- Accurate information regarding the heath risks and behaviors of gay and lesbian youth can be collected.

- Questions regarding sexual orientation and sexual identity and/or same-sex sexual behaviors . . . must be added to (South Carolina's) Youth Risk Behavior Survey instrument. Such information would be invaluable in providing direction regarding the best ways to meet the health needs of gay and lesbian students in the state.

- Health teachers . . . must be trained in the best methods to educate students about the topic of homosexuality, especially within the current confines of STD/HIV instruction.

- Teachers must be provided with specific examples of activities they can use in the classroom, as well as opportunities to build their comfort level in answering questions about this topic.

- Community groups must begin (or continue) to address the health needs of gay and lesbian youths. These young people must have access to safe and supportive environments in which they can openly discuss their sexuality, personal experiences, and health concerns.

Adolescents can be affected by discrimination without being directly victimized. One example of homophobic brutality was the murder of Matthew Shepard, a Wyoming student, because he was gay. The shock of this devastating event on LGBT young people can be great. Many of them are beginning to consciously realize they are gay, lesbian, bisexual, or transgender and are living in a society where a segment may condone or even applaud this horrendous act. The messages many protestors, politicians, and religious leaders send to LGBT adolescents against marriage equality can have a profoundly painful impact. Self-esteem or healthy identity development can suffer living in a culture where youth can be rejected, judged, and hated because of their sexuality.

Childhood atypical gender behavior

"Gender-atypical behavior provokes parents' concern that the youth might be lesbian or gay, and some parents react with efforts to diminish or suppress these behaviors to thwart homosexuality, especially in men" (D'Augelli et al., 2005, p. 658)." Landolt et al. (2004) maintain factors in childhood including gender nonconformity and rejection by parents and peers are correlated with a gay orientation in males.

Their research indicates "gender nonconformity was significantly associated with paternal, maternal, and peer rejection in childhood. Findings highlight the role of gender nonconformity in contributing to childhood rejection and the importance of peer relationships in the socialization of gay men" (Landolt et al., 2004, p. 117).

Parental acceptance and approval is important to adolescents. Living a childhood of overt or covert parental disapproval as LGBT youth can manifest in strong emotions of depression, rejection, isolation, and suicide ideation. These feelings are often compounded by peer rejection for atypical gender behavior, leaving the gay or lesbian youth feeling like they have nowhere to turn. Coupled with societal bias and mental, verbal, or physical abuse, mental health problems easily surface and fester.

Katz (1986) explains:

- "Feminine behavior in young males is considerably less normative than masculine behavior in females . . .
- [it] is more negatively sanctioned" (D'Augelli et al., 2005, p. 658).

Sam was 12 when he realized he made gestures other people appeared to find very offensive and feminine. His Mom turned away in conversation when a movement seemed to disgust her. His dad acted embarrassed by these gestures, constantly challenging Sam by saying, "Can't you stop doing that?" His brother chided him often, "Why are you sitting like that? You look like a girl." Sam began to work at changing this.

"I spent a lot of time trying to hide my gestures. They seemed natural to me, but it felt like it made everyone else feel uncomfortable.

It takes so much energy to hide them."

By age 14, Sam was depressed. His grades dropped. Often, he didn't go to school. He told his friends he hated life. He began giving his things away.

Photograph by Kyna Shilling

Stressors such as gender atypical behaviors emerging in childhood are unique burdens creating factors leading to depression and suicide ideation. D'Augelli's research (2005, p. 657) found "more parental discouragement of childhood gender atypical behavior and more lifetime gay-related verbal abuse were characteristic of attempters." D'Augelli explains many had been called "sissy" or "tomboy" by parents. He found those youth who had a higher likelihood of suicide attempts had experienced more verbal abuse by parents, were seen as having more gender-atypical behaviors by parents, and had parents who made efforts to change gender-atypical behaviors.

In conclusion, Landolt et al. (2004) present the following research findings:

- A link between both gender nonconformity and childhood parental and peer relationship quality to attachment as gay male adults.
- Childhood gender nonconformity predictive of parental and peer rejection.
- Parental and peer rejection predictive of attachment-related anxiety and avoidance in adults.
- Intervention efforts must be geared toward changing attitudes toward gender nonconforming behavior reducing rejection often associated with that behavior shifting the developmental pathway toward greater attachment security as an adult. (Landolt et al., 2004, p. 126)

Cultural diversity along with being lesbian, gay, bisexual, or transgender

Rutter and Soucar (2002, p. 290) report the following research findings:

"For racial minorities who are also gay or lesbian, rates of suicidal activity are suspected to be even higher [than their heterosexual counterparts]."

"[This] may reflect prejudice toward both sexual orientation and race. Several researchers suggest that bisexual and questioning youth may be at higher risk for suicidal behavior than self-identified homosexual youth."

Photograph by Kyna Shilling

 # Working With LGBT Diverse Cultures

Therapists and counselors working with culturally diverse groups, including African-American, Native American, and Asian LGBT clients, need to be cognizant of both gender role identity and racial identity issues, and the impact they have on one another. A client facing economic or relational difficulties may well benefit by exploring the situation in relation to the interaction of their gender role identity and racial identity as factors impacting life circumstances. Normalizing family life and creating openness in family portrayal is a key element to openness for parents and children of LGBT youth.

AFRICAN AMERICANS

Research by Wester, Vogel, Wei, and McLain (2006) highlights the plight of the African-American gay male. Their conclusions indicate research is limited on the interaction of male *gender role conflict* (GRC), racial identity, and psychological distress. However, their study explored aspects of racial identity and the relationship between GRC and psychological distress. Results demonstrated that racial identity attitudes often reflected internalized racism or self-hatred. This internalization was amplified by the relationship between gender role conflict (GRC) and psychological distress.

Men of color are often overlooked in current literature in terms of cultural background influencing the experience of male gender role within society. Wester et al. (2006) suggest that the connection of race and gender may cause minority men to be particularly vulnerable to gender role identity distress.

Pressures experienced by men to live up to their prescribed gender role can lead to a myriad of negative psychological outcomes. African-American men's GRC scores predicted psychological distress.

Wester et al. cite Lazur and Majors (2006), and present data on the impact of male gender roles for African-American men as more complex because "to be a man of color means confrontation between ethnic identity and [gender role] demands from the popular culture" (p. 419). For some African-American men, racial identity practically created the effects of GRC on psychological distress and the adoption of exaggerated forms of Euro-American masculinity, often producing negative outcomes. "Research indicates men who internalized a racist understanding of themselves as men of color suffered more from their attempts to navigate the male gender role than did men who internalize a racial identity based on an appreciation of their own African American heritage" (Wester et al., 2006, pp. 425–426).

© Gigi Kaeser from the exhibit and book, *Love Makes a Family: Portraits of Lesbian, Gay, Bisexual and Transgender Parents and Their Families.* 1999.

Savin-Williams (2005) states that research supports "Levels of self-acceptance and 'outness' among African American young men are reflected in whether they are in a same-sex romantic relationship with a white or a black man. If they are dating a white man, their primary allegiance tends to be with the gay rather then the black community, and as a result they experience less family and ethnic community support. If they are dating a black man, they tend to feel alienated from the gay community, but more connected to their ethnic heritage. An underground culture exists among contemporary African American young men who maintain strict hyper-masculine behavior, heterosexual identity, and same-sex behavior fearing they will 'let down the whole black community'" (pp. 77–78).

The book *Love Makes a Family* (1999), edited by Peggie Gillespie, presents photographs and stories that allow the reader to come face-to-face with LGBT people. In a very positive and visible way, this resource portrays the loving and caring of these families exemplified by the Elsasser/Robinson family. Michael Elsasser explains, "When people see Doug and me, some of them say, 'Oh look, there's a gay couple, and I have problems with gay couples.' Others say, 'Oh, there's an interracial couple and I have problems with interracial relationships.' We strike up a lot of interest as a family because we tap into other people's fears and prejudices just by our existence" (p. 84).

> *I always draw parallels between my experience growing up in the fifties and sixties as an African American and being gay in America in the nineties. The most important thing is for every gay person in this country to come out. Straight people would be really shocked to see how many of us there are, and where we are. We are their neighbors.*

> (Doug Robinson, in *Love Makes A Family,* 1999, p. 83)

NATIVE AMERICANS

Modern Native American tribes often have complex relationships with homosexuality. Brian Gilley, author of *Becoming Two-Spirit: Gay Acceptance in Indian Country,* explains that the term for Two-Spirit people is different in each tribal language, but the practices and traditional social positions are usually consistent. Gilley (LeLand, 2006, pp. 1, 6) explains, "in tribal tradition when children exhibited interest in activities not associated with their gender—for boys, typically cooking or sewing: for girls, hunting or combat—they were singled out as inhabited by dual spirits." Some tribes considered these young people spiritually gifted, often being chosen for their presumed powers, usefulness in raising children, or to accompany war parties as surrogate wives. Gilley added, "It was never about sexuality. It was about your role in the community."

The ninth annual Montana "Two-Spirit Gathering" (2006) was held as a weekend retreat for American Indians who define themselves as embodying both male and female spirits. Many were ostracized gay and lesbian young people who found an accepting identify as gay or lesbian, a third or fourth gender, or combining male and female aspects. Steven Barrios is a Native American open about his sexual orientation since adolescence. "A lot of our tribal leaders have their minds blocked and don't even know the history of Two-Spirit people," Barrios explains (Leland, 2006, pp. 1, 6), and cites anthological evidence suggesting before Christian missionaries arrived many tribes considered Two-Spirit people to be spiritually gifted and socially valuable.

Mr. Bane, an attendee of the gathering, told his story. After disclosing to his parents he was gay, his sense of rejection was so great he left home and school. Bane lived on the street selling his body, using heroin, and having little connection to his Indian heritage. "When I went to the gathering there was a sense of acceptance I had never felt before. The mistakes I made in my past didn't matter. What mattered was I came home. It goes beyond sexuality to a cultural role. That was important to me" (Leland, 2006, pp. 1, 6).

In *Love Makes a Family* (1999), The Burning Cloud/Sisson Native American family is featured. Consuelo's son Falcon, an eighth grader, explains the following about his experience of having a Native American lesbian mom (p. 49).

"When my mom told me she was gay, I didn't really mind. I thought that it was her decision, not mine. I can't change it, so I was happy for her. She was still my mother!"

"Everyone on the reservation knows that my mom is gay. Other kids here used to call me names. Sticks and stones may break your bones, but words do hurt."

"Prejudice exists because people are scared of what they don't know. People don't really sit down and talk with gay people and consider them as individuals."

"If someone asked me what it's like to have a lesbian mom, I'd say, "It's fun. I get to talk to her about girls!"

© Gigi Kaeser from the exhibit and book, *Love Makes a Family: Portraits of Lesbian, Gay, Bisexual and Transgender Parents and Their Families.* 1999.

> *I kept looking for my Two-Spirit sisters and brothers, which is our name for gay and lesbian people. . . . If our people would read their history, they would know that Two-Spirit people have been here since the beginning of time.*
>
> (Consuelo Burning Cloud, in *Love Makes a Family,* 1999, p. 45)

LATINO AMERICANS

In many Latino Communities, machismo and Catholicism contribute to homophobic attitudes that hamper efforts to reach Latino gay and bisexual youth with HIV prevention information.

U.S. Conference of Mayors,
HIV Prevention Programs Targeting Gay/Bisexual Men of Color, 1996

The Lavandier family is featured in the book *Love Makes a Family* (1999). Miriam Lavandier is an English professor, activist, and poet. She explains the hardships endured in her Latino community as a lesbian mom. "In the Hispanic community, there's a lot of verbal and physical violence against gays and lesbians. People are thrown out of their families. Most Hispanics are Catholic, and they are raised to think that gay people are very bad in every sense. That's why there's rampant homophobia in the Hispanic Community. Rampant. The priests are constantly saying bad things about us. They say, 'Keep away from those people. They're bad. They're sinners. They're damned, and they're all going to hell.' And people do listen to what the priests say" (p. 171).

Pedro Romero, in his journal article "Impact of Racism, Homophobia and Poverty on Suicidal Ideation among Latino Gay Men" (1999), explains his data analysis of

Latino gay men's tendency for high-risk HIV sexual behavior and suicidal ideation. His findings suggest "that experiences of racism, poverty and homophobia are strongly related to Latino gay men's suicidal ideation." Romero's review of the literature indicates Latino gay men not only experience homophobia but also other risk factors of homophobia as well as sexual abuse, family rejection, and alcoholism.

Romero stresses Latino gay men also struggle against their *double jeopardy* status because they are members of both ethnic and sexual minority groups.

Romero (1999) reports one-fifth of gay bisexual Latino men in his study have had suicidal thoughts at least once within a six-month period. His findings indicate a high prevalence of racism, poverty, homophobia, and suicide among Latino gay men, demonstrating these are important

Photograph by Kyna Shilling

factors to address clinically and preventively in counseling programs. He advocates programs implementing guidelines addressing sexual orientation, racism, and poverty in the Latino community. Romero stresses the physical and verbal abuse Latino gay men experience in schools growing up may be a factor in suicide ideation, and emphasizes the need for suicide awareness programs on the school, family, and community level, with a special emphasis on Latino gay, bisexual, and lesbian youth.

> *Most of the students in the college where I teach are Hispanic. After they get to know me, and they see I'm a wholesome, normal human being, I come out to them. Then they say, "Oh wow. How could that be? It's impossible. It's true. I have a girlfriend, and I have my children and a very good, healthy family." That's my way of fighting homophobia in my community. My students also say, "You look like a normal person." I tell them, "Lesbians are normal people. The one and only difference is that we love women instead of men."*
>
> (Miriam Lavandier, in *Love Makes a Family,* 1999, p. 169)

ASIAN AMERICANS

Twenty-one-year-old Kim Lee responded to the LGBT Youth Questionnaire (chapter 5) with an important emphasis on her cultural background as an inhibiting factor in disclosing her sexual orientation as lesbian to her parents. In the following response, Kim relays the impact of traditional values on parental acceptance or rejection, and the anxiety and fear of abandonment because of implied cultural conceptions.

Question: If you haven't come out to your parents, why not?

"I came out to friends and teachers my senior year of high school. I have just recently come out to my 19-year-old brother a few months ago. I am not out to my parents. It's a long story. I was very close to my parents when I was young. They are the most loving and devoted parents anyone could have. I have no doubt about that.

They grew up very poor in China and we immigrated to the U.S. when I was a toddler.

They tried to raise me very traditionally.

They preferred I have other Chinese friends and be the typical good Chinese daughter (I'm sure you can assume the gist of what that is).

Of course I rebelled in my own way like all kids do. I resented my parents for not being like my American friends' parents. I always did well in school until my junior year of high school. About the same time I really accepted being gay. My grades plummeted all the way into college.

I devoted most of my energy into finding other people like me. My friends in school never shunned me but didn't relate to me either. I ended up picking an all-girls college to be far away from my family and bury myself in an alternative culture. I loved it but ignored my studies. I spent all the time joining political activist groups, mostly feminist and queer.

I ended up dropping out and traveling. I was depressed and did a lot of drugs. Waiting tables to make money. My parents were devastated. Eventually I realized I was walking a dangerous line toward ruining my life permanently so I moved back to my home town.

I am not a psychiatrist or anything but I looked back on that time in my life and realized a few things. I knew if I came out to my parents they would be so disappointed and hurt. It would ruin them. I knew eventually this would have to happen so why try to be somebody or make something of myself when I know no matter how successful I am the time will come when they find out and none of that will matter. They will hate me.

I think I resented them for that and it made me depressed and self destructive. Of course it wasn't just that but this issue has always weighed heavily on my heart.

It hurts me that I went through a lot of my life being closed off and distancing myself from my parents because of this.

I know it hurts them too.

I don't resent my parents anymore. I haven't even given them a chance.

My biggest fear now is not that they will disown me or stop loving me. I know they will still love me no matter what. But I feel sorry for them. I know it will be very painful for them and there is nothing I can do to change that.

They won't drop dead or anything and eventually they might even accept it (after a very long, long and grueling time) but I think it will truly break their hearts. Anyway I'm still working on this one.

Also another issue is my parent's concept of homosexuality. They are very traditional Chinese. A culture even less tolerant of gays than the U.S.

I did research when I was young on support groups for Asian queer youth who deal with other cultural issues on top of just being gay. It helped a little but there really isn't much out there when it comes to that kind of support.

I would love to talk more about this subject of being queer and Asian. I related more to stories of other minorities (Asian, black, Hispanic) about being queer."

Kim's sensitive and thoughtful story underscores the role that traditional Asian values held in her resistance to come out to her parents. Fan (2007) reports in her *Washington Post* article that many gays in China are having fake heterosexual marriages to ease parental pressure. Although China decriminalized homosexuality in 1997, and removed it from the list of mental illness in 2002, LGBT Chinese report one of their biggest obstacles is parental pressure to marry. One gay man explained, "The most difficult people to deal with are not the police. . . . It's your parents." "I'm an only child, and my parents put all their hopes on me," said a young woman Beijing software engineer. "They only graduated from high school, and they suffered a lot, so they really think I should live happily. To their mind that means a husband, a happy family and a good job" (p. 12). Many pursue a marriage of convenience because it is the most important thing to their parents to have a conventional relationship. These fake heterosexual marriages allow them to make their parents happy and still live an independent gay life.

Kim's reticence to disclose her sexual orientation to her traditional Asian parents becomes very understandable as is her need to find support in the queer Asian community which is highlighted in her journaling. Perceiving this cultural issue as compounding her feelings of isolation, Kim sought to connect with others who have experienced similar circumstances.

Loves Makes a Family (1999) served as a wonderful resource for Kim. The following picture of the JANG/OTTO family proved supportive to Kim. The quote by Crystal Jang helped Kim feel not so alone.

© Gigi Kaeser from the exhibit and book, *Love Makes a Family: Portraits of Lesbian, Gay, Bisexual and Transgender Parents and Their Families.* 1999.

I came out over twenty years ago at a time when Asians didn't have any gay role models. I began speaking out in public so that other gay and lesbian Asians would know that we existed. As an Asian lesbian, it is very important to be out there. Our young people need to know that they aren't alone.

(Crystal, in *Love Makes a Family,* 1999, p. 141)

 # Interventions for LGBT Youth

The following interventions are helpful in working with LGBT youth. They each address the stated goals of counseling by establishing a safe and supporting environment that promotes increased self-esteem and aspirations for the future.

Social, emotional, and spiritual considerations are highlighted to aid in resolving internal conflicts. Separating sexual orientation and gender identity from societal homophobic prejudice is underscored. Sharing meaningful resources and supports helps to broaden realistic hopes for comfort in the present and future.

- Enhancing self-image by separating stereotyping from self-identity
- Resolving religious and spiritual conflicts
- Releasing stigma of internalizing homophobic slurs

- Grieving the loss of the idealized self, family, and future
- Presenting at-risk tools
- Interventions for expression
- Blending social and political constructs allowing activism
- Youth advocacy
- Finding the right counselor
- Internet connectedness, resource, and cautioning
- Educating on sexually transmitted infections (STI)
- Support groups
- Materials and community resources

Incorporating Interventions Within Counseling Goals

With a basic understanding of the nature of adolescence, and a deeper understanding of the complex issues facing LGBT youth or children of LGBT partners, it is essential the therapeutic environment become an oasis of safety. It must incorporate knowledge of the loss of the idealized self and future, the internalization of homophobia, the complex minority struggles, and the inherent possibilities of depression, risky behaviors and suicide ideation of LGBT teens. The counselor can best serve the homosexual adolescent by helping to separate stereotyping from self-identity, providing fact-based information, offering resources and mentorship, and allowing expression of all feelings and thoughts without judgment.

The following goals create a framework for deepening the therapeutic relationship. They emphasize *stereotypical prejudice is a function of society* and not the individual. They stress the importance of helping LGBT young people *process thoughts and feelings about gender identity and sexual orientation*. And they require the *creation of safety* in the homes, schools, and communities for these teenagers. The foundation of all counseling is the principle that homosexual and heterosexual adolescents are offered equal rights, privileges, and respect.

GOAL 1

To recognize that this is a societal problem. It is imposed as a prison of bigotry on too many of our youth. This is manifested by the injustice of not seeing these young people or their families as human beings who must be respected for their ability to love in their own way.

Enhancing Self-Image: Separating Stereotyping From Self-Identity

Clearly, the next step in self-acceptance is developing a positive inner stance against the backdrop of social contradictions. Adolescents can begin to *separate* the barrage of stereotyping they have been inundated with from the essence of who they are as people.

Michael, a college freshman, felt disconnected from his parents, especially his dad. His father was enraged with him because he wouldn't go to therapy to help him "change his mind about being gay." He explained his deep hurt over Dad's ignorance to his disclosure. "Why can't he understand? No one would choose this. No one would want the pain of judgment and stereotyping."

Michael began to find other young people that did understand by joining clubs on campus and national organizations that supported LGBT students and began to become more politically active. He became more politically involved and developed an active participation in promoting legalities against sexual harassment and supporting marriage equality. "I felt inspired to be a part of a cause I could put energy into and believe in." Living with rejection from many family members, Michael felt a sense of identity and belonging by joining with others that shared and understood his passion.

In the continuously evolving development of self-acceptance, gay teens can demonstrate positive behaviors and actions in society. This expressive exhibition of *accomplishments* reinforces self-empowerment on many levels. These levels include forming new friendships, creating deep bonds with community, and gaining a sense of partnership with *"a larger whole"* working toward a common cause.

An important piece of the counseling process is blending social and political constructs.

This allows young people to become proactive.

Photograph by Kyna Shilling

Resolving Religious and Spiritual Conflicts

Conflict involving religious beliefs often manifests for the LGBT adolescent. Internalized concepts of sin and rejection by God for being homosexual can create anxiety, self-hatred, depression, and alienation from familiar religious groups.

Doris, a 17-year-old teen, explained her deepest fear after coming out. "I wasn't scared that people would hate me, I was scared God would hate me." She struggled with her feelings toward God and the messages from a strong fundamentalist religious background relaying that she and her supporters are sinners and would go to hell. Doris's parents had rejected her after her disclosure as a lesbian, and she rarely communicated with them. Doris would contact them, but they didn't contact her.

Doris began to value her innate spiritual belief system. She reframed her concept of God as one of a purely loving and accepting being. Internalizing this image of God, she experienced more self-love and acceptance. Exploring the support of her extended family of friends, she began to realize she wasn't alone in the world and had many others to rely upon. Although saddened by the estrangement, she began to have compassion for her family's difficulty in accepting her homosexuality.

A new understanding emerged.
Her parents' rejection was a function of *their* homophobia and fear.
It was not her fault.

Photograph by Kyna Shilling

Doris also missed her spiritual community and began investigating welcoming religious affiliates for gay and lesbian youth (see chapter 12). Attending services and volunteering at a nearby religious youth group led by a gay male clergy with homosexual and straight membership was affirming. A new sense of community and spirituality surfaced as Doris created another piece of a larger extended family.

Releasing Stigma of Internalizing Homophobic Slurs

Constant stereotyping and homophobic slurs are a part of the world of the homosexual adolescent. Balancing this bias with a healthy self-image can be difficult. An initial step toward this goal is *expression* of reaction to harmful slander, and confronting the ignorance of bigotry. Hurtful as it is, the foundational concept lies in society's misplaced projections of gender and not in individual worth.

Josh was an 18-year-old senior in high school. He had disclosed to his parents that he was gay, and found their response affirming. His dad explained, "We love you and will always support who you are." Relieved and reassured of their acceptance, he was able to disclose to others as well. One person was his Aunt Jane, and he had assumed he would be greeted with the same positive response.

Yet, he overheard a disturbing conversation Aunt Jane had with his mother. He kept it hidden for quite some time. His aunt and Mom were talking about Josh being gay. Aunt Jane asked,

Photograph by Kyna Shilling

"What do you think parents would do if an amniocentesis would show gayness? Do you think they would have an abortion?"

Josh burst into tears in the other room, stunned to think anyone would consider annihilating him for being homosexual. Unfortunately, he heard his mom have the same response he had to this extreme remark. Obviously, this aunt was ignorant to her existing prejudice, and Mom expressed her alarm about any concept inferring "a great kid like Josh should be eradicated for his *gayness*. This was clearly unconscionable."

His mother's total support helped to diffuse the hurt of this question ever being brought into existence. By sharing feelings about this experience, Josh realized the depth of hidden prejudice. "I wonder if Aunt Jane would have asked that question before she knew I was gay. I am still the same person." Once he could share this encounter, he could begin to process it as her homophobia, and see that as separate from his own self-identity.

Internalizing Shame and Stigma: The Child of an LGBT Parent

Sometimes therapeutic interventions are helpful, not only for LGBT youths but also for children of lesbian and gay parents. They, too, are exposed to ridicule and judgment, and may internalize cultural homophobia. This can result in another form of isolation, as child rejects parents because of the shame and stigma associated with homosexuality.

Joel was 16 when his dad told him he was gay, and Joel was disgusted. Embarrassed and ashamed, he didn't know what to tell people. He was teased by his peers and even a teacher at school. His parents got divorced. Dad eventually lived as a couple with his partner, Greg, in a long-term relationship. Everyone in the community knew, and taunting by all too many kids persisted. "Your dad is gay. Your family is weird. Something is wrong with your family. They're not normal!" Joel refused to have any contact with his dad, although Dad often tried to speak with him. He had internalized society's homophobic projections onto himself and his dad, resulting in hating himself and Dad. Unfortunately, Dad contracted AIDS and became very ill. His Mom and Greg nursed him until his death.

At the funeral, the clergy asked the family and Greg what they would like him to say about Dad. Joel blurted out.

"I can't believe you would do this for a faggot." He walked out of the room.

At the funeral Joel sat in the last row, expressionless. The room was filled to capacity with people who wanted to honor his father. Dad's partner gained the courage to speak about Joel's dad at the end of the service. He began sharing his life and then looked directly at Joel in the back seat as he relayed the following sentiments. "The only regret he had was not having a relationship with his son Joel. He talked about you all the time and how much he loved you." Joel suddenly got off of his seat, walked to the front of the room, got on his knees in front of Greg. He began to sob and sob uncontrollably. "Please forgive me, please forgive me," was all he could say.

This catharsis was the beginning of his release from the internalization of shame and stigma surrounding homosexuality. Seeing his dad honored by a room filled with loving friends and family and hearing of his father's love for him opened his heart. Joel began to forgive Dad and himself for being caught in the web of stereotypical social slandering and was able to grieve his dad as a much-respected human being and loving father.

GOAL 2

To help LGBT youth process their myriad of feelings with the recognition of their gender identity or sexual orientation. By creating methods that provide a safe passage for them to come out they can share themselves in the most protected way.

Grieving the Loss of the Idealized Self, Family, and Future Hopes

Another aspect in counseling LGBT youth involves a grief and loss process. Adolescents may grieve the loss of being identified as a part of a mainstream heterosexual society, often living as a heterosexual by pretending to be straight or unsure of their sexual identity. Some may grieve the loss of the relationship they thought they had with friends or family. Some may feel relieved not to carry on the charade. Still others are saddened by the perception of difficulties and limited future potential for marriage and family life with a loved partner.

Amelia had an extremely close relationship with her mom. She grew up feeling that she was different, but she could never find the words to relay this to her mother.

When she realized that she was a lesbian and could articulate her attraction to other females, she was excited to share her inner discovery with her mother, never thinking it wouldn't be accepted.

To her astonishment, her mom was enraged, and exploded with anger to her great disappointment and emotional devastation. She and her mother became distant from that point on, and the loss of her idealized mother created deep wounds and intense suffering.

Seventeen-year-old Ralph dated many girls in high school. He even would say to his dad, "We have the same taste in girls." He would talk to his mom about when he got married and how many children he wanted to have. When he came out, he feared this future might not be possible. His hopes and dreams were dim.

Photograph by Kyna Shilling

Although Ralph clearly knew he was gay, the dream he had maintained of having a family seemed far more complicated after coming out. For some time, he felt a void in his life as he searched for new ways to proceed with his sexual orientation and also manifest his goal of family. Through researching facts about same-sex partnership, adoption, and the increase of two-mom and two-dad homes, Ralph began to realize he could hold the hope and dream a family life for himself. This renewed hope allowed him to feel alive again.

Adam knew his mom had always wanted grandchildren. He was an only child. One of the great fears he held in coming out was the disappointment it would be for his parents at the unlikely prospect they would have biological grandchildren. As he discussed this fear, he began to realize he was partially projecting this on his mom and dad as he discovered, "I probably won't be able to have my own children. That is so sad for me, too."

He became aware of his own grief issues surrounding future parenting.

Awareness of his desire to raise children led him to explore the present options for same-sex parenting.

Poster courtesy of OUR HOUSE: A REAL DOCUMENTARY ABOUT KIDS OF GAY & LESBIAN PARENTS, directed & produced by Meema Spadola, originally broadcast on PBS in 2000. Available on VHS and DVD from www.frif.com. *Photos © James Crnkovich and Donna De Cesare.*

Advocacy for LGBT Rights: Creating Resilience

An important intervention to enhance self-esteem is active engagement in activities promoting education and demonstrating advocacy in protecting civil liberties. As LGBT youths feel their voice is heard within school systems, communities, religious affiliations, and political venues, they will incorporate self-expression as a viable means to create change. Their natural abilities to manifest productive action in society are enhanced.

This advocacy enables the actualization of goals that recognize LGBT youth are not different but are fellow human beings. It challenges society's stereotypical perceptions and encourages the elimination of prejudice and limitation.

Day of Silence: Remembering Victims of Homophobia

GLSEN or Gay, Lesbian, and Straight Education Network, announced unprecedented numbers of students participating in the 10th annual *Day of Silence* on April 16, 2006. Using silence to voice the truth about anti-LBGT bullying and harassment in the schools, 500,000 students from 4,000 schools took part in the day.

Director Kevin Jennings explains: "The tremendous numbers of students who take part in the *Day of Silence* is cause for celebration and a loud message from America's students that we must work harder to ensure safe and effective schools for every child" (GLSEN 2006a).

The *Day of Silence* allows young people to actively take a group stand against homophobia and slander, and speak to its extinction. It gives all adolescents a sense of *empowerment* to make a difference by branding injustice. The project is a collaboration between GLSEN and the United States Student Association (USSA).

This national youth-led day of action creates a forum for students to recognize and protest against lesbian, gay, bisexual, and transgender (LGBT) bullying and harassment. It underscores that bigotry is unacceptable. The following picture is a commemoration ceremony at a California college to highlight the silence surrounding harassment against LGBT students and the climate of silence that perpetuates abuse.

The ceremony is for the *Day of Silence*.
Photograph by Kyna Shilling

Throughout the day, students coordinate programs and activities to participate in and voice their truth. They pledge nine hours of silence in taking a stand of silence against discrimination of LGBT peers. It is a day to remember all those victimized by homophobic hate crimes.

The *Day of Silence* was founded by a high school teen named Jessie Gilliam, who had experienced harassment as a LGBT student. Her advocacy led her to become cofounder of this day and a role model to others. Jessie exemplifies that one can make a difference and have their voice heard if they are willing to take a stand and create change.

Advocate for Gay–Straight Alliance

Kelli Peterson was a 17-year-old student from Salt Lake City, Utah, determined to make a difference to end discrimination for LGBT students. She bravely created the history-making experience of forming the first Gay–Straight Alliance in her high school. Kelli fought the battle against bigotry through demonstrating, educating, and protecting the rights of homosexual Americans in our schools. Her protests and legislative battles serve as a foundation for today's human rights movement. Kelli explains why her commitment is so strong and unbending. The following are her words from a public rally in support of the Gay–Straight Alliance as she explains her cause is to:

> End the misery and isolation of being gay in high school.
> We must keep fighting, keep teaching,
> and keep faith in what is right!

Advocate of the Year: Kerry Pacer

Many teens are becoming proactive, and refusing to accept the status quo of exclusion. In high schools and colleges throughout our nation LGBT youth are emerging as powerful forces making their voices heard. Their resilience, perseverance, and drive for social action have made them leaders in the war against intolerance. One shining example is Kerry, who made history as a teen.

She was the youngest person ever to earn the honor of *The Advocate*'s Person of the Year.

Kerry, her friends, and family challenged her Cleveland, Georgia, high school after they were denied the right to create a Gay–Straight Alliance (GSA). Through a series of challenges and court encounters, the students eventually triumphed. These young people are "the face of the younger generation who are learning that with the support of families and friends they can—will—move forward" (PFLAG, 2006a, p. 11).

Permission by *The Advocate*

The incredible courage of this lesbian teen and her community of support achieved a successful outcome by establishing a GSA at her school. Kerry sent a potent message to her fellow LGBT peers that *it is possible* through determination and resolution of purpose to create the justice and equality they so well deserve.

GOAL 3

To create safe homes, schools, and communities. This offers the LGBT youth all the rights, privileges, and respect deemed worthy to any other young person their age.

Finding the Right Counselor

There are a variety of conventional and alternative therapies for young people with LGBT issues to choose. They range from working with therapists of their same sex, specialists in sexual issues of youth, straight or gay therapists, or alternative methods such as "reparative" or conversion therapy. The essential issue is to give the teen the choice of who to work with. Only they can decide what therapeutic environment is comfortable and what philosophy resonates with their own ideology.

Within the varying modes of therapeutic environments, there remain certain constant interventions for counseling gay adolescents. They include:

- Exploring the internal process
- Grieving the absence of their heterosexuality
- Anticipating partners, sex, future
- Creating safety behaviors
- Joining clubs and supporting advocacy
- Shaping life as an LGBT person
- Relating with friends and family

LGBT or Heterosexual Therapist

Max was a senior in high school. He had good grades and lots of friends throughout his school career. He excelled in science and played an excellent game of soccer. His coming out was a surprise to many. For many months he had been depressed, and his mom implored him to get some help, someone to talk to. Finally he said okay.

Two weeks later, he came home from counseling and explained to his parents that he had something to say.

"I think I am gay."

Max's therapist was excellent in helping him recognize and come to terms with his sexual identity, and served as a support for his coming out process. Yet, after his disclosure, Max realized he needed extra guidance in ways to navigate uncharted territory in the gay community. He was encouraged to seek a gay male therapist and felt comfortable learning about and sharing this new dimension of his life. Both therapists were extremely effective, each helping Max to accept and adjust to his new life patterns.

Once a teen feels comfortable with his or her sexual orientation or gender identity, often he or she can make the choice of going to a gay or straight therapist. Angela, a 21-year-old, enjoyed a meaningful relationship with her heterosexual therapist for years. She had accepted being a lesbian before entering therapy. Her issues were not gender confusion, but relational. She experienced distress over childhood issues around parental acceptance, incidences of harassment at school, and relationship issues with her partner Jessica. "No one understands me like you do," she confided to her therapist. Her depth of inner understanding grew from this therapeutic experience.

Ron Lawrence, a therapist with an expertise in providing therapy and training regarding minority issues, is also gay. Lawrence, the executive director of the Community Counseling Center, encourages gay youth to work with gay therapists because he feels there is often a "certain empathy point where a heterosexual therapist can't go."

Confusion About Gender Roles

"Many parents bring their children to me thinking they could be gay. A typical example was a 9-year-old boy named Henry who rejected sports, avoided conflict, and didn't relate to physical force or violence. His level of sensitivity and depth of understanding was way beyond his years. His art ability was outstanding. Henry rejected the stereotypical boy behaviors. These were all indicators he could be gay." At 15, Henry came back to Ron and said, "I am gay." Ron Lawrence was not surprised (Lawrence, interview, 2006).

Nathan, age 6, drew the following picture. He shared he wanted to be a baker or artist when he grew up. Many boys this age dream of becoming police officers or football stars. Nathan already perceived his livelihood as one that was representative of atypical culturally defined masculine roles.

Sometimes having atypical gender behaviors can be difficult for elementary school students. Billy was a very artistic and creative 10-year-old. He loved drawing, writing, and had a wonderful sense of humor. He even liked to sew. LeRoy was a boy in his class who continually shouted insults during gym like "You're a fag." and "Boys don't sew!" He began to learn to hide some of his interests from other children to stop the teasing.

Each person in Billy's class was asked to create a book on a special topic. The following was the book he created. The theme was being called a wimp by friends and how cruel that can be. He created a scenario in which the main character, Willy, perceived verbal abuse by his friends Blar and Ralph—only to happily realize it had been a misunderstanding.

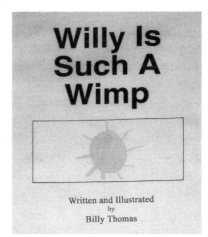

The story was light-hearted, and ended with a comic twist.

Yet it still underscores the damage name-calling relating to sexual stereotyping can create.

The following few pages present the story line Billy created. Through words, imagery, and wit, the message is apparent. Words can hurt.

Self-expression and the creative arts allowed Billy to take a difficult life situation and transform it into *levity with a lesson.*

"...at break [Willy] hid behind the bushes and heard Ralph say, Will.......wimp."

"Willy jumped out and unfortunately landed on his head"

His teacher gave him an A+ and commented, "What a moving story that left me laughing."

The story ends with a realization that the entire incident was a misunderstanding of what he thought he had heard. Willy realizes his friends were talking about a TV show called *The Will Show.* Will, the starring character in the show, was the one being called a wimp. However, all of the boys recognized how disturbing it is to label a friend in a way and how bad it can feel.

Many parents expose children with these gender traits to more masculine activities which may include sports or karate, with the hopes of a change back to societal norms. Some psychotherapists attempt to create this change therapeutically. Other caring adults become advocates against gender stereotyping for children by creating situations whereby young girls and boys don't feel boxed in to prescribed ways of being. Encouraging same-sex friendships and activities like board games can help ease rigid gender roles.

Eric, a 17-year-old, also wondered if he were gay. From an early age, he explained to his therapist he had always felt different. He didn't follow the gender norms prescribed by his parents and school. "When I was a young kid," he shared, "I never understood or related to sports. My father had an interest in sports and would sometimes watch boxing. He would get excited at what seemed to me an ugly and stupid display of senseless brutality. I remember at seven walking to school and bumping into a tree and feeling I should 'apologize.' I was creative and artistic and found escape from a life that felt very alien to me by using my imagination."

Clearly, Eric shared common themes with Billy and Nathan. These themes ranged from sensitivity, creativity, disinterest in sports, and lack of stereotypic rough and tumbling boy behavior. All three boys were unskilled and disinterested athletes and were given the underlying message of inadequacy for not excelling.

The following cartoon spoofs the often exaggerated parental pressure to form gender norms of sports expertise for boys.

©*Baby Blues Partnership: King Feature Syndicate. Reprinted with permission.*

Eric came to therapy confused and overwhelmed about issues of sexual orientation. "I just don't know if I'm gay or not," he would say with great puzzlement. He continued to share his earlier life experiences. "Growing up, girls were an attractive mystery to me. Dating started late and was at best only marginally successful. I was never quite sure of how it was all supposed to go. My sense of my own masculinity was pretty shaky. I usually was picked last for a sports team and teased at school for my sensitive ways."

The anguish and doubt he felt about his sexual identity was finally quieted by his decision to see how he felt being with another boy. He chose Adam, who he knew was openly gay, and they went to dinner and talked for hours. Being with Adam helped him to realize he really was not attracted to men, just very unsure of his heterosexuality due to gender stereotyping and gender norms. He soon began dating Alice and they have been dating for over a year. His inner work with a heterosexual therapist proved very effective. Eric had come to realize he was heterosexual and his therapist was not surprised.

It is important to emphasize that although some girls and boys do exhibit atypical gender behaviors such as the described lack of interest in sports, and so on. They can be heterosexual. The broader range of attributes of maleness and femaleness associated with gender identity and sexual orientation should not be limited to any stereotyping. As the section on role models (see chapter 2) illustrates, professional sports stars with all of the qualities of strength, masculinity, and sports expertise can also be gay, as are many members of the military. Our LGBT population exhibits a wide range of masculine and feminine traits that allow for athletes and chefs to be gay and police officers and fashion models to be lesbian.

A Word About Conversion or "Reparative" Therapy

Conversion or "reparative therapy" is a type of counseling based on "repairing" the LGBT young person to become nonhomosexual. Its very name implies this person is broken and needing of repair. It eliminates the idea that sexual orientation is not a choice but an inherent part of one's being.

Photograph by Kyna Shilling

Mathew went to a therapist to understand his feelings about being an LGBT youth.
After the second session the therapist told him he needed to "go to church and learn about morals."
Mathew decided that this therapist was not right for him.

Some young people are confused about their sexual orientation and gender identity and need time and experience to unravel the questioning of their uncertainty about these issues. In this respect, a counseling environment that allows exploration of all dimensions in question can enable teenagers to come to the decision that best fits who they feel they really are. This needs to be a conclusion they come to, not one forced on them as their only alternative.

The National Gay and Lesbian Task Force Policy Institute released a report (2006) on gay prevention programs. This report accused several religious organizations of harming teens by offering parents therapies to keep children from becoming gay. The Task Force questioned whether the therapies are ethical or effective and urged greater state and federal oversight when these programs are aimed at youth. Task Force Executive Director Matt Foreman stated the necessity of those offering such therapies be licensed. Foreman adds, "This deserves attention and to be regulated" (Wides-Munoz, 2006). He added he would like to see more long-term studies on the effectiveness of the treatment.

Chuck Bright (2004), in the *Clinical Social Work Journal,* provides an abstract for social work clinicians to create an informed opinion about the use of reparative therapy for homosexuality. Bright defines reparative therapy "as a process through which reparative therapists believe they can and should make heterosexuals out of homosexuals" (p. 471). He states most professional regulation bodies have banned its use and it is not supported by reliable quantitative or qualitative studies.

Reparative therapists are often promoted by social political and religious organizations that champion the cause of creating former homosexuals. Those who identify as former homosexuals advocate the use of reparative therapy with faith-based religious counseling. Yet, Bright maintains reparative therapists represent homosexuality as a pathological and curable mental illness, even though most professional regulating bodies have banned its use and the notion homosexuality is a mental disorder. The following are relevant examples.

Major medical and mental health professional organizations have expressed viewpoints on the practice of "reparative therapy." They include the American Psychiatric Association, the American Psychological Association, and the American Medical Association.

- In 1973, the American Psychiatric Association removed the term "homosexuality" from the list of mental and emotional disorders. Sexual orientation is not a disorder; therefore, it does not need to be cured.

- In 1990, the American Psychological Association stated that scientific evidence shows that reparative therapy does not work and that it can do more harm than good.

- In 1998, the American Psychiatric Association stated it was opposed to reparative therapy, stating "psychiatric literature strongly demonstrates that treatment attempts to change sexual orientation are ineffective. However, the potential risks are great, including depression, anxiety and self-destructive [suicidal] behavior..."

- The American Medical Association states in its policy number H-160.991 that it "opposes, the use of 'reparative' or 'conversion' therapy that is based upon the assumption that homosexuality per se is a mental disorder or based upon the a priori assumption that the patient should change his/her homosexual orientation."

- In 2001, The U.S. Surgeon General's *Call to Action to Promote Sexual Health and Responsible Sexual Behavior* asserted that homosexuality is not "a reversible life choice."

PFLAG: "Ex-Gay Ministries and Reparative Therapy"
http://www.pflag.org/index.php/id=280 4/8/06

Internet: Connectedness, Resource, Caution

The Internet and its virtues and vices are an integral part of the world of adolescence. Young people can access an enormous amount of help and accurate information online about homosexual issues. Purchasing books and videos on sexual issues through commercial Web sites is commonplace. Misinformation and danger also can be present on the Internet, with facts skewed to fit the viewpoint of whoever is writing them. Prudence is an important caveat for adolescents when surfing the Web, using reputable Web sites from respected organizations for information. Helpful Web sites for LGBT teens are given in chapter 12. It is important to emphasize that any connecting links are not necessarily endorsed.

Often, LGBT youth can feel isolated, with no support groups or school clubs available for them. Online communication can be a valuable tool to reach out and connect with others going through similar life issues, through online support groups, chat rooms, and blogs relating to youth and homosexuality.

Seventeen-year-old Tyrone was a gay young man living in a community with open hostility toward homosexuals. He dared not tell friends, family, or religious acquaintances that he was gay for fear of great reprisal.

He kept the secret, feeling isolated with no outlet for sharing, until he discovered the value of the Internet. The following was his response to one of the questions on the LGBT Youth Questionnaire in chapter 5.

Question: What has helped you the most to accept being LGBT?

Photograph by Kyna Shilling

"I guess when I was coming to terms with my sexuality the biggest help was the Internet. I knew I was different in middle school because I would get crushes on boys. I thought I just wanted to be their friend but I realized later on what it really was. I had no gay friends that I knew of and no one to talk to so I started researching on the Internet. I found tons of information from support groups for gay teens, chat rooms, and even gay artists, musicians, and performers who I could look to as role models.

Through the Internet I found out that the next city (to where I was living) had a gay and lesbian community center that had an after school support group for gay teens. This was my first chance to actually meet other gay teens. At first it felt like I was living two separate lives. I was happy and outgoing with my new friends with the group, but secretive and closed with my friends at school. But eventually I gained the confidence to come out to my school friends."

Tyrone's response valued the Internet's capacity to create connections with others. It allowed him access to people and information stimulating a network of understanding and community and eventually an opening to be a part of a gay and lesbian support group. Yet, it is imperative to educate LGBT teens to use the Internet cautiously, especially when engaging in a discussion group to meet other teens.

Online profiles can be bogus, and it is difficult to tell who is being truthful. The all-too-real possibility exists that someone may want to take advantage of a young person and pursue meeting them.

Informing young people never to give their full name, telephone number, or home address, or agree to meet someone they met online without being accompanied by another person in a public place is imperative in their counseling process.

Knowledge and Education:
Sexually Transmitted Infections (STIs)

An essential piece of the counseling program is informing LGBT youth about sexually transmitted infections (STIs). The following statistics confirm they are more at risk than many of their heterosexual counterparts for these diseases. Serious emphasis on the *real dangers* of unprotected sex is mandatory.

> In the United States, sexually active teens experience high rates of sexually transmitted infections (STIs), and some populations of youth face excessive risk—African American youth, young women, abused youth, homeless youth, young men who have sex with men (YMSM), and gay, lesbian, bisexual, and transgender (GLBT) youth. The STI epidemic is a global phenomenon, and wherever they live, youth in high risk situations also face a heightened risk of STIs.
>
> (Alford, Advocates for Youth, 2003)

> Experts estimate that more than 15 million sexually transmitted infections occur annually in the United States, nearly four million among teens and over six million among youth ages 20 to 24. Moreover, rates of curable STIs in the United States are the highest in the developed world.
>
> (Alford, Advocates for Youth, 2003)

> Likelihood of a gay man acquiring HIV infection by the age of 20 years old: 20%. Likelihood by the age of 50: 50%.
>
> (OutProud, 2007)

Awareness of the very nature of the adolescent mind is its impulsivity and predisposition to ignore consequences. Richard, age 17, explained to his friend after he disclosed an unsafe sexual encounter: "Nothing will go wrong and so what, if just this one time I didn't use anything, it won't matter." This attitude can lead to devastating consequences. A short time later, he was in excruciating pain, and, after several unsuccessful diagnoses, he was finally told that he had syphilis. The shock was great, the fear was greater . . . yet it was a needed wakeup call that lack of sexual protection can be life-threatening in today's world. It turned out to be a painfully helpful lesson in that it may well have prevented a future infection of AIDS or hepatitis.

Counseling Techniques

The following are suggestions for helping professionals in working therapeutically with gay youth to build a positive framework for self-esteem and empowerment. They incorporate the provision of accurate information, creating supports, and enhancement of their self-esteem. All techniques emphasize separating homophobic stereotyping as an external societal assumption and not an inner identity.

1. Gain knowledge and education about homosexual life.

2. Use the words lesbian, gay, bisexual, and transgender positively in general conversation.

3. Assume everyone might not necessarily be heterosexual but might be LGBT.

4. Explore the comfort of one's own sexuality and any hidden homophobic judgments or prejudices. (See chapter 2)

5. Identify and challenge homosexual stereotypes and create language to explore open discussion. (See chapter 1)

6. Provide role play and story telling that encourages scenarios about LGBT issues. (See chapter 6)

7. Remember all adolescents have issues appropriate to their developmental age as teens. Everyday problems may be those naturally attributed to young people and may not necessarily be a "gay" issue.

8. Allow the LGBT teen to take the lead on the issues he or she needs to deal with, and resist projecting one's own values or "quick fixes" in a patronizing or overly inquisitive style. (See chapter 8)

9. Become aware of the many issues involving gay youth, and the tremendous amount of energy these young people expel in dealing with issues like coming out, dating, partnering issues, heterosexual discrimination, parents, friends, societal acceptance, and finding safe supports at home, school, and in the community. (See chapter 3)

10. Communicate an atmosphere of acceptance and respect that encourages spontaneous expression of many repressed, denied, or uncomfortable feelings and thoughts. (See chapter 5)

11. Offer community supports and resources for the adolescent client as well as their family to create a network of support and a sense of understanding and normalization. (See chapter 9)

12. Maintain an environment that includes language conducive to sharing sexuality. Johnson and Johnson (2000, p. 632) suggest "even small things, such as inquiring whether the client has a partner rather than a boyfriend or a girlfriend; can indicate to clients it is safe to open up about oneself."

13. Educate youth on cautions, preventions, and information on Internet use and sexually transmitted diseases.

14. Provide information and resources on prominent LGBT role models.

 # Conclusion

These kids have overcome so many obstacles. They shouldn't be called "gay" teens, they should be called "gifted" teens.

Kevin Jennings, executive director of GLSEN, on *The Ricki Lake Show*

Seventeen-year-old Anthony entered therapy overwhelmed with sexual orientation issues. Terrified to come out to friends and family, he would repeatedly ask with great distress, "Why would anyone think this is a choice. Who would want this?"

We worked together for quite some time. He first came out to his sister and she was very accepting. His mom cried and was initially grief-stricken. His dad wouldn't speak about it. Anthony began to accept his identity and work with family members to transform difficult feelings into acceptance. A year later, Anthony came out to his friends as well and was amazed at their acceptance. He also established new friendships in the LGBT and straight community.

It seemed Anthony had finally achieved inner acceptance of his sexual orientation. It was reflected in all parts of his life. Often, he would speak of his spiritual belief system and his belief in reincarnation. One day, I asked him if he thought he would be gay in his next lifetime. He sat back, thought about it for a minute, and said, "I hope so!"

Through the love of family and friends, Anthony created congruency in his relationships and within himself. The ultimate goal of humanity is the dissolving of multiple, separate factions to create the oneness of unity. Discordance of polarized issues represented by religious fundamentalist antihomosexual activism versus gay marriage is only a surface manifestation of a deeper theme. These issues appear to be black or white, yet they push toward the understanding of a new paradigm. Although this larger truth has not yet revealed itself as a common thought form in society, it is the essence of democracy itself. As Anthony left my office he turned to me and smiled. "I love being gay and totally support gay marriage. After all, we live in America, and *everyone* deserves to be equal and free."

> *Helping LGBT youths to achieve the necessary balance of separateness/connectedness—to master the developmental tasks of adolescence—will serve to enhance their opportunity to celebrate diversity while rediscovering the many ways we are all reassuringly similar.*

(Johnson and Johnson, 2000, p. 624)

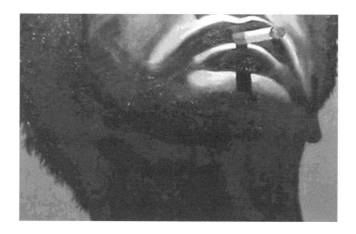

C H A P T E R 5

Speak Up and Share: Self-Expression and the Creative Arts

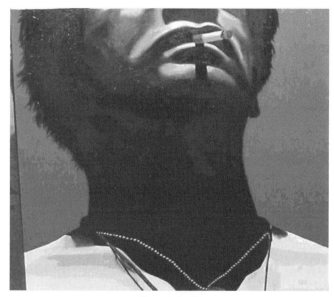

Jon, Age 19

THE NATURE OF SELF-EXPRESSION • TEEN VOICES
CREATIVE ARTS • JOURNALING
QUESTIONNAIRE • ARTWORK • MUSIC
POETRY • HUMOR • DRESS • DRAMA
PEER SUPPORT • ADVOCACY

"Where are my allies?
I don't need to know you are my ally;
I need you to BE an ally."

Jane, age 15

The Nature of Self-Expression

One of the most effective interventions in allowing LGBT youth or the children of same-sex parents to process their issues around sexual orientation and gender identity is to create an oasis of safety and protection for self-expression. These safe havens can evolve from compassionate adults and loving friends, LGBT support groups, school clubs, alliances, and assemblies on LGBT issues. Community agencies and nonprofit organizations such as PFLAG and the Family Pride Coalition allow a forum for expression for parents and children. Giving voice to feelings and issues releases suppression of ideas and establishes a firm commitment to openness of dialogue and of willingness to connect with others.

 # Voices of LGBT Youth

Antigay or lesbian derogatory language manifests homophobic ideology within a society and reinforces notions of the social inferiority of the LGBT youth. Through the internalization of these notions, the LGBT adolescent and young adult is marginalized from the normal heterosexual society and denied sovereignty over the construction of their identity and self-representation. They need their voices to be heard to create new language and meaning to their inner and outer plight.

> *I am sorry, but I can no longer remain quiet. I can no longer remain complicit with the conservative-valued politically correct and the oppressive status quo. I will say it, and it is vital that we all do. I am racist. I am a chauvinist. I am a (self-hating) homophobe. BUT, I am these things only in the sense that my brain is filled with mainstream values that, frankly, are hateful and hurtful. I hope that these ideas in my head, which I constantly and actively try to eradicate, never interfere with my social interactions. If I am hurtful myself, it is out of ignorance, and I hope you correct me.*
>
> James, age 18

I focus on gay marriage because gay marriage is really the heart of the gay/lesbian struggle. It is a legal acceptance and protection of our freedom to love. Is that too much to ask?

Leslie, age 20

Photograph by Kyna Shilling

My deep disappointment is with American society right now. There is something deeply disturbing to me, the fact that in America to this day certain rights are given to a certain portion of the population, while the same right is denied to another.

Alison, age 15

I love being gay and I totally support gay marriage. After all, we live in America, and everyone deserves to be equal and free.

Corina, age 17

Photograph by Kyna Shilling

I gave a "coming out party" for all of my friends. I was so happy!

Amanda, age 18

Photograph by Kyna Shilling

Gay marriage is essential and nonnegotiable. I will not stand by to be a second-class citizen in my own nation. There are no excuses. There are no rebuttals to gay marriage. I was born to love men, and I will raise my family with one. If you want to hate me for it, fine. But you have no right to impose your moral values on me when it denies me equal rights with the person I love.

Mathew, age 19

This war is domestic. It is not a gay and lesbian issue, but an American issue. Do not be complicit. Stand for equal rights.

Eric, age 16

Vote for equality and do not let a homophobic moment go by. Correct them. Change their minds. They speak from ignorance, as they probably have never really interacted with a gay person before.

Tommy, age 20

I am too hurt and frustrated with my subpar status. This is too important. The revolution has begun, even if it only exists in my heart for the time being. I will not be treated less-than when the stakes are this high. I am the soldier of freedom.

George, age 21

I am not going to change or apologize for who I am. It's the society that needs to change. (Mastoon, 1997, p. 112)

Leah, age 21

Expression Through the Creative Arts: Promoting Well-Being

Artwork, poetry, music, writing, and other forms of journaling allow expression through the creative arts. They help young people release stored, underground notions that become an endless groundswell of turbulence until they can be sorted out and shared.

 # Journaling

Often, young people find it useful to journal by expressing ideas about situations through language. Providing tools such as the following LGBT questionnaire is helpful in allowing teens to convey thoughts and feelings. This can create a forum for discussion, an avenue of expression, and a vehicle to normalize difficult issues through sharing with others.

 # LGBT Youth Questionnaire

1. What has helped you the most to accept being gay?
2. What has been the most hurtful?
3. If you have come out . . . what were your parents' reactions?
   How did you feel about their reactions?
   Were they what you expected?
4. If you haven't come out, why not?
5. Is there an incident you recall about sexual orientation or gender identity which stands out in your mind?

6. What have you said or done when you heard a prejudicial remark?

7. Where have you felt the most comfortable?

8. What advice do you have for young people who have not yet come out?

9. Is there any TV, movie, or music or art portrayal you found the most offensive? Was there one you found the most helpful?

10. Is there any public figure who served as a mentor for you in the LGBT community?

TANYA'S QUESTIONNAIRE

Tanya, age 17, shared a few of her answers to the questionnaire. She explained, "I liked working on this. It made me think about some things I hadn't addressed before." Writing about the loving acceptance of friends and the ignorance of society highlighted the extremes she had been living with as an LGBT youth.

Question: What has helped the most to accept being LGBT?

Answer: "I never had a problem accepting it myself. But having great, open-minded friends around made it really easy to come out."

Question: What has been the most hurtful?

Answer: "Society's ignorance regarding homosexuals and equal rights were the most hurtful."

Question: If you have come out . . . What were your parents' reactions? How did you feel about their reactions? Were they what you expected?

Photograph by Kyna Shilling

Answer: "My mom said she had figured it out a while ago. My dad said, it wasn't the life he would have chosen for me but, whatever makes me happy. I pretty much expected both of the reactions."

A few weeks after responding to this questionnaire, Tanya began to realize her dad's response had felt hurtful. The message was that *she wasn't good enough.* Feeling she needed to tell her father, Tanya called him and shared her discomfort with his words. He listened carefully and then responded. "I'm so sorry. I never meant to hurt you. I love you just the way you are." By journaling thoughts and feelings, Tanya was able to recognize hidden hurts, process them, and reframe them into a positive experience with her dad.

MARIE'S QUESTIONNAIRE

Marie is a 21-year old who came out as a lesbian when she was 17. She answered the following questions about a particular incident involving sexual orientation or prejudicial remarks in the following way.

Question: Is there an incident you recall about your sexual orientation or gender identity which stands out in your mind?

Answer: "I guess you could call me asexual when I was in high school. All of my friends had boyfriends and their lives revolved around relationships and dating. I felt uncomfortable because I wasn't interested in boys and thought it would make my friends uncomfortable if I talked about girls so I just remained the funny asexual friend to goof off with. This changed when my senior prom came. Everyone was so excited including me. I decided to take a girl so I did and everyone, to my surprise, supported me. Even though I went to a private Catholic school which had a rule against taking another girl to a dance function, the teachers and faculty supported me. During the dance, a few girls were saying homophobic remarks behind my back and my friends stuck up for me. I wasn't expecting this and it really touched me."

Question: What have you said or done when you heard a prejudicial remark?

Answer: "If I don't know the person I usually won't say anything. I guess I feel like I won't be able to change their minds on the subject and they are just stupid bigots who aren't worth my time. My good friend once made a homophobic remark about gay male sex after watching a movie. She is very supportive of the queer cause but still held some stereotypes (which we all do) but I confronted her by saying even though I am a gay woman it still offended me."

Her response opened a discussion on where judgments come from and how each person is different. She realized many bias statements come from ignorance, cultural bias, and misinformation. Marie explained "I still have prejudice inside of me. I can understand why others do too."

Marie acknowledged that she had a choice in the way she did or did not respond to friends or acquaintances.

She recognized her active participation at the prom helped diminish negativity and gain support. These concepts became an avenue of exploration of her inner homophobia and that of others. We began to form the following list of levels of participation in counteracting stereotyping.

Levels of Participation Against Prejudice

1. *Directly supporting bias slurs* by joining in jokes or harassment. This joining with the prejudice may be a way to avoid being perceived as gay.

2. *Being inactive to respond* to prejudice by ignoring it. This creates an unspoken acceptance of the homophobic situation.

3. *Awareness of inappropriate comments.* Not joining the homophobic remark by not saying anything, but having an inner awareness of its harm.

4. *Recognizing and becoming active* in stopping the oppressive remark by saying something.

5. *Decision to learn more* about the LGBT population, whether homosexual or straight. Many prejudicial remarks and abuses come from ignorance and lack of understanding.

6. *Creating dialogue and questioning* to open discussion. Bringing misconceptions and accurate information into the open can help formulate new awareness.

7. *Maintaining activism* by supporting and encouraging others in a change of mindset about intolerance and bigotry (examples: joining clubs, alliances, organizations).

8. *Initiating preventative interventions* to stop LGBT bias in educational, community, and national forums.

Artwork

Jon was a young gay man with great artistic talent. He began to create paintings that allowed for self-expression of his sexual orientation. The freedom these paintings created for him was enormous.

Jon was able to manifest his vision of sexuality through the arts.

He shared his vision in a medium that went beyond the intellect for the onlooker.

Jon, Age 20

Jon explained how difficult it was to live the life of a gay young man, not being free to share affection for a loved one of the same sex safely in public. It seems unthinkable to most in the heterosexual world to imagine not holding hands, touching, or displaying any open show of emotional caring for fear of being ridiculed. Jon's painting underscores the necessity of demystifying a kiss or an embrace from those of the same gender. He reminds us that everyone has the need for intimacy, affection, and genuine expression of human contact, regardless of their sexual orientation.

 # Music

Susan, a high school junior, felt the song "All I Really Want" by Alanis Morissette had great meaning for her when she came out to friends and family as bisexual. She shared that this music, "although slightly bitter, was blatantly honest," and helpful in validating her inner state and expressing this state to others. Susan explained the lyrics spoke of feeling restricted and lonely. The words conveyed a longing for a soul mate and for freedom to find some peace, comfort, and justice with others on the same wavelength.

Leona, an 18-year old high school student, found music to be her media for expression, too. She had struggled with "coming out" as a lesbian for years and spontaneously disclosed to her lacrosse team by singing one of her original songs. It began like this:

> "I'm running away from time
> I'm running away from this cage of mine"

("Keeping Kids Healthy," *Parenting Gay Teens,* 2003)

After she finished singing, she was frozen in fear, terrified of any reaction. She stared at the floor and started to cry. Leona said "I'm gay." The response to her honesty was enormous encouragement as her teammates began showering her with warm hugs and words of support and acceptance. Many teammates comforted her by saying, "You will be okay."

Ben, a college sophomore, often used journaling and music as a vehicle to express feelings and thoughts, many about being a gay male. The following was a journal entry describing the importance of music for his self-expression, identification, and ability to relate.

> *I feel like gays and lesbians are really unique. We have our own culture and I think it goes beyond that. Gay men are different than straight men and lesbians are different than straight women, in more than the obvious. It's much deeper. It's kind of like separate genders. It's just different. The song "Fuel" by Ani Difranco speaks to accepting many options in searching for love and that it is okay to be who you are. Maybe others can hear what I mean, maybe not. Her lyrics seem to disregard labels and remind us not to limit options in life. She has a feel that most singers couldn't capture, maybe like how a white woman can't capture a black woman's feel in a song. Just some food for thought.*

"Fuel" Ani DiFranco

> "how 'bout we put up a wall
> between the houses and the highway
> and then you can go your way
> and i can go my way"

(Lyrics by Ani DiFranco from the album *Little Plastic Castle.*
© 1998 Righteous Babe Music. Permission grated.)

Anna explained that she related to music a lot before and after she came out as a lesbian when she was 16.

"Growing up I listened to a lot of feminist and queer music (Ani Difranco!). She sang about things I could really relate to."

Photograph by Kyna Shilling

Poetry

All too often, young people struggle with the most courageous act of their young lives. This is the prospect of *coming out* and telling friends and family that they are gay, lesbian, bisexual, or transgender. Many gay youth have kept this identity buried deep inside, under layers of false pretenses and societal conformities until they feel they can no longer carry the burden. The secret becomes too large and it can be all-consuming.

Raymond was a senior in high school, struggling with the unfathomable need to share his sexual orientation and the terror of being rejected for doing so. He also spoke of knowing that once this secret became known his life would change, as he began to live outwardly what had remained hidden for so long.

The following poem is Raymond's attempt to express his weariness and overwhelmed state of living with the weight of pretense and not yet finding the way to be free from this self-imposed prison. His drawing indicates a sliver of light he expresses in his poem that holds the hope of escaping.

JAIL BREAK

By Raymond, Age 17

Only in the darkest times of the day,
Can I see where I am?
Grey structures engulfs me,
A constant digestion

A sliver of light comes in from high above,
Only to illuminate the darkness,
It shines in constantly to remind me
That it is my undoing

I can only find sleep in the cold,
Fluorescent glow of my cell,
But, lately, the lights have been
Turned off, and I do not get any sleep.

I stir in discomfort, overwhelmed
By the beam of sunlight above,
I've tried covering it, but I can't reach
I must live with it.

I am so tired. Still afraid of the
Light, but more scared of this
World of darkness
I resolve on change.

My past actions led to this incarceration.
I am not mad at my captures,
Only weary of this suppression.
From the light

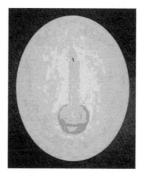

Where is God?
Where is Allah?
Where is Adonai?
It is time to go.

After courageously coming out to friends, family, and teachers, Raymond was confronted with an unexpected realization of how life was forever changed. He had bravely established *"who he was"* in the world. Now he realized he had begun a long journey and felt unsure about the new life he was embarking on. Entering uncharted territory, Raymond felt weary from this travel. The depth of his soul searching is conveyed in the following poem and his accompanying photograph. His spiritual belief system is expressed and becomes evident as a support for him in maintaining an inner resilience for eventual success on his new path.

ASYLUM

By Raymond, Age 18

At first I am blinded by the light.
Feeling it on my skin is exhilarating.
I float, intoxicated, down the highway.

Suddenly, the road is less defined.
My honesty weighs me down,
And I realize how tired I am.

I sit on a rock off the path,
Light up a cigarette, and look for God.

I sit on this rock for a long time.
The road has moved somewhere else,
And I am lost.

I move to other rocks,
Sometimes I find an old tree stump,
Aimlessly exploring my world

I light another cigarette,
And I see just how big the sky really is,
Brilliant light spreads out before me.

God is everywhere,
directionless,
I can go anywhere
without moving.
I will just sit where I am.

Expression Through Dress and Humor

Jeff came out as a gay male in his junior year of high school. To his amazement, he was overwhelmingly accepted by friends and faculty at his school. His best friend was Alex, one of his closest friends since fourth grade. They remained just as close after his disclosure.

Jeff's degree of comfort was so great at school he decided to wear his favorite T-shirt on senior day.

It was received with great humor from most of his peers. He felt good about wearing it.

Tara was 17 and had come out to friends and family the previous year. One of the lucky ones with great support, she soon felt comfortable enough being a lesbian to display a keen sense of humor about sexual orientation and stereotyping. She freely shared jokes with others, often shaking the very roots of the gender binary she was so accustomed to hearing. The following was one of her favorites.

> A young guy from Nebraska walked into a bar and sat down next to a beautiful red-haired young woman. His name was Ron and he was naive to many of the ways of the world. He began to talk to this redhead and she suddenly stopped the dialogue. "I want you to know something about me. See that woman over there. I like the way she looks. I would like to get to know her better. Maybe take her to dinner and then back to my apartment and explore a sexual relationship with her. I am a lesbian." This Nebraskan youth looked back at her and replied, "I would like to do the same thing. I guess I am a lesbian too."

Tara said when others laughed and saw the humor of the absurdity of confining norms, it made her feel better.

Photograph by Kyna Shilling

Somehow, the amusement of friends and family who could perceive the funny side of inclusion for many onto a sexual continuum was comforting. It helped Tara feel that she had company in her world.

 # City at Peace: Young People Supporting Each Other

Another aspect important in creating a productive life for gay youth is peer support. LGBT school clubs, national alliances, community support groups, and welcoming spiritual affiliations bridge the gap from isolation to community acceptance. One such peer alliance used theater to express and support relevant social issues.

A diverse group of adolescents in the Washington, DC, area, ages 13–19, spend Wednesdays and Saturdays meeting and sharing their life stories 10–12 hours a week for the entire school year. They came together with a goal of getting young people to be allies for each other through a nonprofit DC youth organization, City at Peace.

This enterprising group of teens created a production entitled *"What Doesn't Kill Me"* in April of 2006. It was a choreographed musical made up of scenarios dealing with contemporary issues including homelessness, death, drug addition, abuse, homophobia, and body image.

The uniqueness of this presentation lies in cast members being assigned roles that are actually based on stories from their peers.

Elly Kugler, (Zara, 2006, p. 1) assistant director and former City at Peace member, describes the process used in developing the scripts as follows.

Permission by City at Peace

"The people who are cast into the roles write the roles and play the roles. They'd have to do a lot of research on the part of whose stories they were depicting to get a sense of what it's like to be in their shoes."

One story line tells of a girl in love with her (female) best friend. The cast was careful not to portray stereotypes. The scene was titled *"I Really Like You"* and depicts two close female friends who have *the perfect relationship.*

It is perfect until one realizes that she has a crush on her friend.
Without a blueprint, she must struggle to find happiness while keeping her friendship.

Permission by *City at Peace*

Another scene was named *"Interfaith."* It presents a group of students brought together to write an article about teens and faith. As lies are exposed and one young person is dragged out of the closet, the group must try to find common ground while writing about religion and sexuality. One 19-year-old actor expressed conflict relating to the religious aspects of coming out, examining the internal struggle of young people feeling they sometimes need to choose between being gay and being religious.

An evaluation is given to every cast member after the performance asking if they can now become an ally for other young people in promoting diversity and resolving conflict in their own lives. Kruger reports the answers are overwhelmingly positive. She explains, "We look at different power imbalances—race and racism, heterosexism and homophobia, and explore the ways those things intersect. A lot of adamantly homophobic people come through these doors. If you're homophobic, let's talk about why. Let's let the GLBTQ kids talk about their life experiences in the same space. We promote that dialogue and let it be transformational" (Zara, 2006, p. 2).

The following quote is representative of the freedom to share and opportunity to help one another provided by *City at Peace.* Adolescents can deal with these life challenges by expressive exploration of inner issues resulting in public presentations.

> *"You can talk it out, debate it out, scream, cry, break down and be supported by a group of people." Tony, age 16, City at Peace member.*
>
> (Zara, 2006, p. 2)

City at Peace serves youth by creating a safe environment to openly discuss issues including physical and sexual abuse, family secrets, a loved one's death, race relations, flirting, homelessness and abandonment, body image, fear of success and failure, and homosexual issues. Through drama, dance, music, and advocacy, young people use this creative forum as a vehicle for self-expression through the arts within their community.

Support Groups for LGBT Teens: A Safe Place to Share

Research indicates forming supportive peer connections enhances self-esteem and reduces attachment anxiety for LGBT individuals as teens and later in adulthood. Creating connectivity with other young people in a welcoming and encouraging environment increases self-acceptance as part of a larger community.

Melvin was 15 and had just come out at home but not at school. Homophobic slurs taunted many of his peers, and the teachers and principal seemed deaf and blind to the continual harassment. Melvin yearned for friendships with freedom to express his sexual orientation, yet was fearful to approach fellow students. The pain of rejection and abuse seemed too great to risk an attempt of disclosure.

"I think I will quit school," he told his mom.
"There is no one to talk to, eat lunch with, or hang out
    with. I hate it there. I wish I could find a friend!"

The *Rainbow Youth Alliance* in Montgomery County, Maryland, is an example of a safe place for LGBT teens and their allies. They can ask questions, find mutual peers, and learn information pertinent to their lives. Meetings include curricula, discussion groups, movies, and games for youth between 14 and 18, regardless of sexual orientation or gender identity. Guest speakers are invited, including a safety issues presentation by the head of the Gay and Lesbian Unit of the DC police force. Projects include *"gay pen pal"* letters, sharing feelings of shame about homosexuality, peer pressure and problem solving, gay history programs, and readings from LGBT authors and poets.

Support groups such as the *Rainbow Youth Alliance* provide a safe forum for homosexual teens and their allies to explore safety issues, a sense of worth, role models, and new alliances with others of their age having the same life concerns. The result is a *bridge of connection* often very difficult to create at school or in other parts of the community.

Self-Expression Through Advocacy

Marina is a 17-year-old nationally recognized LGBT rights activist and leader. She is also the proud daughter of two lesbian moms. Marina was the recipient of the Equality Advocacy Award 2005 in Beverly Hills California, and her instrumental role in establishing new legislation was honored. The groundbreaking fight for equal rights through the passing of the religious freedom and civil marriage protection act by the California legislation was achieved and then later vetoed.

Through speech writing, essays, and poetry, Marina has fought and gained recognition for her perseverance and courage in advocating same-sex rights for marriage equality. The following are a few examples of her work.

Marina's eloquence is evident throughout her writing and poetry.

She explains her goal is not a religious fight, but a struggle for civil rights for all.

MARINA'S SPEECH: "MY FAMILY IS DIFFERENT"

"My name is Marina, I'm 14 years old and I've got two moms. My family is different, not only because I've got two moms, but because our family is filled with unconditional love, acceptance, openness, and strength. Life is a contradiction in many ways because my moms are pretty, they're funny, they're cool, and people like them. Yet, when people realize they are a couple, or that we are a family, many of those same people feel hateful and fearful of them, and of us.

My moms have taught me that you never combat hate with hate. Instead, educate, love, and lead by example. What you can't accept, you change. The greatest differences I think I make, and my family makes, are by just being who we are.

The morning I was to tape [a show] on alternative families, everyone was supposed to meet in the lobby of a hotel. One of my moms and I came down and immediately saw a group of families with moms and dads, some holding Bibles. We walked over, they saw us, and I think the crosses we were wearing around our necks as well. Immediately, they embraced us, befriended us, and welcomed us into their circle of families. We laughed, and joked, and my mom and another mom hung out and talked. Within minutes there were invitations to visit where they lived someday, talks of correspondence, and all the things that our families had in common. They genuinely liked us as people, and as a family.

A couple of hours later during the taping of this show, the host asked me how I felt about having lesbian moms. My mom said that back in the green room, jaws dropped. That was the first time that they realized that we were an "alternative family," and that my mom was gay.

After the show, some of them [those people previously befriended] didn't want to be around us anymore. Most of them, however wanted to take pictures with me, talk and hang out, and that same mom and mine even hugged goodbye. Believe it or not, one of those same boys contacted the producer later, wanting to correspond with me. I'm sure we were the only alternative family that those people had ever met, and my mom probably the only gay person that they've ever knew or been around. But inadvertently, accidentally, without knowing that changes were being made to their hearts and to their subconscious minds, or wanting them made, I believe they were. I think somewhere deep inside, they realized how truly small our differences were.

I like having a pride flag on our house, I like having two moms, even though life isn't always easy for us. At school I'm well liked because I try to like everyone, and befriend the people who need it most. Empathy is something I understand first-hand. I like going to a parochial school and having to explain to my social studies teacher why my family has two women instead of having a man and a woman. I like what we are.

Marina and her moms

That's when I believe people figure out what's really most important, which no matter what kind of family you are, your family is special and wonderful when it is filled with so much love, respect, and happiness."

STAND STRONG

A Poem by Marina

Stand strong against those who oppose
We are a loving and wonder family, and everyone knows

I know it's hard to keep up the fight
But you really must try with all of your might

I will be there to stand by you
Hard times and easy, I will see you through

Keep your head up, and try not to frown
Don't let the ignorance of others get you down

Stand strong, and be proud
Don't be afraid to shout it out loud

I hear you, and feel your pain
Just remember that all of your endeavors are not in vain

I will be here, to walk beside you through this
Your efforts will not go missed

I support you all the way
Even if in the past you have wandered astray

Keep your chin up, and remember to smile
Because this whole time has been worth while

MARINA'S ACTIVISM FOR EQUAL MARRIAGE RIGHTS

Marina was a passionate and accomplished advocate for the historic passing of the California Legislature of Assembly Bill 849—The Religious Freedom & Civil Marriage Protection Act, a bill that would grant marriage licenses to same-sex couples. Although its passing was historical, it was eventually vetoed by the governor of California. She actively engaged legislators in the battle for marriage equality, explaining:

"To those people who don't understand the difference that you can make in the world as just one youth, I can tell you that there is no one more qualified to speak about discrimination than a child directly affected by it."

In her award acceptance, Marina underscores the importance of advocacy and the power of each person to create change. "This was a monumental step forward; it was history in the making, and there is no going back. For every person and every leader that stands up against discrimination and bigotry, we are one step closer to ending it. We must continue to fight for full and complete equality for all people, by educating the world one person at a time. Our greatest gains as a community will continue to be made when as people, as youth, and as families, we stand up visibly and proudly. Each of us must get involved in the fight for equality, and we must encourage others to do the same."

We have the ability to change hearts and minds
  everywhere by sharing our stories with others.
One person can make a difference.
  One person can change the world.

Marina

The goal of self-expression is to gain comfort in being who one really is, inside and out. When LGBT young people and children of LGBT couples can release hurt and shameful feelings, express concerns about civil liberties and gay rights, create a song, a poem, play, or a speech to share images of their journey, paint a picture giving insights into their homosexual world, or merely tell a meaningful joke, we are creating avenues to open up larger vistas of seeing oneself.

Feeling free to openly dress with humor or keeping a private journal is an individual choice and personality preference. Any path of expression that leads our LGBT youth and children of gay and lesbian parents to release difficult feelings and challenging experiences is a means of achieving congruency with their inner self and the world around them.

CHAPTER 6

The School Environment: Creating an Oasis of Safety

SCHOOLS AS SAFE PLACES • OPTIONAL FACULTY TRAINING
SERVICES • SOCIAL SUPPORT
CURRICULUM DEVELOPMENT • ADVOCATING CIVIL
LIBERTIES • ACTIVITIES, DISCUSSION, ROLE-PLAY, AND
PROJECTS ON LGBT ISSUES • CLUBS AND ALLIANCES
ROLE MODELS • NO NAME-CALLING WEEK • ALLY WEEK
HARASSMENT POLICY • FACULTY QUESTIONNAIRE

Cowardice asks "Is it safe?"
Vanity asks "Is it popular?"
Conscience asks "Is it right?"

Martin Luther King Jr.

Schools are our students' homes away from home and the place they spend the majority of their time. LGBT adolescents need to be guaranteed their environment is safe. All students deserve to learn in an environment that is supportive and friendly.

Prejudice against homosexuality impacts the school and its educational goals, as well as the mental and emotional health of the students exposed to it. Van Wormer & McKinney (2003) confirm in their research that "failure to take a proactive stance [within the school environment] to help youth with gender identity issues is a major cause of psychological problems, leading in some cases to alcohol, drug abuse, homelessness, depression and suicide (p. 409).

> *A safe space is one where there are student and adult allies who can help shape a program or school culture that is accepting of all people, regardless of sexual orientation, gender identity, expression, or any other difference.*

(Defined by KidsPeace Institute)

 # Statistics on LGBT Youth Safety in Schools

The following statistics underscore the need for love, friendship, acceptance, advocacy, and safety in our schools. In today's world, this mission has not been accomplished. Young people have not yet attained the freedom to an education without terror of harassment or violence.

- "GLBTQ youth feel they have nowhere to turn—4 out of 5 surveyed said they do not know one supportive adult at school.

- Approximately 70% of GLBTQ students surveyed faced verbal, sexual or physical harassment, or physical assault while at school.

- Twenty-five percent of teachers see nothing wrong with bullying or put-downs, and intervene in only 4% of bullying incidents.

- Studies including GLBTQ youth indicate that they are at a higher risk of dropping out of school, homelessness, and mental health issues related to chronic stress associated with harassment by peers and family members."

(PFLAG, 2005c)

Research: Perceieved Social Support of LGBT Students in School

Mufioz-Plaza, Quinn, and Rounds (2002) present research findings indicating "significant gaps in the social support available to participants from peers, school personnel and family" (p. 60). The social isolation of LGBT youth falls into three types of categories: cognitive, social, and emotional (Mufioz-Plaza et al., citing Martin and Hetrick, 2002).

Cognitive isolation was experienced because many felt they had very limited access to accurate information on issues related to sexual orientation. Emotional isolation can result from constant negative messages about LGBT issues from students, educators, and family. The homosexual research group indicated their feelings seemed wrong to others.

These adolescents felt socially isolated by friends, peers, teachers, and family, regardless of their homosexual disclosure.

Photograph by Kyna Shilling

"Most participants expressed a sense that their own sexuality was not adequately conveyed using commonly accepted terms and described a more fluid sexuality than that which is implied by contemporary definitions of sexual orientation. Increased institutional support in schools will ensure the LGBT students continue to develop positive self-images into adulthood" (Mufioz-Plaza, Quinn, and Rounds, 2002, p. 61).

In other words, our gay youth are asking for a common language to be developed devoid of sexual stereotyping. Through educating the educators, we lay a foundation of trust based on accurate and unified information throughout a school system. The faculty becomes *a team of support* that encourages inclusion and greater self-esteem for their LGBT population.

Reactivity in the
School Community

Schools have a legal responsibility to adopt guidelines about sexual harassment that are inclusive of sexual orientation.

(PFLAG, 1997)

Fifteen-year-old Rebecca came out as a lesbian to the students and faculty in her school.

Her favorite English teacher, Mr. Clark, was the adult she projected would be her staunchest ally. To her deepest disappointment, she was devastated by his complete rejection of her as a lesbian. His distressing response challenged her new voice by his urging. "I don't believe you are a lesbian. I really want you to think about it carefully."

Rebecca only thought to herself, "How could he *not understand* how much I have thought about it. Why doesn't he understand?"

Photograph by Kyna Shilling

Had Mr. Clark received optional educational training for faculty on LGBT issues, perhaps Rebecca's hurt could have been avoided. Presenting reliable information and dialogue for acceptance to educators *strengthens* their ability to facilitate support for the gay student.

Muñoz-Plaza, Quinn, and Rounds (2002, p. 61) suggest four categories for supporting LGBT students, including increased awareness, professional training, services, and curriculum development. The scenario between Mr. Clark and Rebecca could have been transformed into a deeper understanding of her coming out. The school system's incorporation of the following categories of support would have been helpful in broadening the scope of the school as a safe and inclusive environment for LGBT youth.

Catagories for Supporting LGBT Students

It is important to create a balanced perspective supporting LGBT students as well as others with varying perspectives. *The Equal Access Act* explains schools should not create clubs, GSAs, and so on, as they must be fully student-initiated and student-led. Schools can present optional but not mandatory training on same-sex relationship issues that not only include advocacy but also focus on bullying and harassment impacting all students. Assemblies offered to the student body in keeping with first amendment issues can share outlooks that educate students about a variety of standpoints. This includes conservative religious views as well as positive information about homosexuality. Any school-sponsored program must be balanced in fairness to all points of view with respect for all. The following support categories are listed with these understandings in mind.

1. INCREASE AWARENESS AND SENSITIVITY

Display information on LGBT issues throughout school.

Create a no-tolerance policy for sexual harassment.

Nondiscrimination policies include sexual orientation fairness and conservative religious views.

Assemblies, dances, and guest speakers to enrich diversity on a variety of perspectives and views.

Support gay faculty as visible rolemodels.

2. PROFESSIONAL TRAINING FOR EDUCATORS AND SCHOOL PERSONNEL

Create optional training and courses for educators from elementary school through college.

Make optional sensitivity training available for everyone on all levels of the school staff.

3. SERVICES

Allow clubs, gay–straight alliances, and school functions for LGBT students.

Offer counseling within the school and recommend community resources.

Health services must be informed on health issues for homosexual students, including both mental health issues and sexually transmitted infections (STIs).

4. CURRICULUM DEVELOPMENT

Expand the sex-ed and social living units in the curriculum to include LGBT issues.

Integrate LGBT issues into English or history classes that involve civil rights movements.

In some school systems development of these support categories has been effectively created. In other schools their implementation has been met with great opposition.

Schools as Safe Zones for LGBT Youth

Schools can no longer ignore the presence of adolescents who identify themselves as gay, lesbian, bisexual, or transgender, or their deep need to at least question their sexuality without judgment. Educators can foster an environment that permits this questioning, and dispels any ideology involving gender bias by assuring these youth have the same opportunities as their heterosexual peers.

Teachers, principals, and counselors can effectively become *a huge social support* by acknowledging the natural attributes of resilience these students assuredly possess, by fully accepting and valuing them as LGBT students. Finding ways to utilize already existing school supports, while developing new ones, is essential for the health and welfare of gay young people. Providing clubs, mentorship, peer support groups, educational curriculum, and open acceptance through language and inclusion is essential for creating comfort for our LGBT youth in our educational system.

School Policy for Eliminating Sexual Harassment

It is essential to create a clear policy which is known, understood, and implemented by students and staff. Schools must develop a strong boundary for identifying any abusive language or behaviors. Providing optional training for teachers and students would be helpful in developing strategies to openly label and actively stop prejudicial incidents as they occur. Support from adult personnel and peers are essential. If individual attempts are unproductive, knowing where to reach for further assistance must be provided for all concerned.

Photograph by Kyna Shilling

Helping Someone Come Out Safely

The following guidelines are adapted from GLSEN Safe Space to provide useful ways to create a nonjudgmental environment for the gay teen to disclose his or her sexual orientation. Through training and assemblies for staff and students, an environment of acceptance can be implemented.

- *Model acceptance for the LGBT individual and others.* They are taking a brave and trusting step to come out.

- *Acknowledge the person's bravery and trust.* Let them know you appreciate and respect their faith in sharing with you and that you will reconnect with them soon.

- *Show compassion through interest.* Ask questions about time span of knowing they are LGBT, difficulties in keeping this secret, and what is helpful or hurtful.

- *Listen to the entire story.* The story of coming out may be involved and lengthy. Giving a sympathetic and patient environment without judgment facilitates a positive experience of disclosing.

- *Offer outside help if needed.* Be educated in community agencies, hotlines, school clubs, counselors, and support groups that might be needed.

- *Uphold confidentiality.* This person may only want to disclose to you. Be sure they know that their choice to come out to others when they are ready will be upheld.

- *Provide availability for others.* Offer yourself as a resource for others coming out.

- *Maintain humor.* Create a feeling of lightness around this challenging disclosure.

Photograph by Kyna Shilling

The Legalities of Sexual Harassment

School personnel have long understood that a fair and inclusive education is threatened when students' physical and emotional security is endangered. The hostile environment that exists for LGBT youth in many of our schools is all too apparent. School officials that know about harassment and do nothing must be held responsible. This harassment should be dealt with in an even-handed and balanced way to include any infringement on equal rights for all students regardless of their point of view.

The clash between *freedom* and *safety* not only prevails in the school environment, but the legal system as well. On May 24, 1999, the U.S. Supreme Court in *Davis v. Monroe County Board of Education* imposed a ruling with far-reaching and positive implications for LGBT students. As Stone (2004) explains, this case "established that public schools can be forced to pay damages for failing to stop student-on-student sexual harassment" (p. 6). This landmark case can support school personnel in heightening awareness and consequences of sexual persecution, developing a respectful school climate, and serving as a source of strength for equality for all students.

For the process to enable agreement from all sides, the school environment must be devoid of taking sides. Charles Haynes, senior scholar at the First Amendment Center (2006b), refers to this volatile school arena as "the culture war over homosexuality" and has initiated agreement on policies that bring the community together rather than separate them.

The following legal decisions exemplify fairness for both sides of the polarized groups. A junior high school student in Arkansas complained that because he was openly gay, school officials harassed him and punished him, forcing him to read aloud Bible verses and prayers. A lawsuit was filed, and the school district settled by paying damages and apologizing. Another high school student in Michigan had an issue on the opposite side of the spectrum. In 2002, she challenged her school district for censoring her religious views against homosexuality. She was prevented by her school from sharing her religious views during "Diversity Week," as they were seen as negative. This young girl also filed a lawsuit, and the courts ruled in her favor that her free speech rights had been violated. Both cases solidify the concept that educators cannot impose their religious view of homosexuality, nor can they censor the religious beliefs of their students.

The clash of ideology extends to dress code. In many schools, students wear T-shirts proclaiming "Gay Pride" counteracted by T-shirts professing "Straight Pride." The U.S. Circuit Court of Appeals ruled a Poway, California, high school was justified in barring a student from wearing a T-shirt reading "Homosexuality is Shameful" on one side and "Be Ashamed, Our School Embraced What God Has Condemned" on the other.

The court's decision dictated the shirts interfered with the rights of others, especially freedom from harassment for gay and lesbian students. Haynes (2006b, p. 1) explains: "If courts in other parts of the country follow this line of reasoning, this decision could have far-reaching implications for student rights in public schools." Haynes suggests that solutions be found for the common good. He calls on conservative Christians to acknowledge that many GLBTQ students in public schools are more frequently bullied and harassed. By contrast, he asks gay-rights proponents to extend the concept of freedom of speech rights to the religious conservatives in public school by allowing expression of their conviction about homosexuality or other issues in class discussion, religious clubs, and other arenas.

Public Schools and Sexual Orientation: A First Amendment Framework for Finding Common Ground (2006, published by the First Amendment Center and endorsed by GLSEN and Christian Educators Association International) advises school districts to hear from all sides in the process of decision-making. But curriculum content is a decision made by the school board based on many factors including sound science. The consensus guide proposes a process for decision-making, not a prescription for what the decision should be. The advice offered by the guide is excellent; however it is being misrepresented by some ex-gay groups to mean that their perspective must be included in the curriculum. This is not the intent of the guidelines. There are many viewpoints that school districts will and should hear during a fair and open process to develop curriculum. Not all of these viewpoints will be approved by the district for inclusion in the curriculum.

> *Can we win the peace? Yes, but only by affirming that public schools belong to all Americans. And only by insisting on schools that are both safe and free places where all members of the school community commit to address religious and political differences with civility and respect.*
>
> *A safe school is free of bullying and harassment. And a free school is safe for student speech even about issues that deeply divide us.*
>
> (Haynes, 2006b, p. 3)

Speaking About LGBT Issues in School

Many parents, educators, clergy, and even health care professionals may not see the importance of why schools need to address LGBT issues with young children. It is important for adults caring for children to rethink these assumptions.

One assumption is that this creates discussion of sexuality when in fact lessons are based on prejudice, harassment, misinformation, and respect for all. The younger we begin planting the seeds of understanding and inclusion, the easier our next generation of kids can grow into becoming more open-minded and compassionate adults with the understanding that homosexuality is a natural part of the human spectrum.

With this caveat, it is essential to underscore that any lesson to young people should contain the space for freedom of speech with the educator holding the awareness all viewpoints are acceptable without judgment. If 7-year-old Sami says, "My aunt says all gay people are sinners," it is an accurate statement of the religious view of many people. Sami cannot be corrected by her teacher that this is wrong without violating her First Amendment rights. Her teacher can only say, "Many people believe that to be true, while many others do not."

What is age-appropriate for children regarding LGBT issues is a difficult question. For most schools in most parts of the nation, the focus in the early grades is combating bullying, name-calling, and doing as much as possible to promote a caring atmosphere for all students that respects diversity in individuals and families. The challenge is to do that *without ignoring or attacking* the religious views of many parents and students.

Core Inclusion Concepts for Educators

So much of the information our children hold comes from peers, siblings, parents, and the media. All too often, this information is filled with bias, criticism, and stereotyping.

Schools can appropriately address these sensitive issues and see the value in prevention of violence. Our school systems have an invaluable opportunity to accurately teach their students the differences between prejudice and fact, compassion and hatred, and the essential quality of equal rights for all.

Educators can promote inclusion by discussion, activities, and modeling core concepts about stereotyping and bias that can build throughout a student's lifetime from preschool through high school. The following is a broad outlook of the paradigms that can be instilled in children and teens at different stages of development.

INCLUSION CONCEPTS FOR EARLY CHILDHOOD

- Name calling and teasing are never okay.
- There are no such things as "girl colors and boy colors" or "girl games and boy games."
- Boys and girls don't have to act, dress, or talk a certain way.
- Everyone is different and that is okay.
- Families are different, too. They come in all shapes, sizes, and configurations.
- Loving and taking care of each other is what makes a family.

INCLUSION CONCEPTS FOR MIDDLE SCHOOL

- Define words such as bias, stereotyping, discrimination, and prejudice.
- Discuss stereotype based on sex, gender, and sexual orientation.
- Introduce myths related to groups subject to prejudice and include LGBT.
- Provide information on all kinds of families including LGBT.

INCLUSION CONCEPTS FOR HIGH SCHOOL

- Highlight contributions to society made by LGBT individuals and LGBT families.

- Provide specific information on gender, sexual, and family diversity within a comprehensive sex education program.

- Educate students about laws against discrimination including LGBT citizens.

- Provide information about the history of these laws and the struggle for social justice.

 # Suggested Activities Involving Prejudice or Stereotyping

DISCUSSIONS

(1, 2, and 3 adapted from *It's Elementary*, 1996)

1. Uncover through discussion preconceived ideas children have on gay/lesbian issues.

A fourth-grade class was asked to share the first thing that came to mind when they heard the word gay or lesbian. They were told anything they said was okay. They responded in the following way.

cross-dressing	pair	naked	couple	a boy
getting married	sick	private	someone	fun
gay pride day	pervert	disgusting	love	nasty
TV	movie	yucky	couples	a sin
kissing	together	peep shows	walking funny	

2. Students related to thoughts about discrimination and prejudice. Children gave their ideas and opinions, allowing all ideas without correction or judgment.

"When I think of gay, I think of someone like a boy walking funny, like a girl."

"I think of gay pride day."

"It's like that they are in love with a boy. That a boy is in love with a boy or a girl is in love with a girl. Or else they could just be teasing or something."

"I don't think people should be strict about them, because if they were gay, they wouldn't want to be getting beat up and stuff."

"That's how their life is. They're gay. So what."

3. Locate the source of their information for establishing any misconceptions and faulty understandings. Then present the facts.

These fourth graders were then asked where they got this information. Their response was mainly TV and the news. A girl explained that her parents and aunts and uncles were always saying gay is wrong and that's just the way it is. Another boy commented he gets his information from talk shows and heard homosexuality is bad.

Many of these children also get their information from movies such as *Kindergarten Cop*, which includes a scene where the male kindergarten teacher is called gay for teaching young children. A second film discussed was *Ace Ventura*, where a child recalled a man was so disgusted by accidentally kissing another man he vomited and burned his clothes. One student retold a news item about a gay guy that walked into a bar and got beat up.

4. Dispelling stereotyping about LGBT families

Ursula Ferro, educator, child development consultant, and author suggests several ideas to use with children on the topic of many types of families including LGBT familiies. Prior to reaching adolescence, she explains, young children gather information about what is "normal" or "accepted" within their culture. Without consciously realizing it, the young child is influenced by images and stories, developing both positive and negative biases. In her series of early chapter books, *Tanny's Meow, Wishing for Kittens,* and *Mother's Day on Martha's Vineyard,* she provides experiences that teach values embracing all kinds of families and many ways of being. Ferro explains the primary focus is *not* LGBT issues, but rather the story or adventure that captures the imagination. The LGBT issues are quietly present while the pictures and story model caring and respectful family relationships. The child learns that having two moms or dads is "normal." After reading *Tanny's Meow*, a seven-year-old with two moms said, "I want to read that book about *me* again." Ferro also recommends reading stories in which only one parent is present and then creating discussions such as: "I wonder if this is a family with a child and a dad. Or maybe the child has two dads. Or there might be a dad and a mom. What do you think? There are so many kinds of families."

5. Share the film *Oliver Button Is a Star.*

Tomie DePaola tells the story of Oliver Button, a boy who is called *sissy* for dressing up and tap dancing. Music is sung by the Twin Cities Gay Men's Chorus. Interviews with adults (for adults only) harassed as children for sexual stereotyping are poignantly presented. Young children in the movie respond to their teacher on issues of name-calling and stereotyping in thoughtful and candid ways. These segments are appropriate for elementary age children.

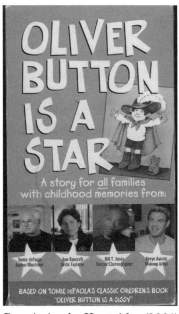

"I'll say something and you say if it is a boy or girl thing."

playing with dolls (girls) painting and building (boys)
shopping (girls, moms) fixing cars (boys)

"Think of put-down names you have heard, been called or you called someone." (retard, idiot, dumbbell, cry baby)

Permission by Huntvideo (2001)

ROLE-PLAY

6. Create exercises for children to become empathetic to anyone treated unkindly or excluded for who they are. This can include "being gay" and called a name or "being straight" and called gay or any other form of bullying and harassment.

Creating role-plays and projective dialogue can be a vehicle for enhancing deeper understanding of the hurt and low self-esteem prejudicial stereotyping brings. It is important that children realize the harasser, the victim, and the onlooker have individual roles.

Scenario One: Michael was 7 years old.

He lived in a lesbian family with two moms.

Peter teased him all the time.

"You are so weird.
You have two moms.
Your moms are lesbians.
There is something wrong with them."

Photograph by Kyna Shilling

He would often start crying on the playground as Peter shouted these mean words when many others could hear. Tony and Alice saw what happened and watched Michael alone and sad. They didn't know what to do. Suggest questions for individual and interactive discussions.

What would you do if you were Peter, Michael, Tony, and Alice?
How do you think each person feels?
What could each person do differently to change the bigoted comments?

Scenario Two: Ralph was a 10-year-old boy who loved gardening and cooking. He didn't like team sports and tended to enjoy artistic hobbies of painting and sculpture. While the rest of the boys in his class were playing basketball at lunch, he would sketch a beautiful scene. Mark, one of the players, walked by him, and causally knocked down his drawing, stepping on it as if it was an accident.

"You are such a fag! Why don't you go play with the girls?"

Ralph picked up the destroyed drawing on the ground and threw it in the trash. He didn't say a word. He just walked away. Leroy and Mario were watching. They had stopped playing ball when this happened. They felt bad for Ralph, but Mark was their friend. They didn't know what to do. A helpful discussion could include:

What would you do if you were Ralph, Mark, and
  Leroy and Mario?
How do you think each person feels?
What could each person do differently to change the
  bigoted comments?

ACTIVITIES

7. Involve children in activities to highlight their feelings on LGBT issues and gay/lesbian family life.

Activity: A method of introducing discussion on LGBT issues in a classroom is to ask the children what they think gay or lesbian means. This can be recorded on the blackboard and then categorized as facts and fiction. (Adapted from *It's Elementary,* 1996.)

It is a beginning step to separate culturally learned bias from the realities of LGBT life. These stereotypes are constantly reinforced to our children, over and over again. By talking about it, misinformation and bias can be appropriately corrected. The following ideas were given by fourth and fifth graders.

"I think . . . one meaning of gay is happy. And you
  know, how like if you have someone you like, and
  they like you, you're usually happy. I think that might
  be the reason."
"I mostly get it from my parents and my aunts and
  uncles. Because they are always talking about it,
  saying it's wrong, and that you shouldn't do it."
"People say I act like a girl and sometimes I do."

It can be difficult for a teacher to respond to such comments. Often the value of the exercise is simply for the children to *"hear themselves"* and contrast their own thoughts with their classmates. They may have never questioned automatic responses to these issues before, and now can begin new internal awareness and thoughtfulness.

Activity: A third-grade class began a discussion by creating a WEB, a basic starting point that builds common knowledge of students' preconceived ideas and leads them to a next step of understanding. The word gay or lesbian was placed in the center of a circle. Children's negative and positive attitudes were expressed and placed as separate branches on the WEB. It was visually, intellectually, and emotionally very powerful to watch the complex web of often contrasting and conflicting thoughts expand across the entire blackboard. What seemed like a simple idea grew into so much more to think about.

The WEB: Children's Ideas on the Words Gay and Lesbian

gay and lesbian are   discrimination

the same as real people   homophobia and fear

it's ok to be gay   **Gay and Lesbian**   calling names

people are mean to gay people   weird to be gay and lesbian

we are all the same   Hitler and Nazis

The discussion that followed uncovered many extreme ideas which existed previous to the WEB building. The children began to realize that name-calling and judgments sometimes were unconscious, and that they hurt. They also realized they had a choice in what they said and thought. (Adapted from *It's Elementary,* 1996.)

Activity: Invite students to participate in an activity entitled *"Outside the Box,"* which highlights gender stereotyping. Students can be asked to draw a big box and put inside everything that was okay for girls to be or do. Students can also draw a big box and put everything that was okay for boys to be or do. The following are discussion questions:

What is okay for you to do or be that fits in the box (as a girl or as a boy)?
What kinds of things are you or do you do that fit outside the box?
What makes it hard to be outside the box? What makes you go back inside the box?

Children can list lots of things girls could do or be inside the box. Some are playing with dolls, dressing up, wearing pink, and having a pony tail. Many girls feel it is hard when people tease them for not wearing dresses, forcing some to wear skirts even when it feels uncomfortable. The following exercise can be used for boys and girls to identify things okay (inside the box) or not okay (outside the box). This example is for girls.

Outside the Box		Inside the Box
wear blue		*wear pink*
play sports		*be a ballerina*
be a firefighter		*wear dresses*
coach football		*use fingernail polish*

Photograph by Kyna Shilling

This is an exercise adapted from the *Let's Get Real Curriculum Guide,* 2004, Women's Educational Media, which was adapted from "Making Friends: A Curriculum for Making Peace in Middle School" by Hugh Vasquez, M. Neil Myhand & Allan Creighton with Todos Institute (Hunter House Publishers, 2003).

PROJECTS

8. Create projects that demonstrate there are lots of ways people and families can be.

Teachers can share books, videos, and posters with classes on related topics. They can explore famous LGBT role models and invite some as guest speakers to their class. Classes can present plays on different family units, make a booklet such as "A Book about Gay and Lesbian People," invite LGBT parents to speak on family life, and display a photo gallery of "Different Kinds of Families." Posters can be shared by teachers and counselors to motivate discussion. This poster, *Respect All Families,* from the COLAGE organization, is an excellent example:

Permission by COLAGE

Project: One school system advocating instructing in gay issues hosted a photo exhibit. This exhibit was entitled *"Love Makes a Family: Living in Lesbian and Gay Families."* Beautiful photographs of gay and lesbian people, family, culture, and life were displayed, and these everyday images helped to normalize negative visual conditioning. Although this project was at first met with controversy, the school challenged the questioning and welcomed community attendance. (Adapted from *It's Elementary,* 1996.)

Project: Another project for early childhood education is for children to discuss what is similar and different about their families. They can then complete a chart similar to the one below and share with their classmates in a discussion.

How My Family Is the Same   How My Family Is Different

_____   _____

_____   _____

_____   _____

_____   _____

_____   _____

(Adapted from That's A Family! Viewing Guide, 2002, Women's Educational Media)

Project: One second-grade class in *It's Elementary* created a class booklet with words and illustrations and the title was *"Everyone is equal: A book about gay and lesbian people."* The introduction to the book explained, "We made this book to tell people to respect gays and lesbian people and to try to stop kids who are making fun of gay and lesbians." One page read, "Just because two boys and girls hang out with each other does not mean they are gay." Another said, "Name calling is not OK." One child wrote about going to the Capitol with her mom to "march with people that like gay people." (Adapted from *It's Elementary,* 1996.)

One little boy even wrote a poem for the booklet and drew a picture to explain it. He perceives his classmate as a normal kid with two moms and discusses homophobia and the fear of gay people.

He feels "It's got to go!"

Reprinted with permission from "Rethinking Schools"
Vol. 11 #2. http://www.rethinkingschools.org

CLUBS AND ALLIANCES

9. Develop clubs and alliances within the school.

One middle school girl, Andrea, had begun to feel very isolated keeping her inner secret of being a lesbian. She came out at the end of the school year and by the next fall had decided she wanted to create a gay–straight alliance in her school. Andrea formulated a plan and her school supported her 100%. Her goal was to create a forum for straight and LGBT kids to come together, get to know each other, and have fun, and just *"get past the gayness."* The alliance met at lunchtime and friendships grew. They even created a school dance and a "gay–straight" day at school.

Andrea and other members of the gay–straight alliance were told of a local church preaching for LGBT children and teens to become heterosexual. Andrea and a group of straight friends decided to protest, carrying the slogan, "We are straight, but we don't need to hate" (*Keeping Kids Healthy,* 2003). Andrea explained that she was very grateful for the support.

She said it helped her to feel normal and eased her path to join in traditional school activities such as going to the prom.

ROLE MODELS

10. Invite guest speakers.

Invite guest speakers in the community who are openly LGBT to speak to the class not only about their sexual orientation but also the active and prominent role they play in the community. These speakers can include a teacher in the school, a parent, a community helper such as a firefighter or police officer, or a politician, physician, or religious leader. Allow time for the children to ask questions.

11. Create discussion about well-known LGBT role models.

> *If it weren't for homosexuals, there would be no culture. We can trace that back thousands of years. So many of the great musicians, the great painters, were homosexual. Without their input, it would be an entirely different, flat world.*
>
> Elizabeth Taylor (Carlson, 2007, p. C7)

Use quotes such as this one to create discussions about respected homosexual persons who serve as role models. Present a broad spectrum of individuals, emphasizing what kind of people they are and their impact on society and contribution to the world. The following are role models in the political, entertainment, sports, and religious arena: Ellen DeGeneres, Representative Barney Frank, Reverend Gene Robinson, John Amaechi, Sgt. Eric Alva, Esera Tuaolo, Lance Bass, Billie Jean King, Harvey Milk, and Senator Rich Madaleno.

 # No Name-Calling Week

More than 5,000 educators and administrators officially registered to take part in the *No Name-Calling Week* campaign, January 2006, a project of GLSEN and Simon & Shuster Children's publishing, inspired by the book *The Misfits,* by James Howe. This program was done in collaboration with more than 40 educational organizations, and has become a nationwide effort to stop name-calling in the schools. Although the project is geared toward grades five to eight, it can be modified for varying grade levels.

The *No Name-Calling Week* program has gained national recognition as a vehicle that addresses the problems associated with verbal slander and the tools educators and other caring adults can use to combat it. This program includes a manual and video and free lesson plans that can be downloaded from the Internet (http://www.nonamecallingweek.org) to help create dialogue about ways to eliminate name-calling in our homes, schools, and community.

Results from surveys of the impact of the past two years of its existence indicate that in "2004 bullying surveys in schools report a significant decrease in the amount of bullying and harassment in school after taking part in the first *No Name-Calling Week* and its activities . . . [GLSEN Executive Director Kevin Jennings explains] "Every week should and can be a No Name-Calling Week and every school should be a place where students feel safe and protected."

(GLSEN, 2006b)

 # No Name-Calling Week: Creative Expression Contest

No Name-Calling Week Creative Expression Contest had one third of its participants aged 8–18 submitting original artwork, music, poetry, videos, and essays. The contributions of these young people share an intimate understanding of name-calling and its negative impact on themselves and others. Their work displays valuable insights into deeper compassion and understanding, resilience, and creative problem-solving approaches to this challenging problem. The following are examples of the materials presented.

The first is the Creative Expression Contest Grand Prize Winner 2006 awarded to Chrisopher, age 8.

Christopher's collage in mixed media is entitled "Junky Words Belong in the Trash Can." He explains through imagery that hurtful words should be thrown away.

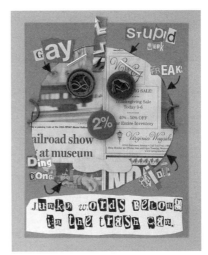

Permission by GLSEN

The third-place Creative Expression Contest Winner 2006 was Lara, age 13. Her poem, "New Beginnings," discusses the aspects of all sides of name-calling and bullying, the victim, the bully and the onlooker, and presents positive alternatives to work with this problem for each group.

PART ONE: TO THE VICTIM

Stand strong
What they say isn't true
The names will only hurt
If you let them get to you

Don't be afraid
They just don't have a clue
It's nothing personal
They just happened to pick on you

If you permit them to make you a victim
Of all the "games" they play
They will have won
And will do it everyday

Don't let the name-calling hold you back
For that is what it's meant to do
If you ignore them
They won't ever bother with you

The time is ripe
To start anew
Anything is possible
This is too

PART TWO: TO THE WITNESS

Don't just be a witness
One who sees, but doesn't do
What is happening to the victims
Could just as easily happen to you

Don't snicker as you walk by
And encourage them to strike
They will feel overlooked
And that they won't like

Don't be the audience
Of their cruelty and evil
Just walk away
And they will look uncivil

Be part of the solution, not of the problem
Make the victim your friend
Be welcoming
Setting a new trend

The time is ripe
To start anew
Anything is possible
This is too

PART THREE: TO THE BULLY

Why? Is all I have to say
In disgrace, in dismay
Why pick on someone day after day
Can't you think of a better way?

Why do you name call?
Envy is one possibility
Why not admire the person instead
Is that beyond your capability?

Name-calling is not the way
And bullying is hardly the tool
That can carry you forward
And make you feel "cool"

Be recognized and respected
By doing good things proudly for all to see
Things that are meaningful
And will help you model be

The time is ripe
To start anew
Anything is possible
This is too

Permission by GLSEN

The last two pieces are examples of artwork given Creative Expression Contest Honorable Mention 2006 awards. They illustrate the magnitude of name-calling that exists in school and its repercussions for all students.

The first by Michelle, age 12, is entitled "Untitled." She shares an image of a multitude of words that slur, defame, and hurt surrounding any child.

Permission by GLSEN

The second-prize honorable mention drawing is by Alexia, age 13. It is called "Don't Be the One Who Tears Kids Apart."

This picture creates an image of the way name-calling can tear one's self-image apart. Words can stick on kids and they then are forced to carry them wherever they go.

One word on her picture was gay.

Permission by GLSEN

Ally Week

GLSEN began a nationwide project in the schools named Ally Week. This is a one-week action seeking "to empower straight students, faculty and administration to be allies in making anti-lesbian, gay bisexual and transgender (LGBT) name calling, bullying and harassment unacceptable in K–12 schools."

Executive director and founder of GLSEN, Kevin Jennings explains that "Allies have always been an integral part of the safer schools movement and this project seeks to encourage straight allies to make a visible stand, and celebrates their key role in ensuring safer schools for students" (Students Across the Country take "Pledge" to be Allies, September, 19, 2005).

Over 300 clubs throughout the United States have registered to become an ally.

Many students wear buttons and share stickers to show their commitment to becoming an ally for one year against bullying, harassment, and name-calling.

Permission by GLSEN

Permission by GLSEN

"What do you think? A group exercise to increase heterosexual ally behavior" is a group exercise. It was adapted form Social Norms Theory and the work of the Gay Alliance of the Genesse Valley (Tanya Smolinsky, GLSEN, 2001.)

This exercise encourages empowerment for children and teenagers to act as allies toward LGBT people by correcting misconceptions of peer attitudes and then be free to perceive themselves as allies. Each person is given the following survey and instructions.

 # What Do We Think?

For each of the statements below, circle the number most closely corresponding with both your own belief and the belief you feel is typically held by members of your peer group.

1 = strongly disagree; 2 = disagree; 3 = unsure; 4 = agree; 5 = strongly agree

1. *Being lesbian, gay, bisexual or transgender (LGBT) is healthy and normal.*
   a. Your peers' typical response   1   2   3   4   5
   b. Your response   1   2   3   4   5

2. *I would be accepting towards a close friend or family member who is LGBT.*
   a. Your peers' typical response   1   2   3   4   5
   b. Your response   1   2   3   4   5

3. *LGBT people should have the same rights as straight people.*
   a. Your peers' typical response   1   2   3   4   5
   b. Your response   1   2   3   4   5

Survey Results

Social norms are beliefs about attitudes acceptable or expectable in a social context. Sometimes, people misperceive the norms of their peer group, and use these inaccurate perceptions to choose to engage in behaviors they believe to be a part of these false peer norms. With regard to the above survey, most people misperceived their peers' attitudes, presuming their peers were less accepting of LGBT people than they were themselves.

This leads many young people to avoid becoming an ally because they mistakenly fear the lack of peer support. Sometimes this misperception can be so great that one may internalize the preconceived prejudice or harass LGBT students. In a study of 240 undergraduate dormitory residents, research found that students' personal attitudes toward LGBT people were significantly more positive than the attitudes they thought their friends and fellow students held.

Students are encouraged to sign the following pledge. This pledge becomes a commitment to extend themselves as an ally by intervening in bullying or harassment throughout the year.

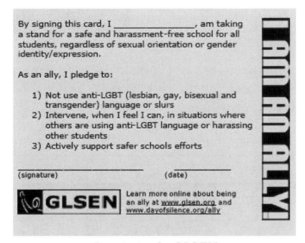

By signing this card, I _____, am taking a stand for a safe and harassment-free school for all students, regardless of sexual orientation or gender identity/expression.

As an ally, I pledge to:

1) Not use anti-LGBT (lesbian, gay, bisexual and transgender) language or slurs
2) Intervene, when I feel I can, in situations where others are using anti-LGBT language or harassing other students
3) Actively support safer schools efforts

_____   _____
(signature)   (date)

GLSEN   Learn more online about being an ally at www.glsen.org and www.dayofsilence.org/ally

I AM AN ALLY!

Permission by GLSEN

The faculty is encouraged to reward allies for their courage and commitment. The goal of Ally Week is to not use anti-LGBT language or slurs and to get involved whenever possible in situations where students are being mistreated. The emphasis is the dramatic impact active involvement has on diminishing stereotyping and exclusion.

Exploring Feelings

A 2005 study conducted by Harris Interactive found that nearly half of students (47%) and a majority of teachers (64%) in junior high/middle schools consider harassment a serious problem.

(GLSEN, 2006b, p. 2)

Teachers, counselors, principals, school nurses, school psychologists, and social workers may find it helpful to explore their own feelings and perceptions related to gay issues. Their role as mentors and supporters is crucial for the health and well-being of their students. Many educators may feel uncomfortable exploring this subject with youth.

It is helpful for *any member* of the school staff to look inward.

By reflecting on their own attitudes toward LGBT young people, they will be better able to support them.

Photograph by Kyna Shilling

The following questionnaire can provide insights to normalize common ideas. It can be used as a tool for creating dialogue and exploring self-understanding and awareness of school staff regarding their LGBT population.

 # Educator Questionnaire Regarding LGBT Students

1. Have you ever had an LGBT student in your classroom?

2. What was your attitude toward him or her?

3. Did you do anything to facilitate their comfort as a LGBT student? Their discomfort?

4. Are you aware of your school's harassment policies?

5. What would you do if an LGBT student was being harassed?

6. Has this ever happened in your school?

7. Does your school create an open environment for clubs, bulletin board displays, and speakers for LGBT students?

8. Do you personally feel it is right or wrong to be LGBT? Why?

9. What resources are you aware of in your school library on these issues?

10. Is there a peer support program for LGBT students at your school? If not, what community resources are you aware of for adolescents and their families?

 # What Can the School System Do to Advocate Civil Liberties for All Students?

Every young person has the right to a sense of self-respect and dignity. In public education, we serve the needs of all our students. Some are gay and lesbian and we need to serve them, too. We're supposed to be teaching them to live in an increasingly diverse society. This shouldn't be a place where prejudice is fostered. It's where discrimination should be fought.

(Dr. Virginia Uribe, Founder, Project 10, *LA Times Interview,* 1984)

1. Schools can not assume heterosexuality. LGBT people can be students, faculty, and friends.

2. Schools can use the words lesbian, gay, bisexual, and transgender in positive ways in daily conversation.

3. Schools can include the significance of LGBT role models in lessons and class discussions, highlighting famous people known to be homosexual.

4. Schools can invite LGBT guest speakers that can serve as role models of respected citizens.

5. Schools can teach methods to stop homophobic harassment to students and faculty. They can request it be stopped by explaining these words are hurtful and wrong.

6. Schools can promote inclusive library collections of literature so students have places to find accurate information about gender identity and sexual orientation.

7. Schools can educate athletic staff and students to reduce bias and bullying so often found in locker rooms and gymnasiums.

8. Schools can create dances, proms, and social programming inclusive of the entire LGBT and heterosexual community.

9. Schools can collaborate with staff to address prejudice in all forms of diversity and oppression and create a united front.

10. Schools can recognize and value the role of heterosexual allies in helping to create a change in school climate extinguishing LGBT harassment.

11. Schools can provide appropriate health education that addresses the needs of LGBT youth, and affirms similar issues shared with straight peers.

12. Schools can celebrate LGBT History Month by recognizing the struggles, contributions, and victories of this community with special lessons, events, displays, and assemblies.

13. Schools can allow students to create a GSA group for a time and place to dialogue about LGBT issues and recognize the value of open dialoguing that leads to healing.

14. Schools can support inclusive antidiscrimination policies in order for the gay and lesbian community to know that their school values equality and they are protected against discrimination. These policies include zero tolerance for homophobic slurs or actions with clear boundaries and consequences being strongly implemented into the school program.

15. Schools can establish a "safe zone," with a familiar sticker or poster on the door of a guidance counselor, school nurse, coach, or administrator.

    This safe zone sticker or poster signifies to heterosexual and gay and lesbian students that this is a person with whom I can share feelings about LGBT issues, LGBT harassment, and from whom I can gain accurate information on the subject.

16. Schools can provide a bulletin board to display written information and brochures detailing support groups, the school policy and implications on sexual harass-
Permission by GLSEN
ment, legislation, and community activities for the homosexual community. (Adapted from GLSEN, 2003, p. 34)

Conclusion

The rights of every man are diminished when the rights of any man are diminished.

President John F. Kennedy

Teaching children about gay and lesbian issues in the school system can provide an objective forum to dispel myths, identify and extinguish homophobia, and incorporate concepts of equality for all. Some parents and educators feel these are worthy topics to include in their curriculum. Others feel it is far too liberal, not at all the school's business, and sending the wrong message to our children.

We do know change is needed and that change begins with educating youth. The earlier that young people can integrate the universal concept that "people are different and that they are all entitled to equal rights and dignity," the sooner our society as a whole can reach new levels of respect for one another.

Photograph by Kyna Shilling

Possibilities for LGBT Participation in Daily Life: Evolving Relationships and Communities

CHAPTER 7

Parenting LGBT Children:
A Foundation
for Love and Support

Photograph by Kyna Shilling

PARENTAL REACTION • ACCEPTANCE
REJECTION AND ALIENATION • MEDIA DEPICTION
STEREOTYPICAL PARENTAL RESPONSE
A PARENT'S PROCESS
A MOTHER'S LOVE • A DAD'S STORY
THE POWER OF POSITIVE RESPONSE
EXPLORING FEELINGS • PARENT QUESTIONNAIRE
SAFE SPACES • INTERVENTIONS

"One never loves enough."

Aldous Huxley

Hearing the words *"Mom I think I am gay, lesbian, bisexual, or transgender"* can be life-changing for many parents. Within an instant of hearing these words, their preconceived image, dreams, and future expectations of their child are dramatically reshaped.

Yet, parents can choose to be supportive.

It is still the same child they have always loved.

Parents can grow with him or her as they venture into lives with LGBT relationships.

All too often, young people look to parents to be their ultimate support. Many times, parents cannot overcome the hurdles of prejudice. Ultimately, many mothers and fathers distance, alienate, and disown their daughters or sons because of their sexual orientation or gender identity.

Some young people would choose isolation or death rather than disclose to their parents; others feel they are the only people they *can* turn to. The level of trust is immense as a child who has inwardly struggled with sexual orientation or gender identity decides to confide in his or her parents. The very fact a son or daughter brings their truth into the open creates fertile ground for the growth of great pride in terms of parental trust, for they have exemplified courage and honesty that most would run from. And, for this, LGBT youth need to be commended and not rejected.

 # The Range of Parental Response

Significant numbers of lesbian and gay youth still face rejection and abuse from their parents and relatives; and more than one quarter of them is forced to leave home due to conflicts over sexual orientation.

(The National Youth Advocacy Coalition, 2003)

The range of parental response to a child's gay disclosure can range on a continuum from complete rejection to extreme activism. Points on this continuum vary, grow, and evolve as the nature of the relationship and deeper understandings emerge. Parental alienation can reinforce self-hatred, isolation, and suicide ideation.

Parental rejection can be life-threatening.

Parental support can increase self-confidence and growth.

The humor of this cartoon is apparent. It illustrates the timelessness of parental disappointment over the loss of the idealized child.

FLYING MCCOYS©2006 Glenn and Gary McCoy. Dist. by UNIVERSAL PRESS SYNDICATE. Reprinted with Permission. All rights reserved.

 # Stereotypical Parental Responses

1. Disbelief: "I don't believe you. "It's a phase. You'll pass through it."
2. Self-blame: "It's my fault. I was too protective. I should have pushed harder. I have to blame someone; I might as well blame myself."
3. Denial: "You are not gay! You are not. It is out of the question."

4. Anger and depression: "Talk some sense into him! Don't be ridiculous!"

(Adapted from Bernstein, 2003, p. 71.)

Sue at age 16 had struggled for over a year for the courage to tell her parents she was a lesbian. She was frightened that her mother and father would stop loving her. To her delight, her dad's first response was, "I love you. I want to do whatever I can to understand." Sue felt safe and reassured by her parent's love.

Wayne's dad threw him out of the house the night he confided in him he was gay. His father shouted, "I never want to see you again!" and slammed the door in his face. Wayne was 18. Now he is 26 and his dad still refuses to recognize his existence.

Tish was 13 when she told her dad she was bisexual. His only words were, "You are too young to engage in sex." Her sexual orientation was never discussed again.

Sally told her dad she was a lesbian and hoped he would be accepting.
Instead, his response was hurtful beyond understanding, as he shouted, "I'd rather you were mentally retarded than a lesbian."

Photograph by Kyna Shilling

 # Media Depiction of Parental Response

Huff, a new series on Showtime TV, depicted an episode of a young gay teen, Sam, coming out to his parents. Terrified by his parents' response, he explains to the therapist his father's unconscionable reaction, which was, "You would be better off dead!" His mother immediately slapped him across the face and started crying as she demanded, "You tell me what I did wrong!" Sam became so frustrated with his perceived minimization by his therapist that he immediately took out a gun and shot himself in the therapist's office.

The Power of Positive Response

These dramatic scenarios underscore the depth of importance of the parental response and its capacity to devastate or uplift their children through their coming out. An understanding of the following process parents experience is essential in helping them facilitate a healthy acceptance and a shift in vision as this new phase of their life with their child emerges.

A Parent's Process

For other parents, like myself, it is important to take a stand by joining the cause and marching in the parade. As the slogan goes, "Equality through visibility." The more visible our gay sons and daughters are, and the more visible we are as supportive family members, the better we will be able to help them achieve equality.

(Betty Degeneres [Ellen's mom], 1999, p. 326)

- Family members may experience a wide range of feelings that include self-blame, grief over the perceived loss of grandchildren and traditional marriage, fear for their child's happiness, health and safety, and anger, shame, or disbelief.

- Family members may have had an awareness of their child's homosexuality and tried to discourage the child or create a supportive environment.

- The impact of learning a child is gay can result in crisis.

- Family adjustment may begin with a period of mourning the loss of their perceived heterosexual youth and the beginning of the awareness of their own prejudices and their resolve to dispelling them.

Photograph by Kyna Shilling

- The family members begin a process of integration, which is ongoing and continually changing as life presents challenges and rewards in the moving toward positive acceptance of a young person's identity and orientation. Parental support groups are an effective intervention for dialogue and normalization for the family.

 # Open Acknowledgment: A Mother's Love

Mary was the mother of a gay son. She explained that although it was initially a shocking reality for her to hear her son was gay, she miraculously and thankfully began understanding more of her son's world as he patiently shared thoughts and feelings to maintain and strengthen their all-important relationship of deep communication. Although many times he expressed he never thought she could really understand, it seems as though through time Paul came to the realization she does.

Mary explained to friends and family at Paul's college graduation party her tender love and true respect for this wonderful young man. He had always been a fine person and a hard-working individual, and was becoming even more so as he approached that special day. She was very proud.

"Ever since I have heard that Paul was gay, I have tried very hard to learn more about what *it is* to be gay. Because anything that is a part of Paul is something I want to understand. I was born with a given sexual orientation, and could be no other—I know it is the same for Paul. The strength, depth of character, sensitivity, and appreciation of life that Paul possesses is part of his being homosexual."

"I prayed very hard for a wonderful son.
"My prayers were answered in this beautiful soul, my son Paul.
"I am eternally grateful."

A Child Comes Out: A Dad's Story

Susan Salezberg (2004, pp. 112–114) presents common themes experienced by parents after disclosure of being gay by a child. They include awareness of difference, knowing with certainty after coming out, emotional detachment, fears of estrangement, and adjustment and education. She describes parental patterns after disclosure as commonly including *coming out* as a defining moment, feeling a parental disconnect, and eventually reorganizing the parenting structure. These patterns may not be linear as mothers and fathers weave in and out of phases as new aspects of family life emerge.

Joe was a parent of a gay son. He had attended several support group meetings for parents of gay or lesbian children and decided to express his journey through writing. He realized it was cathartic in his evolving process of parenting an LGBT youth, and enlightening in conceptualizing his sensitive internal and external experience. The following is his story of his son Brad's coming out, and the impact it had on him and his wife. Several of the pre-mentioned common themes and parental patterns by Susan Salzberg are highlighted in Joe's story.

I'VE GOT SOMETHING TO TELL YOU. . . DISCLOSURE AS A DEFINING MOMENT

"I still remember the night my wife and I were relaxing in bed—feeling good, watching TV and talking about how we should be able to slip effortlessly into the retirement stage of our life within the next several years. We were happy to note that our home was just about paid for, retirement funding was, while not everything we might have dreamed of, pretty decent for a couple with fairly simple needs, college funds had been secured and with one semester of high school to go, our son, Brad, seemed on his way. Honor roll, friends, and a car that ran reasonably well. It seemed. . . well, *made in the shade,* as we used to say when I was Brad's age.

I hardly noticed that Brad had calmly walked into our bedroom and sat down. He had been a bit moody lately, but we chalked that up to normal 'growing pains' for a seventeen-year-old boy. He was always a sensitive kid and took everything pretty seriously. He took himself seriously. It's not as if he was obsessed by what was on his mind, but if he thought something was important enough to give it his time, he wanted it to be done well. That went with just about everything. His hobbies, his friendships, his music collection and the way he dressed—a delicate balance of preppy and homeboy that he created as his own unique and comfortable style. His room was another story. . . sort of like Hurricane City! In a way we were happy about his room. . . it seemed so normal and appropriate for a boy his age.

Anyway, after a while he said he had something important to tell us, adding 'don't worry, it's nothing bad. . . .' What could it possibly be we wondered for what seemed a long time? "I think I'm gay," he said flatly, and then time stopped. Time stopped, I think, for a long time. It felt like an eternity. My mind was numb. I didn't know how to react. I didn't know what I was feeling, or if I were feeling anything!"

AWARENESS OF DIFFERENCE

"Then my brain-fog cleared like how clarity comes in moments of crisis and all sorts of thoughts came rushing in. We had wondered would he be gay when he was five and play-acted a female role in a little one-minute impromptu play he happily made up for us in our den. Had I been involved enough during his childhood? What had I done wrong as a dad? I remembered early in my life thinking maybe I was gay because it didn't seem to work out with girls the way I thought it was supposed to. I remembered how awkward and painful growing up was at times for me. I thought this must be what he is experiencing.

Surely it would resolve itself for him just as it did for me. He's just jumping to premature conclusions, right? It'll be fine, right? Just don't panic—stay calm. Reassure him. Love him. He's a great kid, just confused, right? He was apparently still talking but I hadn't heard any more of it; my own inner dialog was too loud and distracting to listen to him. What's that he was saying?

He was saying how he had known he was gay since he was 12! How could that be? How could we not have known? He said he was sure! Sure? What exactly did 'sure' mean? Panic alternated with compassion. Back and forth. Surely this was a dream reenactment of some *Outer Limits* show I had seen.

No, he was SURE."

EMOTIONAL DETACHMENT

"For the next several days my wife, Ellen, and I worked hard to stay as normal as we could but our world had been shaken. We weren't even entirely sure why or how, but suddenly the earth's axis had shifted for us. Our fantasy about the future, grandchildren, our sense of what it means to be a family, our son's future happiness. . . and safety . . . all of these things and too many more suddenly went from securely predetermined and bankable to totally up in the air, scary and unknown. We were literally 'blown away.' Our minds were glazed over. We kept functioning outwardly. Nobody knew what a jumbled mess of thoughts and feelings we were inside. For a while it was just putting one foot in front of the other to get through the day."

THE LOSS OF THE IDEALIZED CHILD AND FUTURE

"With the imagined loss of our future goals and plans and expectations, life seemed to deflate and lose its organization and meaning, like a beach ball with the air let out. A fog of depression and confusion took the place of earlier satisfaction and pride. Gradually, we began to come to terms with this new reality we had not anticipated or desired. Ellen and I talked to a therapist a few times and we talked a lot to each other. We had an enormous amount of work to do, to get up to speed, as they say, if we were to be able to relate in a genuine and loving way to each other as a family. While we were acquainted with the word 'gay' and had some preconceptions of what gay was all about, we now knew we knew nothing about it. Not when it is about your own son. Somehow it was easier and abstract when it was about other people's kids, but this, THIS was something else again."

REORGANIZING THE PARENTING STRUCTURE

"Over the next months calm seemed to come over us, an uneasy calm at first, but then gradually, a resolve and sense of purpose and strength grew. Brad was offered the opportunity to talk to a therapist that works with adolescents. That was helpful and he made good use of his time with the therapist. Later, we found a gay male therapist that helped him make his next internal and external adjustments that were necessary. This therapist also represented a kind of mentor/role model for Brad. He saw a healthy example of someone living a purposeful, productive life, openly gay and feeling good about himself. I guess we felt that if Brad is gay, at least he should have the opportunity to feel good about who and what he is, and not have to hide in shame by going underground."

ADJUSTMENT AND EDUCATION

"That process of learning, developing resolve and strength and purpose, continues to this day and is still growing. Ellen and I have just recently gotten involved in PFLAG (Parents, Families, and Friends of Lesbians and Gays). We have become more educated about gay and related issues and we have come to understand so much more about ourselves and our culture and about how young people like our son, Brad, are being wounded daily by careless and narrow thought patterns so prevalent in our society—and not just by obviously bigoted folks, but even by well-meaning people who pride themselves in thinking they are pretty liberal and broad-minded.

As we work on our inner knowing, our dedication to enlarging the thought forms of others relative to sexual orientation and gender identification issues is growing steadily. We see ourselves as very parallel to early civil-rights activists always pressing uphill against the tide of group stereotypic thought. We happily notice little and large victories that indicate that the culture is changing. Movies like *Brokeback Mountain* and *The Family Stone,* and TV shows such as *Brothers and Sisters,* are well-received by many. As a result there is a gradual shift in perception. Gay and lesbian people are beginning to be seen less as bizarre and alien phenomena, and more as a living, feeling facet of a complex cultural range of human beings, comprising a significant portion of just about any family around.

Our greatest teacher in all of this, of course, is our son, Brad. We love him more than ever."

Exploring Parental Feelings

As parents begin to become an integral part of their child's disclosure of being gay, it is important they examine their own feelings and thoughts. Many mothers and fathers, even the most liberal, are surprised at their hidden prejudice and challenging ideas, as they felt they were devoid of bigotry until they found their own child to be homosexual.

Some are confused by mixed emotions of shame, disbelief, sadness, anger, relief, acceptance, and love they may experience during this new phase of relationship. Some may immediately accept or reject their sons and daughters, while others may need time and even outside help to integrate their child's coming out. Exploring new ways of thinking openly can help parents normalize difficult attitudes as they begin to realize many reactions are very common.

LGBT Parent Questionnaire

1. What was your first reaction to your child's coming out?
2. How did he or she tell you?
3. Did you ever think your child was gay before they told you? Why?
4. How have you continued to react to your child's coming out process?
5. In what ways have you been helpful or not helpful?
6. Did you ever feel it was your fault? Why?
7. Did you ever feel there was something wrong with you or your child? What?
8. Have you shared your child's coming out with friends or family? Why or why not?
9. Have you discovered any hidden prejudices? What are they?
10. How do you see society accepting and/or rejecting your LGBT child (friends, relatives, teachers, media, etc.)?

11. Has your relationship with your child changed? In what ways?

12. Have you reached out for outside help, counseling, clergy, support groups, etc.? If so, have they been helpful?

 # Parent Support Groups

Mei-Ling's son Mike had recently disclosed he was gay. Mei-Ling was overwhelmed with the information. As an Asian American, she desperately wanted to relate to people of her own culture. She explained her feelings as follows.

"I have no one to talk to about my son being gay. None of my friends have gay kids. I hear a lot of prejudice that stops me from sharing. I need to speak to other Moms and Dads with LGBT children. Where can I go?"

Asian PFLAG members:
Permission by PFLAG

So often, parents feel alone, as they assume no other friends, relatives, or mothers and fathers of their child's friends are living the experience of having an LGBT child. Finding a support group with other parents is of great help. They begin to see many of their thoughts and feelings are very common, and they have companions who understand. Organizations such as PFLAG (Parents, Families and Friends of Lesbian and Gays) are explored in depth in chapter 9.

Parents Can Create a Safe Environment

Parental support can be a major force in a child's well-being as they step out and reveal with others their son or daughter is gay, lesbian, bisexual, or transgender. The enormous trust that children display in sharing what had been hidden for so long is a powerful tool in building a strong bond.

PFLAG'S program reinforces the message for parents to *stay close* to their children.

The following are interventions adults can create to facilitate a comfortable and safe atmosphere. Their ability to create a secure environment is paramount for their child's well-being.

Participants in this program include Cyndi Lauper, with her sister Elen, and Congressman Gregory Meeks (D-N.Y.), with his brother John. Photograph permission by PFLAG

Helpful Parent Interventions

- *Create* a supportive environment. Clearly show love and respect without judgment. Promote open discussions, and advocate for equal rights express a desire to learn and understand your child's journey.

- *Educate* parents, students, school personnel, and community and health professionals. Contribute articles, books, films, and other helpful resources.

- *Develop* a sense of community. Become involved with LGBT-related organizations. Share your experience of parenting an LGBT child with other parents.

- *Engage* LGBT role models as identifiable supports and mentors for gay youth. This could be a teacher at school or a friend at work.

- *Maintain* firm boundaries and clear limits against any slurs or abusive words or actions. Become an advocate for your child and speak up with family members and friends, educators, and people throughout the community.

- *Distinguish* between simplistic and negative media stereotyping and supportive films, TV, newspaper articles, and music portraying LGBT relationships in a real and thoughtful way. Discuss with your child.

- *Construct* language that elicits acceptance and understanding of LGBT issues and expresses equality.

C H A P T E R   8

"Coming In":
LGBT Family Life

LIFE CHOICES • SPEAKING OUT • SHARING
PARENTAL INVOLVEMENT • INVITATIONS
COMMUNITY • LGBT PARTNERSHIP
MARRIAGE EQUALITY • LGBT PARENTING
ENVIRONMENT • A CRUISE • LEGAL BARRIERS
WORK ENVIRONMENT • VOICES • POLITICS
ADVOCACY • CIVIL LIBERTIES
SUPPORT GROUPS FOR CHILDREN OF LGBT PARENTS
INTERNET

"All kinds of love can create a family."

Richardon and Parnell

The importance of writing a chapter which integrates an LGBT family life into the mainstream is twofold. Chapter 7 first presented a picture of a family system with heterosexual moms and dads successfully parenting LGBT children. This picture holds the ever-evolving process of parenting, as it unfolds for a family after they learn that their child is gay, lesbian, bisexual or transgender. Mothers and fathers may find new issues challenging, but also very rewarding. Communication can bridge the gaps that limit understanding and openness in sharing new ways of supporting and nurturing their sons and daughters. It is not only possible but often gratifying to remain a loving parent and ally as well.

The second premise for creating this chapter on *LGBT family life* is to recognize new family systems that include marriage equality and parenting by two moms or two dads with gay parents and heterosexual children. LGBT youth often question how it will be possible to step into a future while presently living the impact of today's ever-changing climate on gay issues. These young people wonder how they can create a successful life. It is essential to understand the emotional and physical environment they now live in, in order to help them create the potential for partnership, family, and children. We can examine their frequently asked questions about the future based on the ever-changing range of bigotry and acceptance that engulf their world.

"The 2000 Census is showing huge increases in the number of same-sex couples sharing households in the District and the nation, reflecting a decade's worth of political and social gains that have made gay men and lesbians far more willing to report their living arrangements . . . with census figures showing more than 3,500 same-sex couples living in the city (Washington, DC), a 66 percent increase over the figures reported in the 1990 Census" (Cohn, 2001).

 Life Choices

There are 601,209 same-sex couples in the United States and Puerto Rico.

(2000 5% PUMS file,
http://www.gaydemographics.org/USA/PUMS/nationalintor.htm)

Of all lesbians and gay men, 45.1% and 52.7% live in urban areas respectively, while 33.1% and 31.7% live in suburbs, respectively.

(http://www.pflagupstatesc.org/statistics.htm)

The 7 largest concentrations of the lesbian and gay population in the United States are:

New York City
San Francisco
Boston/Cambridge
Seattle, Washington
Oakland/Berkley
Washington, DC
Chicago/Evanston

(PFLAG Upstate SC, Copyright 1995–2005,
http://www.pflagupstatesc.org/statistics.htm)

Too many LGBT young people fear their future. Once they have "come out," they begin the struggle of "coming in"—coming into a life where they can maintain and enjoy successful love and family relationships and become partners and parents if they choose. They have many questions with which this chapter will deal.

How can I live productively in a LGBT relationship?
Where will I live?
Can I be a parent?
What are my rights legally?
What would be the rights of my future children?

 # Parents Speak Out: Straight Parenting of LGBT Youth

As parents we must send the message that discrimination of our loved ones is not OK. Our voices must ring out loud and clear and echo throughout the land that hate and bigotry, under any guise, are unacceptable. Speak up. Let's make all our voices heard.

(Bernstein [citing DeGeneres], 2003, Foreword)

Parenting an LGBT son or daughter is a special gift to be viewed as almost magical in creating a bond and solidifying the pure love that exists between a child and his or her parent. Parents can imprint the stamina and courage it takes for their children to live in a society where they may be hated by some who don't even know them. It gives a father and mother the opportunity to be as courageous and brave as their children as they enter a new frontier of advocacy for equal rights and normality in existence for all, especially their children.

Sharing With Others

The only way to stop homophobia is to know someone who is gay, lesbian, bisexual or transgender and realize that he or she is just a person like I am.

An anonymous teen

Being a mom, a sister, a babysitter, or a teacher of a beloved child who has disclosed their *gayness* allows these caring friends and family members a new role of informing others that gay young people *are the same human beings* they were before they came out. This helps to reestablish their inherent status as productive members of society.

When family and friends *come out,* too, they are creating a larger forum of understanding.

For all who know and respect them as well, a broader base is created for LGBT youths to *come in* and remain a part of the larger community.

Photograph by Kyna Shilling

Parental Involvement: Joining In

Many gay young people are apprehensive to include friends and parents into their life. They may fear ridicule, judgment, or abandonment. When a child reaches out to a parent to join them in an activity, it is usually done after much contemplation, resolute trust, and courage. The following scenario portrays such bravery expressed in a simple email extending an invitation for parents to join in a Family Pride parade and "come in" to her experience. Seizing the moment, and responding with enthusiastic acceptance was a key factor in widening this lesbian adolescent's spectrum of life possibilities with her family and deepening her feelings of well-being.

AN INVITATION

Nancy was 16 when she told her parents, Audrey and Tom, she was a lesbian. Although stunned and shaken by the sudden disclosure, her mother and father quickly embraced their daughter and maintained a loving relationship. The next few years were difficult for Nancy, as she began to find her way into the LGBT community and form solid relationships, eventually partnering. She shared her inner world with her mom and dad as comfort permitted. One day Audrey received an e-mail from Nancy, an invitation to enter another part of her emerging world.

"Dear Mom,

Here are some pictures of *The Pride* that took place this past summer. The most moving part of the whole parade was PFLAG. Also pictures of my friends there—gay and straight. And friends we made during the day. You'll have to come next year. But eat a hearty breakfast and take it slow.

Love yah,

Your daughter"

Photograph by Kyna Shilling

Audrey and Tom were touched with the initiation for inclusion and the sensitivity of their daughter, as this gesture opened up for them a new piece of Nancy's life they could be a part of. They seized the moment and responded immediately.

"Dear Nancy,

We would love to come next year. And we can all have a hearty breakfast together before we go. We love you too.

Your Mom and Dad"

FEELING PART OF A COMMUNITY

Nancy had explained to her parents in a previous e-mail why participation in *The Pride* was so meaningful. Her sense of belonging and feeling protected and comfortable with gay and straight friends and families was highlighted in this e-mail. The importance of feeling safe from homophobia in a community became apparent to her parents. They realized it was also important to Nancy for them to join her in this experience.

"The cool part of the whole day about the Gay Pride parade was all of the families and children running around. It's pretty cool.

You get to dismiss the way the majority of the world feels about you for the day.

Everything that surrounds you is safe."

Nancy

 # Ways That Parents Can Become Involved

Parental involvement is as varied as individual parents vary. Some are comfortable talking to their children, some seek information, many look for support, and still others speak out. All efforts are important and helpful to their sons and daughters. Many mothers and fathers have found being involved in some way with fresh life patterns of their children can be cathartic. It is very difficult to become comfortable with something you do not know or understand. Understanding increases with participation, whether it is a family trip or a day together at an LGBT event.

- Read books, participate in seminars, become educated.
- Find out the sexual harassment policies at your child's school.
- Discover if schools provide clubs for LGBT students.

- Use the creative arts for self expression—draw, write, create poetry, etc.
- Talk with other parents of LGBT children.
- Talk to your children and their friends.
- Ask questions and show interest.
- Be honest.
- Share your journey, too.
- Seek information.
- Join a support group.
- Speak out against homophobic slurs.
- Challenge conventional stereotyping.
- Become involved at the organizational level.
- Disclose you are a parent of an LGBT child.
- Advocate for legislation and join the political process.
- Spend time together through events and travel.

 # Welcoming Travel for Families: Gay-Friendly Bed and Breakfasts

Gay-friendly inns are spreading throughout the country. Straight and LGBT travelers are welcomed, allowing parents to join children comfortably. In Gary Lee's *Washington Post* article, "Gay Stays in Virginia" (2007), he explains that one guest house in Virginia permits "gay men and lesbian travelers to know this is a welcoming haven" (p. C2). DeRoach, the owner, explains, "I don't want to be concerned about how people will react if I walk around holding my partner's hand . . . so I don't want guests here to worry about that either."

Domestic or LGBT Partnership: A Long-Term Relationship

A domestic partnership is a relationship between two people who may or may not be the same gender. In this relationship, LGBT couples can live together and mutually support each other as spouses.

This is not a civil union or legal marriage, although some couples enter into domestic partnership agreements to legalize contracts involving property, finance, inheritance, and health care. Domestic partnerships do not grant the same rights and benefits as a civil union or legal marriage.

Ron and Mac met when they were very young and have lived a long-term, committed relationship. Both men are accomplished in their fields, and are open about their homosexuality. Their commitment to each other is evident. They serve as an inspiration to young gay men, modeling that long-term same-sex relationships *can and do* exist. The following is Ron's sharing of his life journey with Mac.

"Mac and I met while we were in undergraduate school. I was a senior and he was a freshman. But it wasn't until three years later that we 're-found' each other and settled into a relationship. Since I came from a divorced home, I had made up my mind that when I fell in love that I would do my best to make that relationship work for the rest of my life. Loving Mac is a very easy thing to do."

"As I look back on the 34 years that we have been together, it has been very much like a marriage in every sense of the word. We pool our resources as most married couples do. We solve problems as most married couples do."

"But, since we are gay, there has been much that we have to deal with that married couples do not—having to explain why you bring a man instead of a woman to a work function, having to figure our taxes ten different ways so that we can get the maximum return for our money, having to make sure that legal matters are in place in case something happens to either of us, etc."

"But, our life together has been a phenomenal journey that I would not change for anything. We have marvelous friends (both gay and straight) that mean the world to us. We have supporting and caring families."

"But, most importantly, we have each other.
That is what life and love is all about."

 # Toward Marriage Equality

Two people meet and fall in love. Over time, their relationship grows and they decide to spend the rest of their lives together. They plan a wedding, a formal binding into a permanent relationship with family and friends on hand as witnesses to solemn but beautiful vows. It's an occasion people dream about for most of their lives, though it is often joked that the wedding is more for the parents than the children.

But what if they are gay?

Book Jacket, *The Wedding*, Wythe, Merling, Merling, and Merling, 2000

Photograph with permission
by David Sternfeld/Freestyle Photo

Douglas and Andrew and Andrew's parents chronicle their intimate journey in deciding, implementing, and enjoying their wedding as a married couple. This chronicle is presented in their book, *The Wedding*. Douglas and Andrew share the importance of this ritual in their lives to underscore the sacredness of their loving relationship.

Religious ceremonies regarding gay marriage stir controversy in many denominations. Cooperman (2006), explains that Conservative rabbis gave permission for same-sex commitment ceremonies and ordination of gays within Conservative Judaism. A backlash to affirming gay congregants is also present. In Cooperman's and Whoriskey's article (2006), the Presbyterian Church's (USA) stance of putting a minister on trial for conducting a marriage ceremony for two women is also presented. The National Roman Catholic Bishops (Baltimore meeting, 2006) stated "Catholics with a homosexual inclination should be encouraged to chastity and to firmly adhere to the church's teaching that same-sex attractions are *disordered*" (Cooperman & Whoriskey, 2006, p. A1).

 # Marriage and Civil Unions

LGBT couples can decide to marry in a civil ceremony, a religious ceremony, or both. They also may choose to unite in a civil union. Civil unions provide legal protections and rights. They are currently recognized in Vermont, Connecticut, New Jersey, and New Hampshire (2008).

> *Civil marriage* is a legal status established through a license issued by a state government. This marriage grants legal rights to, and imposes legal obligation on the two married partners.
>
> *Religious marriage* is considered to be a sacrament or solemnization of two persons recognized by the clergy of a religious group.
>
> A *civil union* is a legal mechanism, sanctioned by civil authority, intended to grant same-gender couples legal status in a similar way to civil marriage.
>
> (Pawelski et al., 2006, p. 360)

Reactions to LGBT unions can be varied and extreme. Ann and Cindy created a religious ceremony. They were lesbians. They invited friends and family to attend. Ann's sister Sue refused to come. She wrote Ann she was living in sin and would go to hell.

Tyler's mom was told by e-mail he was gay, and she was shocked to hear that not only was he gay but that he had a partner, Justin, as well. They were in a committed relationship and wanted very much to marry in their church. Their clergy were very supportive.

With parental support and a welcoming spiritual community, Tyler and Justin married. They have remained in a partnership of respect and caring for six years.

Religious marriage is a powerful affirmation of a commitment to another human being with God's blessing. Civil marriage also validates that commitment legally.

Photograph by Kyna Shilling

 # Creating Marriage Equality

Marriage Equality is the goal. It provides legal recognition of same-sex marriage on both state and federal levels with the same rights, priviledges, and protections as legal heterosexual marriage.

The creation of marriage equality has become a global issue as well as one raised in America. In the United States, Massachusetts is the single state to recognize marriage equality on a state level, but not on a federal level. The Defense of Marriage Act (DOMA) 1996, defines marriage as a union of one man and one woman for the purposes of federal law.

The most recent country to overwhelmingly approve legislation recognizing marriage equality is South Africa (2006). South Africa was the first country globally to prohibit discrimination on the basis of sexual orientation in 1994. Home Affairs Minister Nosiviwe Mapisa-Nqakula said to his National Assembly, "When we attained our democracy, we sought to distinguish ourselves from an unjust painful past, by declaring that never again shall it be that any South African will be discriminated against on the basis of color, creed, culture and sex" (Nullis, 2006, p. A15). The bill does not specify heterosexual or homosexual relationships. It presents the "voluntary union of two persons, which is solemnized and registered by either a marriage or civil union" (Nullis, 2006, A15).

The following countries have legalized marriage equality:

S. Africa—2006, Canada—2005, Spain—2005, Belgium—2003, Netherlands—2001 (Nullis, 2006, p. A15)

> *Civil marriage is a legal status that promotes healthy families by conferring a powerful set of rights, benefits, and protections that cannot be obtained by other means . . . fostering financial and legal security, psychosocial stability, and an augmented sense of societal acceptance and support.*

(Pawelski et al., 2006, p. 391)

 # Parenting as an LGBT Couple

> *According to the 2000 census, 99% of counties in the United States have self-identified cohabiting same-sex (LGBT) couples, and many of them already have children or will have children in the future.*

(Griffith, 2005, p. 46)

Parenting is a difficult, rewarding, and full-time experience. Parenting by gay couples creates unique issues for this population that add to the basic rewards and challenges of being mothers and fathers. "Millions of gay Americans with children face uncertainty fueled by a sea of ever-changing state laws and statutes that affect everything from who is a legal parent to who may have what when a loved one dies" (Griffith, 2005, p. 43).

The American Academy of Pediatrics (AAP) presents a view that seems to have *less to do with gender issues of parents* but more to do with the finances, health, legalities, and stability of the child. "The AAP is committed to calling attention to the inextricable link between the health and well being of all children, the support and encouragement of all parents, and the protection of strong family relationships.... Civil marriage is a legal status that promotes healthy families.... Children raised by civilly married parents benefit from the legal status granted to their parents" (Pawelski et al., 2006, p. 361). Their data concludes children raised by same-gender parents do as well as those raised by *straight* parents with no more risk to children growing up with an LGBT parent.

Conscientious and nurturing adults, whether they are men or women, hetero-sexual or homosexual, can be excellent parents. The rights, benefits, and protections of civil marriage can further strengthen these families.

(Pawelski et al., 2006, p. 361)

Voices of LGBT Parents

"My last name is Simson now, the same as my partner's. I changed it because people would ask each one of us, 'Who is the real mother?'"

All three of us have the same last name now including our daughter Sophie. We haven't had this intrusive question asked since then.

Maria goes to a private school now. She makes cards for both of us on Mothers' Day but she doesn't talk about having two moms as being unusual—it's cool to have two moms.

Photograph by Kyna Shilling

I am one of two moms in a lesbian family. We take our daughter to a program for children with gay and lesbian parents. It was a big turn for her (in her life) when we took her to an event last summer where over 100 moms and moms and dads and dads with more than 200 children rented a hotel and had music, videos, and food. This event was for kids 8 and older. There was babysitting and play for the little ones along with a lot of fun.

In my daughter's school she is the only one with a mom and mom but we talked to the principal before the school year began, and our concerns were that of typical parents.

I spoke last week on a radio show about having programs for gay and lesbian parents. We probably have more than for heterosexual couples (I said on the air). But we do not discriminate, however, if a heterosexual couple wanted to join our group I would check, but I didn't think it would be a problem. I'm laughing now anyway, I hope this helps."

A Place to Live

Aunt June was explaining to her niece Catherine that someone in the neighborhood had actually talked to two lesbians. They had just moved down the street.

"Can you imagine in our neighborhood—
such a thing—lesbians—could live in *our*
neighborhood."
Catherine was the mom of a lesbian
daughter, Erika.

Photograph by Kyna Shilling

The locale of the parenting process and the safe zone of a particular school system can greatly influence parenting abilities. A mom or dad who feels secure in one state may feel at danger in another due to the wide variance of laws on LGBT partnership and marriage equality. LGBT parents can daily face change that fluctuates from friendly inclusion to hostile territory depending on the political climate and legislative actions of the moment. Many two-mom and two-dad families make individual decisions, fight back, or move to friendlier locales, seeking successful integration into a community for themselves and their children.

For families headed by LGBT couples there are questions to consider when seeking a "home." This home needs to be a place where they as a family feel valued and secure. Sometimes these parents not only do extensive research before a move, but engage a lawyer well versed in local legal issues. The following are questions these couples may consider depending on a potential friendly or hostile climate.

Considerations When Seeking a Home

- Can I become a parent?
- Can I take off work if my mate or partner or child gets sick?
- Will I be able to inherit the home we live in or the lifelong assets accrued and leave them to my children?
- Can the children become a part of a community?
- Will I be accepted like any other mom or dad?
- Will our children be accepted by others?

Legal Barriers

The wide variance of law creates an overwhelming tide of obstacles for many LGBT couples. Even the best of research and preparation can't impact the ever-changing legal system and the tide of pro-gay or antigay legislation in a perpetually changing environment. The following are just a few examples of this variance.

Massachusetts: Gay and lesbian married couples have the same rights in state matters as heterosexual couples.

Virginia: The general assembly banned civil union and same-sex couple contracts appearing to give both parties legal privileges of marriage.

Hawaii: The legislature issued a statute allowing couples to register as "reciprocal beneficiaries" that entitled them to many rights and responsibilities given in heterosexual marriages.

Twenty-six states have constitutional amendments explicitly barring the recognition of same-sex marriage, confining civil marriage to a legal union between a man and a woman. Forty-three states have statutes restricting marriage to two persons of the opposite sex.

http://en.wikipedia.org/wiki/Same-sex_marriage_in_the_United_States

One dad of a two-dad family wasn't prepared for the refusal to amend the birth certificate of their daughter to show both men as fathers in the state they had just moved to. They experienced a new state law that disallowed LGBT couples from being adoptive parents (even if they came from another state where they had already been legally recognized) creating for their daughter an "inaccurate birth certificate."

Other states allow LGBT couples to complete a second-parent adoption, making both partners "legal parents." This patchwork means your rights as a parent fluctuate based on geography, explains Carrie Evans, state legislative director for the Human Rights Campaign. "Most gay [and lesbian] parents probably have no idea when they move that [the act of moving] can change the legal status of their family" (Griffith, 2005, p. 44).

New Jersey recently passed a court decision that was a new precedent for that state. A New Jersey lesbian couple registered as domestic partners in New York and legally married in Canada some time later. Asking the court to recognize them as the joint parents of their daughter in the best interest of the child, and not their rights as a couple, Supreme Court Justice Talbert agreed and allowed them to have both of their names listed on the birth certificate. A commentary on a recent news show about this ruling was very heartening. After discussing Justice Talbert's decision, the news commentator exclaimed, "Clearly this is the direction we are going. Why don't we just do it?" These words were very affirming to many viewers.

This decision allowed full parental rights to both women.

One of the mothers, Jeanne (Griffith, 2005, p. 46), explained the ruling "was a real release."
"We always knew that we would be a family, but to have it legally recognized was really great."

Asking the court to consider the best interest of the child rather than to consider their rights as a couple made all the difference.

Photograph by Kyna Shilling

Statements and Policies: Professional Organizations Regarding LGBT Couples and Effects of Civil Union, Marriage, and Partnership Laws on Children

1. The American Academy of Pediatrics (AAP) supports "the right of every child and family to the legal, financial, and psychosocial security that results from having legally recognized parents who are committed to each other and to the welfare of their children."

2. The American Academy of Family Physicians' Congress of Delegates agreed to "establish policy and be supportive of legislation which promotes a safe and nurturing environment, including psychological and legal security for all children, including those of adoptive parents regardless of the parents' sexual orientation."

3. The American Psychological Association (APA) adopted resolutions stating that "the APA believes that it is unfair and discriminatory to deny same-sex couples legal access to civil marriage and to all its attendant benefits, rights, and privileges and shall take a leadership role in opposing all discrimination in legal benefits, rights, and privileges against same-sex couples."

4. The American Psychoanalytic Association position states, "Accumulated evidence suggests the best interest of the child requires attachment to committed, nurturing and competent parents. Evaluation of an individual or couple for these parental qualities should be determined without prejudice regarding sexual orientation. Gay and lesbian individuals and couples are capable of meeting the best interest of the child and should be afforded the same rights and should accept the same responsibilities as heterosexual parents."

5. The National Association of Social Workers (NASW) "encourages the adoption of laws that recognize inheritance, insurance, same-sex marriage, child custody, property and other relationship rights for lesbians, gay and bisexual people."

6. Related policy from the American Academy of Child and Adolescent Psychiatry (AACAP) states, "The basis on which all decisions relating to custody and parental rights should rest is on the best interest of the child. Lesbian, gay, and bisexual individuals historically have faced more rigorous scrutiny than heterosexuals regarding their rights to be or become parents. There is no evidence to suggest or support that parents with a gay, lesbian or bisexual orientation are per se different from or deficient in parenting skills, child-centered concerns and parent-child attachments, when compared with parents with a heterosexual orientation."

7. The American Medical Association (AMA) House of Delegates overwhelmingly endorsed a policy "to support legislation and other efforts to allow adoption of a child by the same-sex partner or an opposite-sex non-married partner who functions as a second parent or co-parent to that child."

8. In May 2005 the Assembly of the American Psychiatric Association (APA) approved a statement in support of legalizing same-gender marriage which was approved in July, 2005. This approval made psychiatry the first medical specialty to publicly support same-gender civil marriage.

The APA policy states, "In the interest of maintaining and promoting mental health, (the APA supports) recognition of same-sex civil marriage with all rights, benefits, and responsibilities conferred by civil marriage, and opposes restrictions to those same rights, benefits, and responsibilities" (Pawelski, 2006, pp. 362–363).

 # Work Environment

One mom of a two-mom family became ill and required many surgeries. Her partner was unable to take family leave to care for her and their children as would have been allowed for a heterosexual married couple in her work environment.

Another gay male couple found that for one father his employee insurance covered his domestic partner but the children could not be covered because the insurance did not extend to children of domestic partners. He researched his next employer and changed positions after finding out this new company offered benefits for the entire family.

After a few months, he was devastated to discover his status as an hourly employee did not have domestic-partner benefits at all, as they were only for salaried workers. This couple again moved to another state, Vermont, and registered as a civil union couple. In this state, this civil union coupling provided them with the same rights as married couples, including automatic rights such as hospital visitation, and being able to make end-of-life decisions for each other.

 # Changing Times in Corporate America

Yet, Amy Joyce (2006) reports that for many gay (LGBT) people doors are opening wider in the business world. Joyce discusses the changing trends in corporate America. Ten years ago, most companies barely acknowledged gay employees. Increasingly, companies offer domestic-partner benefits, support gay pride events, and actively recruit gay employees. The Human Rights Campaign completed a five-year survey (Joyce, 2006) by releasing the Human Rights Campaign's Corporate Equality Index, showing more companies than ever support gay, lesbian, bisexual and transgender (GLBT) workers. Out of 446 companies rated, 138 earned a score of 100%.

Helene Madonick is an openly lesbian partner of 20 years in a well-respected Washington-based law firm, Arnold & Porter, receiving the 100% rating. She explains, "It is certainly one of the reasons I stay here. It's an indicator of the working environment that is inclusive and recognizes individuality" (Joyce, 2006, pp. F1, F6).

Companies are also becoming more aware of the importance of supporting lesbian and gay employees by recognizing that a percentage of their customers may be LGBT. By taking an open stance on domestic-partner benefits, they are sending a powerful message to these constituents that they value their business. Keith

Greene, vice president of member relations at the Society for Human Resource Management, explains that companies "are smart enough to know it is a very competitive market when it comes to acquiring and retaining top quality with the specific skills . . . needed, and their goal is to cast a wide net to find, get, and keep the best people. So it becomes a business decision" (Joyce, 2006, p. F6). As of September 2006, 33 states do not outlaw discrimination based on sexual discrimination. Joyce reports Maryland and the District of Columbia do outlaw discrimination, as do 85% of the Fortune 500 companies.

Supporting LGBT issues may not always have a positive outcome. Joyce (2006, p. F6) reports the impact of homosexual support on Wal-Mart. "When news got out last month that Wal-Mart Stores Inc. had partnered with the National Gay and Lesbian Chamber of Commerce, it created a stir among some religious groups that said they would consider not shopping at the retail giant."

Although some companies have experienced a backlash for their support of gay and lesbian employees and business, others have stepped forward with groundbreaking strides towards nondiscrimination. Boeing is one of the companies receiving the 100% rating. They have offered innovations not done by other groups. Its official equal employment opportunity policy includes a prohibition of discrimination against people based on gender identity. This new term is an addition to previous use of the term sexual orientation, covering not only LGBT employees and those who are transitioning from one sex to another but also any workers verbally harassed about not acting "appropriately" male or female.

I think the corporations are recognizing that in order to be as innovative as we have to be and as competitive as we have to be, we have to avail ourselves of all the talent out there.

Everyone has something to contribute. Wherever the talent is coming from, we want that.

Joyce Tucker, vice president of global diversity and employee rights at Boeing (Joyce, 2006, p. F6)

Photograph by Kyna Shilling

Disney Says "Yes" to Gay Couples

Walt Disney Company has offered partner benefits to employees since 1996. It has achieved a perfect score on the Human Rights Campaign's corporate equality index. For many years, thousands of LGBT tourists have come to Disney World Orlando for an unofficial *gay day* in late spring, although it was neither sponsored nor discouraged by the company. Walt Disney announced in April of 2007 that gay couples can purchase the Fairy Tale Wedding package allowing them to exchange vows at the theme park and on its cruise ship. Although same-sex couples have been allowed to use certain facilities at the park, they now have access to very public elements including commitment ceremonies at one of the park's marriage pavilions with Disney costumed characters at the reception. This policy applies to overseas parks as well. Donn Walker, a Disney spokesman, explains, "We believe this change is consistent with Disney's longstanding policy of welcoming all guests in an inclusive environment" (Ahrens, 2007, p. A6).

The events held for gay couples are same-sex commitment ceremonies and not legal marriage. Human Rights Campaign president Joe Solmonese states, "When an iconic company like the Walt Disney Company recognizes the value of treating all customers fairly, gay or straight, it reaps the benefits" (Ahrens, 2007, A6).

Corporate organizations, educators, parents, business leaders, health professionals, entertainers, clergy, public servants, lawmakers, advocacy groups, LGBT and straight youth, and all other caring citizens must join together as a community of strength. MacNeil emphasizes that "The rights and liberties that our founding fathers wrote into the Declaration of Independence and the Constitution were meant for all people. It is time that our nation realized that a significant portion of our society is today excluded and the laws need to be written and enforced to ensure that lesbians and gays are not discriminated against in employment, public accommodations, and housing" (Bernstein, 2003, p. xv).

The Rights of Parents and Children

The Lambda Legal Defense Fund estimates 6 million to 10 million gay parents are caring for 6 million to 14 million children.

(Lithwick, 2006, p. B2)

One of the arguments for marriage equality is as follows. If LGBT parents were legally allowed to marry, many of the rights inherent to their children would be automatic. Human Rights Campaign's Carrie Evans (Griffith, 2005, p. 46) explains, "Not to allow a child to receive Social Security benefits from a parent who has raised them their entire life and who has paid into the system is just so immoral." In this respect, it is important for LGBT couples with children to give voice to their rights and the needed civil liberties inherent for the children they are raising.

Dahlia Lithwick explains in a *Washington Post* article "whether or not same-sex marriage becomes widely legal in America, same-sex parenting is a done deal" (2006, p. B2). She reports that there is a trend throughout the country to recognize LGBT parenting and apply expanded views of parenting and family. The Delaware Supreme Court (March, 2006) ruled that a lesbian woman could retain joint custody of triplets she co-parented with the biological mother. Lithwick (2006) emphasizes this Delaware court exemplifies the unwillingness of many courts to "reflexively downgrade involved gay [lesbian] parents to third party interlopers" (p. B2).

The trend for the courts to make a determination in the best interest of the child is increasing. Judges are supporting the validity of LGBT parenting arrangements not to exercise political or legal values on gay and lesbian parenting, but to address the concerns of the child rather than their parents' sexual orientation. The idea of the best interest of the child centers around the judiciary's decision as to whether a two-parent home is better than a one-parent home for the child or if it's preferable to have a gay adoptive father rather than none at all. Children love the parents they have and want and need to be with them, regardless if a segment of society is in disagreement about their rights to be parents because they are gay.

How Can LGBT Parents Protect Their Family?

- Seek an LGBT-friendly lawyer.
- Stay up to date on ever-changing legalities through Web sites (see chapter 12) and media information.
- Gain using legal advice documents including power of attorney for decision-making rights to a nonbiological partner, wills, health care proxy statements, and a living will.
- Become informed on custody issues involving children in a heterosexual marriage when after divorce a parent becomes a partner in a same-sex relationship.
- Find supportive LGBT parenting groups.
- Become visible. Talk to friends, relatives, and coworkers about your family.
- Support LGBT-friendly businesses and corporations.
- Inform the educators at your child's school that you are a family. Find out the sexual harassment policy.
- Participate in the school system, as parent involvement breeds success for the child.
- Become active in advocacy to lawmakers and politicians.

A Positive Perspective on LGBT Parenting

Doug wrote the following letter sharing his perspective of a gay male couple raising a child. He maintains a 15-year committed relationship and a successful life raising their son Benjamin.

"Here in Los Angeles, being a gay couple with a child is not really a big deal. Benjamin's friends come from mostly mommy/daddy houses of course—but also mommy/mommy; daddy/daddy; and just mommy families.

Our doctor, our pre-school, our neighbors, other parents at the park, play dates, sleepovers; it's all so boringly normal and great. (So far, anyway!) No more challenging than being an interracial couple or a single parent or having an adopted child. Years ago those were seen as impossibly difficult and even detrimental to the child and now that's not the attitude.

What if a parent doesn't speak English? Or is obese? Or has a disability? Or is widowed or not married? These are challenges families face too and parents do it. Their kids turn out fine. Every family has its unique circumstances; it just requires adapting your parenting skills. Being a gay family is not that big a deal if you have a social framework to support you and your child.

I had another gay father tell me that a friend of his had asked if he was going to raise his son to be gay. His response was: 'My parents raised me to be straight and look how well that turned out.'

My parents didn't know they were raising a gay child. They didn't raise me to be gay (quite the contrary). They didn't do anything to make me gay. Just like my partner and I can't do anything to *make* Benjamin straight or gay. He'll just be whatever he is and that's fine.

If my parents had had a resource, if they'd known more about it, maybe my adolescence wouldn't have been as difficult. What did they know about this alien life? They didn't know any gay people, much less long-term, stable gay relationships. They never dreamed such a thing was possible. They didn't know anything about the gay community; or that gay men aren't all cross dressers; that gay men aren't by definition pedophiles; that gays don't all end up dying of AIDS. In short they thought my life was going to be empty and lonely.

My partner and I have been together 15 years and we have a beautiful four-year-old son. And my life is anything but empty or lonely.

I hope other families rise to the challenge."

Photograph by Daniel Chavkin
and permission by *The Advocate*
(Lehoczky, 2005 .p. 47)

Children Living in Two Worlds

The 2000 Census found that more than 150,000 same-sex couples have at least one child under 18 in the home. . . . Experts believe the census number excludes kids with a gay parent living outside the home. The American Bar Association explains that "including these kids the number is in the millions."

(Johnson and Piore, 2004, p. 53)

Children living with LGBT parents are beginning to be visible in our schools and communities. They are beginning to speak out about their special issues and look for other children in family systems of LGBT partnership to support and share their life. Many feel that they were forced to keep their family structure a secret as they were inundated by negative traditional stereotypes of family systems by friends, extended family, educators, clergy, and other members of their community. They lived with the fear of judgment and ridicule for having two moms or two dads.

Marriage equality and LGBT parenting have become media highlights and political weapons as their focus in the public eye becomes more prevalent. The issue is repeatedly present in campaigning issues for potential politicians and those in office. Many voters face referendums on marriage equality. Many clergy openly voice support or hostility on these matters.

More and more these children and teens and their parents are sharing their particular family unit with others. By becoming more visible they allow others to see, experience, and integrate their world into a continuum of family units that exist in present society.

A Cruise for LGBT Families

Rosie O'Donnell, talk show host and lesbian mom, created a documentary for HBO called *All Aboard! Rosie's Family Cruise* (Lee, 2006). Rosie and her life partner Kelli have four children, and decided to unite gay and lesbian people on a family cruise. She explains, "Maybe people will get a chance to see what they are afraid of. . . . The illusion about gay [and lesbian] people that it's all about sex. What unites us on this cruise is not that we're gay [and lesbian], but that we're parents" (Lee, 2006, p. 1).

Over 1,500 gay/lesbian and straight people engaged in a seven-day-trip to the Caribbean. Rosie's goal was to provide a relaxing place where "nobody would stare or ask stupid questions about two lesbians bringing up a family, or two gay men with a bunch of kids and no woman in sight" (Lee, 2006, p. 1). Throughout the TV special, people told their stories and cameras showed parenting in the most natural ways. At one point, children and parents were confronted with protesters at the Nassau docks, met with signs like "We don't welcome sissies in the Bahamas," and the shouting of homophobic slurs for the children to hear.

Seminars on adoption and discussion groups for children were included. Highlights from the children's discussion groups included the following comments: "The hardest thing is to have to constantly defend your family." Another teen told of being teased about her parents. "Why do you hate me?" She asked them. "I love my parents."

"Some parents told their kids not to play with me because my parents were lesbians."

"This one kid told me I was going to hell because my parents were gay."

Photograph by Kyna Shilling

Parents told their stories as well and commented on the comfort they felt in being with others having similar life scenarios. Rosie commented on a reporter's question that caught her off guard, asking her if she intended to raise her children gay. "I was shocked," she revealed and told the reporter, "I can't raise them to be gay any more than I can raise them to be tall" (Lee, 2006, p. 1).

Near the end of the trip, Charlie and Danny, a gay male couple, were married, and their five adopted children took part in the ceremony. They explained, "It meant more to the kids, than to us. Their friends' parents are all married." Another young mother explained "I've never felt so free" and began to sob. Still others expressed similar views as they were preparing to leave. "I'm going to miss being so safe and wonderful all of the time." And, "We've expanded our awareness of what can be."

LGBT Parents and Children among Easter Egg Roll—2006

About 16,000 families, including 200 gay parents, joined together at the traditional Easter Egg Roll on the White House South Lawn in April 2006. LGBT parents and children openly participated in the event. One lesbian couple shared they ran into coworkers who were unaware of their sexual identity and thanked them for coming. Many of these families wore brightly colored garlands to show their visibility. These leis or rainbow garlands were a simple means of educating the public. One Mom explained, "I thought this was a very subtle, nonviolent, lovely, pleasant way to identify ourselves" (Dvorak, 2006, p. 9).

Protestors rallied as well, shouting slurs comparing gay and lesbian families to the Easter Bunny and Santa Claus and inferring that *all* are make believe. One yelled he hoped that heterosexual families would be punished for participating in an event that included gays and lesbians. Another man with his son on his shoulder told the protestors they were doing the right thing. The children of LGBT parents could see and hear the slurs. Many of these kids were caught in the crossfire of this negativity.

One lesbian mom, Mary, who had come with her partner and 5-year-old daughter, commented, "I think people really got to see the variety of what an American family can look like. In the end, everybody watched their kids have a good time, everybody got wet. If anything, it was an educational event, not a political one" (Dvorak, 2006 p. 9). "Without doubt, the notion that loving gay families exist was evident . . . and the message was clear: GLBT parents and their kids rolling eggs and participating in games on the White House lawn are as American as their straight counterparts" (Huckaby, 2006, p. 1).

Voices of Young People With LGBT Parents

"We might be more open because we grew up taught to love everyone."

"I feel the pressure to be perfect—so you can prove your family is not so bad."

"School is not a place I can talk about my mom being a lesbian."

"I'm a lot more confident," says a 14-year-old. "I don't really care what people think about my family anymore."

"Among straight moms, I still feel like an outsider."

"It's hard. You want people to like you."

"We look like every other family. We do the same things."

"If you don't agree with conservative values, you don't say anything."

"I worry about my friends finding out. Would they still be my friends?"

"I like telling people what it is really like to have two moms."

Photograph by Kyna Shilling

Children Reaching Out

With increasing numbers of children and teens with LGBT parents, the realization arises that this is a population of young people that also have been marginalized. Like a family living with AIDS, all too often the family secret becomes the elephant in their living room. The tide is changing, evolving into greater recognition, education, and communication to equalize decades of silence and shame about a child's basic family unit.

Martin, age 12, was living in New Jersey when the courts ruled both of his lesbian moms were now his legal parents with the same parental rights. He said this decision made him feel safer and worry less. Although Mom Lisa (his biological mother) and Mommy Alice were both his moms, Martin explained,

"Now I really feel closer to Mommy Alice.
  I feel she is my real mom too."

"Same-sex couples and their children are likely to benefit in numerous ways from legal recognition of their families, and providing such recognition through marriage will bestow greater benefits than civil unions or domestic partnerships. (there are) trends in public opinion toward greater support for legal recognition of same-sex couples" (Herek, 2006b, p. 607).

Photograph by Kyna Shilling

Herek emphasizes the point that LGBT parents and their children are at a disadvantage without being recognized legally as married same-sex couples. He concludes his research found no evidence to support any assertions that same-sex couples and heterosexual relationships differ in basic psychosocial components, or that those in LGBT relationship are deficient in parenting abilities. He affirms that the restriction of LGBT couples to an unequal status perpetuates antigay stigma. Given trends toward greater support for sexual minority rights, civil union, and domestic partnership, Herek (2000b) speculates that the trend toward acceptance to support marriage equality will continue in the foreseeable future.

Support Groups

Kyle was a straight 13-year-old with two lesbian moms. He felt he needed to keep this a secret in his early childhood. Friends, adults, teachers, clergy, and even the media had sent him a strong message he could be ridiculed for disclosure. Never bringing kids home, lying on school forms, and shunning Father's Day was a part of his life. He even called one of his moms his aunt in public.

Becoming more and more isolated, his moms found an important support group that was life changing. Kyle participated in a camp for gay and lesbian children. These boys and girls could just have fun being together. They laughed, shared feelings, and learned about each other as people without prejudicial stereotyping. This camp experience became a huge turning point for Kyle, as he expressed his belief, "I just don't feel alone anymore."

Family days were events sponsored by organizations like COLAGE (Children of Lesbian and Gays Everywhere). Such a day was attended by Kyle and his parents. It was inclusive of all types of families and participation was open to all.

Kyle and his moms were welcomed into another supportive group. It felt good to participate and become a part of a larger community on Family Day.

The Internet

The need to reach out and find other children and teens of gay parents led many young people to Internet searching and communication. Despite the dangers of Internet use, if children are well informed by parents not to release personal information, many Web sites can be helpful resources for information, sharing, and advocacy. The Internet becomes a tool for connecting with so many of these youth feeling marginalized.

Josh "surfed" the Web to find sites supportive of children with gay and lesbian parents. He located the COLAGE (Children of Lesbians and Gays Everywhere) Web site. Immediately, he felt he could relate to displays that included the following portrait of a child with LGBT parents. This photograph and writing was part of the COLAGE program "That's So Gay."

So many youth just like him had expressed thoughts and feelings he dared not express.

Josh began to realize there were other young people with gay and lesbian parents.

"My immediate family is my mom, dad and brother and I am half Irish and half Chinese. When people hear about my family they ask, 'if your mom is straight and your dad is gay, how did they make you?' I wish people knew that LGBT families exist and would try and be a little more accepting. I struggle with hearing homophobic slurs because I love my dad and it hurts when my friends don't accept people like him."

Permission by COLAGE

Advocacy Groups for Children of LGBT Parents

Our lives begin to end the day we become silent about things that matter.

Dr. Martin Luther King Jr.

Advocacy groups for children of LGBT parents are emerging. COLAGE is such an advocacy group that explains its membership has increased 19% in 2004. Family Week in Provincetown experienced record high numbers of participants as over 3,000 members of lesbian- and gay-headed families came together. There were similar experiences in Michigan. More books are being written and more fairness in media representation is evolving with real-life examples of these families.

These breakthrough interventions are increasing the self-esteem and confidence of children of LGBT couples as they struggle to be included in the mainstream.

"I have two gay dads and a brother who is 9 years old. The kids in my school sometimes tease me or do not like me because of my family. Even though I have two dads I wish people knew that we are like any other family. We gather one night every week to play games or watch movies and we love each other. I am an activist and like teaching other people about what it's really like to have gay dads."

Permission by COLAGE

Children Become Self-Advocates

Many children of LGBT couples have become their own advocates, creating support groups, writing articles, and sharing pictures. Some have shared with groups the structure of their unique families and the destructive quality of prejudice against them. The following are two examples.

Sally, a junior in high school, explained she lived a lie most of her growing up. She told people her parents had divorced and dad moved far away. Her father's false invisibility plagued her. She decided to spontaneously disclose her love for her dad and his being gay in the middle of her English class.

Sally surprised herself by her sudden announcement of her father's homosexuality. She was even more startled to hear a wave of applause as her classmates stood up and clapped their acknowledgment.

Photograph by Kyna Shilling

Tommy, a 15-year-old son of two gay men, organized a silence day in his school for all of those killed by homophobic violence. Although many in his school supported the project, a small group of dissenters chanted, "It's not okay," throughout the day. His advocacy met with minority defiance, but he successfully created a framework for his peers to understand the danger of bigoted hostility.

 # Issues of Children With LGBT Parents

Most children of LGBT parents are heterosexual. "Research shows that kids of gays are not more likely to be gay themselves" (Johnson and Piore, 2004, p. 53). Yet, they seem to be caught in the crossfire of a cultural war, not feeling like they truly belong to either side. Too often, they are rejected by peers and isolated at school. Many feel shame and discontent about carrying their family secret and are angry about having that burden.

Sometimes, stress comes from inside the home. Many of these youth feel extremely pressured to succeed to prove to the heterosexual world they are okay and their parents can raise highly effective offspring.

Most research indicates few if any significant differences between children reared by LGBT parents and those by "straight" parents.

Judith Stacey and Timothy Biblarz report that "kids of gays have as much self-esteem as those of straights. Sons and daughters of gays [and lesbians] tend not to be as rigid about traditional sex roles. Boys raised by lesbians were found to be more nurturing

Photograph by Kyna Shilling

than their counterparts . . . the girls a bit more aggressive."

(Johnson & Piore, citing Stacey & Biblarz, 2004, p. 54)

 # Conclusion

The trend is rising for more and more children of gay male and lesbian couples to come into mainstream society. These children are finding a voice for themselves and an advocacy for their family system. Having two moms or two dads *is* their life and it is a life *that exists,* will prevail, and is increasing in numbers.

> *What's clear is that these children aren't going to sit quietly. If these kids have a message for the rest of the world, it seems to be this: get over it.*

(Johnson & Piore, 2004, p. 54)

Permission by PFLAG

CHAPTER 9

Community Counts:
A Place for Friends
and Family

COMMUNITY COUNTS • HISTORY OF PFLAG
SUPPORT GROUPS
MARRIAGE EQUALITY EDUCATIONAL AND POLITICAL
PROGRAMS • FAMILIES OF COLOR NETWORK
SCHOLARSHIPS • COLLABORATION WITH
BIG BUSINESS • FEDERAL LEGISLATION • ADVOCACY
CIVIL RIGHTS / LEGAL PROTECTION
EXEMPLARY ORGANIZATIONS

"Love is a medicine for the sickness of the world: a prescription often given, too rarely taken."

Karl A. Menninger

Grassroots efforts can effect progress and change at the highest levels of society through community and political activism. From issues of coming out, creating peer support for LGBT youth, mentorship and scholarship programs, maintaining school safety, promoting legislation for equality, honoring children of LGBT individuals, and establishing welcoming communities for same-sex parenting families, the level of productiveness in creating change is astounding. Community and national organizations have grown and expanded in a way that serves these young people in innovative and exciting ways, crossing the huge divide between isolation and acceptance.

A shining example of a successful and effective national organization dedicated to overcoming the challenges in the lives of LGBT youth is PFLAG (Parents, Families and Friends of Lesbians and Gays). By looking closely at the PFLAG model, we may better see the issues surrounding PFLAG's involvement. Their work serves as an example or template to use in new efforts to create inclusion for the LGBT population and their friends and families.

PFLAG: A Model for LGBT Activism

PFLAG is a national organization with more than 500 local branches composed of the parents, families, and friends of lesbian, gay, bisexual, and transgender persons. PFLAG celebrates diversity and envisions a society that embraces everyone, including those of diverse sexual orientations and gender identities. Its vision is the creation of an environment that offers "respect, dignity and equality for all to reach their fullest potential as human beings, individually and collectively."

For over three decades, the advocacy work of this organization has made positive strides toward equality. Their educational programs have enlightened hundreds of thousands of individuals, organizations, and corporations, and their support work has counseled the GLBT person and his or her parents, families, and friends.

The History of PFLAG

In 1972, Morton Manford was physically attacked at a gay rights protest demonstration in New York City. Morty's parents, Jeanne and Jules Manford, saw the attack on a local newscast and were outraged at the police's failure to intervene. Jeanne Manford started an international movement when she marched with her son in New York's Pride Day parade. They carried a sign saying, *"Parents of Gays: Unite in Support of Our Children."*

Many gays and lesbians approached her during the parade, begging her to talk to their parents. She decided to begin a support group. The first formal meeting took place in March 1973 at a local church, with approximately 20 people attending. Many more chapters sprang up across the country and united, forming the Federation of Parents, Families and Friends of Lesbians and Gays. PFLAG formally incorporated in California in 1982. From one woman's activism a national organization with over 500 chapters and affiliates has grown, representing one of the largest grassroots, chapter-based networks of volunteers in the struggle for LGBT rights (PFLAG, 2005).

Community Goals

GOAL 1: SUPPORT GROUPS FOR GLBTQ FAMILIES AND FRIENDS

Through its network, PFLAG supports, educates, and advocates on behalf of GLBT persons and their families, supporting the work of its chapters by providing extensive training and technical support, publications and materials, and funding for special programs.

It is an organization working nationwide to provide support group meetings—thousands each month—to families with GLBTQ family members.

PFLAG provides a natural and supportive outlet for hetero-sexual allies—parents, other family members, and friends—to join in the fight for GLBTQ rights.

A structure is provided to move people through support services into roles as community educators, activists, and advocates. Members come from a wide range of cultural, geographic, ethnic, and racial backgrounds, and are approximately 50% GLBTQ and 50% non-GLBTQ of all ages.

Permission by PFLAG

 # A PFLAG Mom

One PFLAG mom, Sumi, explained her journey with her daughter being a lesbian. She was told soon after her separation from her husband. Her first reaction was, "This is a sin." Her religious leader explained his position:

Sumi was "welcome to come to worship, but if her daughter, Sandy, and her partner, Kim, came, they would *not be welcome* to worship."
She relayed how difficult, conflicting, and confusing this was for her.
The words, "She is my daughter, I love her so much," constantly echoed from within.

Sumi admired the loving relationship she saw with Sandy and Kim, feeling it epitomized her concept of what a relationship of mutual respect should be like. Yet, she often thought to herself, "They shouldn't have sex." Now she laughs at how ludicrous that sounds, but at the time it was profoundly meaningful. Invited to come to her daughter's wedding, she was advised by clergy in her faith group to ignore the relationship. This mother thought to herself, *this is my daughter,* and she went to the ceremony.

A First PFLAG Meeting

Sumi also decided that she needed support from a community that understood the challenges of parenting a gay child and attended her first PFLAG meeting. She was immediately struck by the acceptance of straight and GLBTQ participants no matter how she felt or what she said. It was a safe space to voice anger, negative and hateful thoughts, and doubts and fears without being judged or contradicted. Sumi found there was not only continued support but also praise and respect for her just being there.

Many GLBTQ youth relayed their stories in the meeting. These were stories of being ignored, scorned, or openly and completely rejected by friends and family. Sumi felt heartbroken for these kids without parental love and protection. She turned to 15-year-old Adam, after he told his story. She hugged him and said, "I'll be your mom!" In one meeting, she was transformed from a self-proclaimed victim to a caring advocate by the power of group communication and acceptance.

A Shining Light

Another mom and dad, Sara and Paul, shared at the meeting how they heard their son Josh was gay. Josh had decided to let his sister, Allie, disclose his homosexuality to the family while he drove around the block. If it went okay, she would signal him by putting the porch light on. Josh called her and asked how it was going and Allie said, "Come in a few minutes, Mom and Dad are doing something." When they heard the plan for the porch light Sara and Paul explained a plan to the rest of the family. "Wait, we need to light every light in the house." Everyone went from the basement to the third floor, putting on the lights as a shining glow of affirmation for their beloved family member Josh. This story served as an inspiration for the entire group.

GOAL 2: NATIONAL PROGRAMS: POLITICAL PROGRAMS FIGHTING FOR ADVOCACY

From Our House to the State House: A PFLAG State-by-State Organizing Initiative

A PFLAG initiative to get more politically proactive, called *From Our House to the State House,* has two major goals. The first goal is to strengthen chapters in order to enhance their delivery of support, education, and advocacy initiatives by fostering greater networking among chapters and allies in the same states and building state leadership teams to coordinate activities.

The second goal is to create stronger and more unified statewide PFLAG family voices to address a multitude of issues.

These issues include making schools safer, engaging diverse racial and ethnic communities, helping faith communities to be more welcoming, dealing with policy matters including parenting rights, marriage equality, employment discrimination, hate crimes, and more.

Democratic former Congressman Richard A. Gephardt with his wife Jane and their daughter Chrissy. Permission by PFLAG

PFLAG National provides strong field staff and logistical support to help build leadership teams. National staff trains leaders, develops materials (including Web-based resources), and coordinates and produces educational workshops, meetings, and state conferences. Remarkably, most of PFLAG's work continues to be provided by volunteers.

Educational Programs: Training, Information, Safety: A PFLAG Priority

From Our House to the Schoolhouse: Safe Schools & Youth

Making schools safe for all youth, but particularly for gay, lesbian, bisexual and transgender (GLBT) young people, has been a top priority for PFLAG. In 2000, *From Our House to the Schoolhouse: Safe Schools Campaign* began with the recognition that schools were at "ground zero" in their efforts to curb homophobia. GLBT youth, or those perceived to be, face unspeakable harassment and abuse in schools and are too often effectively denied access to a safe and equal education opportunity. A school culture that fosters and sustains this hostile environment impacts all students negatively. The average high school student hears many anti-gay slurs daily; a huge percentage of high school students regularly hear homophobic remarks. This harassment takes its toll. LGBT students are more likely to skip classes, drop out of school, and die of suicide.

PFLAG helps make schools safer and systematic change is occurring. Family voices carry tremendous weight in schools. And because PFLAG is in over 500 communities in the nation, its work is localized, reaching even some of the smallest schools in rural America. Numerous chapters also host youth groups or partner with other community organizations that do. Activities range from hosting rap groups to helping coordinate special social events or community projects to partnering with *safe schools* activities.

Scholarship Program

National Scholarships from PFLAG provide an important, positive statement to a group of young people that is often marginalized and subjected to harassment and discrimination. These scholarships also are given to straight allies of GLBTQ students. An anonymous donor expanded the program by donating $25,000, adding an additional 13 scholarships in 2006 for gay, lesbian, bisexual, and transgender high school seniors interested in pursuing careers in science, engineering, business, and finance.

 # Families of Color Network

In late 1999, PFLAG helped to form the *Families of Color Network* (FOCN), which works with people of color.

This network addresses GLBT issues within communities of color in the context of their African-American, Arab-American, Asian/Pacific Islander–American, Latino/a and Native American/American Indian communities.

PFLAG has released two booklets in Spanish to meet the needs of Latino/as and Spanish-speaking families. One of these resources is entitled *Nuestros/as Hijos/as Trans* (2006).

PFLAG also formed a Families of Color Advisory Board who assist in the formation of new FOCN chapters. The Families of Color Network Advisory Board meets monthly to discuss issues related to PFLAG in communities of color.

Permission by PFLAG. This photograph is of *The Families of Color Network* PFLAG Members.

Permission by PFLAG. This photograph is an example of a Native American PFLAG family.

 # Civil Rights and Legal Protections

In addition to the programs that it maintains, PFLAG also advocates and educates the general public about GLBT civil rights and legal protections. Important issues include GLBT family issues (parenting, adoption, marriage equality, custody and visitation), GLBT immigration issues, GLBT workplace issues, GLBT health issues (such as reparative therapy), domestic partnership and benefits issues, GLBT hate crimes, and judicial issues.

 # Federal Legislation Monitoring and Advocacy Program: Bringing the Message Home

This PGLAG program focused on visiting federal legislators in their local offices in the weeks between Mother's Day and Father's Day. There were three key ways in which this effort was unique:

1. The project was not just focused on Capitol Hill in Washington, DC but also was designed to take a message of fairness and inclusion to federal legislators in their home towns. Federal legislators all have district offices in their home towns and PFLAG members have a huge impact by visiting the local offices, and "Bringing the Message Home."

2. The project offered great flexibility by setting up meetings with legislators and/or their staff in their district offices. The time period from Mother's Day through Father's Day was featured for the obvious PFLAG connection to family.

3. PFLAG provided education regarding positions on various matters of concern and did not necessarily support or oppose specific legislation. This was a long range strategy recognizing it may take an extensive time for GLBT legislations to evolve.

 # Marriage

Marriage is a powerful legal and social institution that protects and supports intimate family relationships by providing a unique set of legally recognized rights, privileges, and benefits. Same-sex couples are currently denied the right to marry in every state in the United States with the exception of Massachusetts. Massachusetts was the only state to pass legislation allowing marriage but it was later vetoed by the governor. PFLAG opposed any attempt at either the federal or state level to introduce constitutional amendments restricting marriage to heterosexual couples thereby rendering LGBT people second-class citizens.

PFLAG Parents Rally Against Federal Marriage Amendment

A PFLAG press release, May 1, 2006, suggested the following advocacy campaign for parents to rally against the federal marriage amendment.

"Washington, D.C.—'Dear Senator: All I want for Mother's Day is for you to vote NO on the Federal Marriage Amendment. . .' was the theme of thousands of postcards sent to U.S. Senators from members of Parents, Families and Friends of Lesbians and Gays (PFLAG).

'A no vote on the Federal Marriage Amendment would be the best gift any parent could get this year for Mother's Day or Father's Day,' said Samuel Thoron, National President of PFLAG.

Permission by PFLAG

'This is literally giving the gift of fighting discrimination against our children and there's nothing a parent could want more.'

The 'Dear Senator' campaign was part of a month of high-intensity lobbying by PFLAG members around the United States to fight the Federal Marriage Amendment, which, if passed, would have been the first step in writing discrimination into the U.S. Constitution by denying marriage equality to same-sex individuals. More than 10,000 postcards were sent out to friends and families."

 # Lobbying Congressmen

In addition to the postcard campaign, PFLAG members lobbied their congressional representatives on Capitol Hill regarding the Federal Marriage Amendment and other issues of equality for their gay, lesbian, bisexual, and transgender (GLBT)

loved ones. With family photos in hand, they made more than 50 visits during the day, culminating with an evening reception.

> Our legislators need to see that we believe in family values too, to see our photos of the people we do this for—and to understand why passing legislation that hurts our GLBT loved ones is wrong, un-American, and unacceptable. (PFLAG, press release, May 1, 2006)

Members nationwide took the message of marriage equality and fairness in legislation to their members of Congress at home. More than 500 chapters scheduled in-district meetings as part of their fourth annual *Bringing the Message Home* campaign to remind their elected officials that equality is non-negotiable and that discrimination against their loved ones affects all of us.

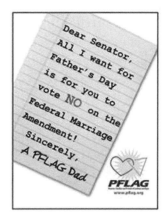

"Our families are everywhere, and we deserve equality," said Thoron.

"It is as simple as that."

"All of our children should have equal treatment, equal protections and equal opportunities and our elected officials need to know it."

Permission by PFLAG

 # Welcoming Faith Communities

A PFLAG initiative supported chapters in recognition of the important intersection of faith and homosexuality. The necessary tools were provided to educate organizations on faith-based issues, mobilize volunteers, and respond to arguments of the religious right and other opposition groups.

The 2006 Faith in Action Award

The Metro DC chapter of PFLAG awarded *The 2006 Faith in Action Award* to Reverends Barbara Gerlach and John Mack for encouraging First Congregation United Church of Christ to be one of the first churches within the denomination to declare being "open and affirming." This provided a strong foundation for other UCC churches in the greater Washington area to follow suit. The statement that "First Church is an Open and Affirming Ministry" is engraved on a plaque outside the church, displayed on a banner above the sanctuary, and printed on the worship bulletins every Sunday. They have led and encouraged many to think beyond the church community to a larger community.

Reverend Mack explained, when asked about negative religious overtones for GLBTQ individuals, that he felt in any and all of the religions "one should be able to find a space for acceptance."

When accepting the *Faith in Action Award,* he ended his speech by saying:

> *"I can taste the day we no longer give awards for these kinds of things."*

A Progressive Judiciary: From Our House to the Court House

Americans can expect to see appointments to many of our country's highest courts including, potentially, three vacancies in the Supreme Court. A progressive judiciary is critical to securing safety and equality of GLBT loved ones. As part of its education and advocacy objectives, PFLAG continued to monitor nominations to federal courts and to alert members of potential judicial nominations threatening to GLBT equality.

Bringing Together Straight Advocates: Straight for Equality

PFLAG's program *Straight for Equality* proposes to bring together more straight advocates for GLBT equality that understand the injustices the GLBT community faces and want to work for equal rights for all people. Participants in *Straight for Equality* will be invaluable in this struggle for equality. Throughout the years, they have been instrumental in getting the message out. An example of a straight ally is Elizabeth Taylor, who influenced the media, government, and society to listen and act as AIDS was decimating mostly gay men two decades ago.

The Role of Big Business

Corporate partnerships are critical in promoting the vision and goals of organizations like PFLAG. Their support enhances strategic educational, advocacy, and support goals by providing much-needed resources including grants, equipment, and technical expertise that lead to the expansion and outreach of programs that underscore diversity and understanding of the GLBTQ community.

IBM

The leadership and involvement by IBM has truly made this company *a hero* of both PFLAG and the entire GLBT community.

IBM has donated over $50,000 within one fiscal year.

Permission by PFLAG

Chris Whelan, Director of Intellectual Assets for IBM's global services businesses and the task force interface to PFLAG, shares IBM's business philosophy of acceptance and equality. "Companies that lead innovation cannot afford to exclude any talented individual and we must create a workplace environment that is welcoming and empowers all of our people."

IBM has not only impacted its employees but many employees in other companies as well. It has become a pioneer for other companies as a model in creating policies of nondiscrimination and diversity in the workplace.

AOL

AOL was a strong supporter of the 2006 Metro DC PFLAG Gala. They stated *diversity* is at the very core of who they were as a company. AOL emphasizes their employees reflect this rich diversity that makes up our country and their millions of members.

This respect for diversity is reflected in the hiring, promotions, design of products and services, and the way people have been treated throughout the AOL organization. Their definition of inclusion (PFLAG GALA Brochure, 2006) was summarized in the following six words:

Honor Similarities . . .
Respect Differences . . .
Celebrate Diversity . . .

PFLAG's mission is apparent in the tremendous role played in promoting the health and well-being of all. This mission is keeping families together. Their vision statement reflects the comprehensive goals and achievements presented in this chapter.

One day society will accept all its members as equals, regardless of their sexual orientation or gender identity.

Until that day, there is PFLAG.

(Metro DC PFLAG's Gala Registration)

Inspiring Models of Organizational Support

Throughout this book, many resources have been highlighted whose work has been *progressive and essential* in producing changes in attitude, safety, and legislation for our GLBTQ population. Although PFLAG is presented as a template for activism in so many ways, other organizations have achieved grand strides in their particular area of advocacy.

Although there are too many groups for each to be described in detail (see chapter 12), several have been chosen as worthy examples of specific areas of advocacy. Each functions as an integral part with its own vision of equality for all, and each has carved a particular niche. They come together as joined partners for the good of all. In the homes, the schools, the workplace, community gatherings, and Congress, GLBT individuals, their children, their friends, relatives, and supporters are nourished by their good works.

The following organizations stand out in particular areas, each with its own particular emphasis—but all creating a cohesive unity. Each one comprises a piece of the support needed to create a network of protection and equality of the GLBT community.

GLSEN (Gay, Lesbian & Straight Education Network) is one of the leading national education organizations focused on ensuring safe schools for all students. Their projects within the schools are numerous and effective. Examples include the *No Name-Calling Week, Ally Week, The Day of Silence, THE GLSEN Lunchbox,* and *GLSEN's Educational Network.* The following gives a brief overview of two of these projects.

The GLSEN Lunchbox is a comprehensive toolkit designed to provide educators with the knowledge, skills, and strategies necessary to make schools safer and more affirming for all students, regardless of sexual orientation or gender identity and expression.

It includes lesson plans, a manual, a video, and worksheets and handouts for school personnel.

Permission by GLSEN

GLSEN was created to help teachers make school a safe place for all students, including GLBT youth.

Members of this network are informed about new and valued educational resources that deal with creating a respectful learning environment devoid of harassment.

Permission by GLSEN

The mission statement of GLSEN is as follows:

The Gay, Lesbian & Straight Education Network strives to assure that each member of every school community is valued and respected regardless of sexual orientation or gender identity/expression.

(GLSEN, http://glsen.org)

COLAGE (Children of Lesbians and Gays Everywhere) is a national organization whose support and activism is by and for people with lesbian, gay, bisexual, and/or transgender parents and families. "COLAGE engages, connects, and empowers people to make the world a better place for (these) children." Activities include youth leadership, support groups, annual conferences and a *just for kids* publication. Programs for their membership comprise pen pals, information and referral, and e-mail discussion groups. They also provide legislative and media advocacy, resource material, and an e-mail action alert and news list.

Permission by COLAGE

Will expresses his feelings about having gay dads and what he would like people to know about his GLBT family.

The mission statement of COLAGE is as follows:

Our mission is to engage, connect, and empower people to make the world a better place for children of lesbian, gay, bisexual, and/or transgender parents and families.

(COLAGE, http://www.colage.org)

FAMILY PRIDE COALITION is a national organization exclusively focused on the particular needs of lesbian, gay, bisexual and transgender parents and their families. This group supports the LGBT community through a diverse array of programs. One major focus is assisting parents in making connections with other families in their communities through nearly 200 local parenting groups across the country. Family Pride also provides information and referrals to parents and those considering parenthood, as well as technical assistance to those interested in making community organizations and events—such as Pride celebrations—more family friendly. Members gather to celebrate family at events like Family Weeks in Provincetown, Massachusetts, and Saugatuck, Michigan; Family Pride Camp: Dads & Kids in the Desert; Gay Day at Disney World in Florida, and Disneyland in California.

Their mission statement exemplifies their goal of comfort and security for GLBT citizens and their families:

> *The mission of the Family Pride Coalition is to advance the well-being of lesbian, gay, bisexual and transgender parents and their families through mutual support, community collaboration and public understanding.*

(Family Pride Coalition, Gathering, Guiding, Growing Brochure)

HUMAN RIGHTS CAMPAIGN (HRC) was named the number one nonunion political organization working in the 2006 elections by the *National Journal*. This organization is dedicated to ensuring every GLBT person in the United States be given their basic equal rights, and can be open and safe at home, work, and in the community. Their strong sponsorship for these equal rights and benefits of the GLBT community *under the law* has increased public support through advocacy, education, and outreach programs. HRC works to secure equal rights at the federal and state levels by lobbying elected officials, mobilizing grassroots support, educating the public, investing strategically to elect fair-minded officials, and partnering with other GLBT organizations.

The National Coming Out Project is an example of the Human Rights Campaign's work in education. HRC has created the *Resource Guide to COMING OUT: For Gay, Lesbian, Bisexual and Transgender Americans,* freely provided to GLBT youth to aid them in their process of *coming out.*

Permission by HRC

This project includes resources and information to support these young people so that no one needs to experience this path alone.

The following is the mission statement of the Human Rights Campaign:

> *The Human Rights Campaign (is) . . . working to achieve gay, lesbian, bisexual and transgender equality. By inspiring and engaging all Americans, HRC strives to end discrimination against GLBT citizens and realize a nation that achieves fundamental fairness and equality for all.*
>
> (HRC, http://www.hrc.org)

From issues of coming out, school safety, legislative advocacy, children of same-sex parents, community acceptance, and legislative empowerment, these organization cover a large spectrum of issues dealt with by our GLBT citizens. The needs and supports of this community are complex and can be approached from many angles. Through the efforts of organizations such as those highlighted, individual visions merge to build a unified larger collage—an evolving paradigm within society regarding sexual orientation and gender identity.

 # Achieving Success

Rather light a candle than complain about the darkness.

Chinese proverb

PFLAG, GLSEN, COLAGE, Family Pride, and the Human Rights Campaign are a few of the many examples of efforts ranging from grassroots levels to government legislation, originating and igniting new possibilities for the GLBT community. Although each of these organizations is strikingly helpful and unique, there are many areas of interconnectedness and overlap. Just as the whole is greater than the sum of its parts, a helpful interaction of all of these resources creates a greater network of safety, support, guidance, and mentorship for the GLBT population and their friends, families, and supporters.

Photograph by Kyna Shilling

These inspiring organizations are indeed outstanding examples of community and national agencies in action. They are resources dedicated to successfully making a difference in the lives of the population of GLBT adolescents and adults and those who care for and support them.

CHAPTER 10

Conclusion:
A Last Look at a
New Beginning

Photograph by Kyna Shilling

A NEW BEGINNING • CREATING A FRESH PARADIGM
LIVING THROUGH TRANSITION • WE ARE ALL ONE

"A mind once expanded by a new idea can never return to its original dimension."

Oliver Wendell Holmes, Supreme Court Justice

We human beings are usually fearful of the unknown, of what is unfamiliar, and tend all too often to project, categorize, and repel what appears foreign to our limited minds. If we join together as a community of like-minded people determined to change the thought forms of society rather than minimize a segment of our youth, we can accomplish the goals of transforming the *terror* of the unfamiliar to the *acceptance* of the familiar.

Creating a Fresh Paradigm

We can create a paradigm whereby individuals of any sexual orientation and gender identity can live with dignity and respect. Our homes, schools, and communities can become safe harbors for these youth to freely be able to live, love, and enjoy relationships with family, friends, and partners in a meaningful and open way.

The essence of this new paradigm is the unification of the inner and outer worlds of all human beings. Humanity has always struggled with the dichotomy between the inner self and the outer world, and it is magnified by the marginalization and stereotyping of gay youth and their subsequent journey toward self-acceptance. Dealing in a positive way with this duality allows for greater change into a larger way of seeing the issues. *Coming Out, Coming In* is a metaphor for us all—to become who we really are inside and relinquish artificial societal projections we send ourselves, are given by others, and we give to others.

We Have a Choice

Creating a stronger ability to unify our inner and outward identities can speed the process of congruency in selfhood not only for LGBT young people but for the heterosexual world as well. The realization that *we have a choice* in accepting into our inner world negative attitudes of others also opens up the idea that *we have a choice* in distinguishing our own projections and attitudes toward others as well. Hopefully, this blend of strengthening our inner image and weakening inaccurate projected constructs will build healthier LGBT and straight youth and a new humanity of self-acceptance for all.

Living Through Transition

We must acknowledge that society is working through a period of transition of incorporating this new paradigm. It would be wrong to presume we can instantly fix a problem so intertwined with false notions and stereotyping.

The solution to LGBT human justice is evolving. The catalyst for transformation lies in uncovering our own narrow thinking and prejudices. Ultimately, we must not merely "accept gayness" as a society but arrive at a position of understanding that the idea of acceptance *is no longer necessary*. Like tallness and smallness, red hair and brown, black-skinned and yellow-skinned, the hope is that being gay will become a normal part of a multifaceted society.

By expanding the vistas of our understanding as human beings, we can gain an insight into the depth of harm prejudice does to everyone. We can begin to experience the cruelty of our own limited minds and the artificial bondage we place on ourselves and those around us that is dehumanizing and suffocating.

Only then can our culture be free from intolerance. Only through knowing, loving, and fully relating to gay, lesbian, bisexual, and transgender youth can we begin to coexist without bigotry and discrimination. Only then can we plant the seeds of self-worth and anchor the belief that all of our young people are true and equal citizens of the world.

PART IV

Creating Equality in Society: Resources and Supports

C H A P T E R   1 1

Resources on LGBT Issues for Youth and Adults: Celebrating Diversity

BOOKS FOR CHILDREN AND ADULTS
CURRICULUM • VIDEOS
EXHIBITS FOR SCHOOLS AND
COMMUNITIES • ORGANIZATIONS
MEDIA FILMS • CURRENT MAGAZINES
FREE PAMPHLETS

"We are all the same when we turn out the light."

Shel Silverstein

Books for Children

ON LGBT ISSUES

Aldrich, A. (2003). *How my family came to be daddy, papa and me.* Oakland, CA: New Family Press Book. This resource clearly addresses for young children the concept of the changing family make-up and families that have two dads. Ages 4–7.

Bryan, J. (2006). *The different dragon.* Ridley Park, PA: Two Lives Publishing. This is a nice story about Noah and his night-time adventure. He lives with two moms. Ages 5–9.

Combs, B. (2000). *ABC: A family alphabet book.* Ridley Park, PA: Two Lives Publishing. This is a family alphabet book that includes family life with two moms or two dads. Ages 5–10.

De Haan, L., & Nijland, S. (2000). *King & king.* Berkeley, CA: Tricycle Press. This is a story about a suitable mate for a prince and a surprise discovery for his choice. Ages 5–8.

Ferro, U. (2005). *Tanny's meow.* West Tisbury, MA: Marti Books. This is a beautiful story about children growing up on a farm with animals, interweaving the theme of family with acceptance of those children that have two moms and two dads. Ages 4–9.

Ferro, U. (2006). *Wishing for kittens.* West Tisbury, MA: Marti Books. This is a wonderful story about kittens that highlights loving, solid relationships between same-sex parents and children. Ages 5–9.

Ferro, U. (2007). *Mother's day on Martha's Vineyard.* West Tisbury, MA: Marti Books. This is a delightful book about two children with two moms celebrating Mother's Day with their grandparents. Ages 5–10.

Garden, N. (2004). *Molly's family.* New York: Farrar Straus Giroux. This is a sweet story about Molly learning that having two moms constitutes a wonderful family. Ages 4–7.

Greenberg, K. (1996). *Zack's story: Growing up with same-sex parents.* Minneapolis, MN: Lerner Publications. This is the story of 11-year-old Zack living with two moms. Age 5–10.

Krakow, Kari. *The Harvey Milk story.* Ridley Park, PA: Two Lives Publishing. This is the story of the first openly elected gay city official in the U.S. Ages 8 & up.

Newman, L. (2000). *Heather has two mommies,* 10th ed. Los Angeles: Alyson Publishing. This book presents families with two moms and speaks to this issue for children. Ages 5–10.

Newman, L. (2002). *Felicia's favorite story.* Ridley, Park: PA: Two Lives Publishing. This is a wonderful story about a little girl living with two moms who loves to hear her favorite bedtime story about being adopted. Ages 5–10.

Richardson, J., & Parnell, P. (2005). *And Tango makes three.* New York: Simon and Schuster. This is a beautiful and true account of two male penguins at the zoo that become a family and creatively raise their own baby penguin. Ages 5 and up.

Willhoite, M. (1990). *Daddy's roommate.* Los Angeles: Alyson. This book provides words to explain a gay male relationship to young children. Ages 5–8.

ON PREJUDICE

Curtis, J., & Cornell, L. (2006). *Is there really a human race?* New York: Harper Collins. This story transforms a child's concept of the literal meaning of *human race* as all humans racing around to all humans loving others and speaking out to help. Ages 4–8.

Heegaard, M. (2003). *Drawing together to accept & respect differences.* Minneapolis: MN. Fairview Press. This workbook helps children to communicate and learn to respect one another. Ages 6–12.

Simon, N. (1976). *Why am I different?* Morton Grove, IL: Albert Whitman & Co. This is a book emphasizing the unique qualities of each person and explores differences. Ages 5–9.

Thomas, P. (2003). *The skin I'm in.* New York: Barron. This is a first look at racial discrimination for very young children. Ages 4–7.

ON STRESS

Moser, A. (1988). *Don't pop your cork on Monday.* Kansas City, MO: Landmark Editions. This children's book explores the causes of stress and techniques to deal with it. Ages 5–8.

Moser, A. (1991). *Don't feed the monster on Tuesday.* Kansas City, MO: Landmark Editions. Dr. Moser offers children information on the importance of knowing their own self-worth and ways to improve self-esteem. Ages 5–8.

ON FAMILY DIVERSITY

Cart, M. (Ed.). (2003). *Necessary noise.* New York: Joanna Cotler Books. This is a compilation of stories that speak of many situations in today's families including a sibling's overdose, life with two mothers, and a dad visiting his son on death row. Ages 10 and up.

Kuklin, S. (2006). *Families.* New York: Hyperion. This book shared 15 interviews with children reflecting family diversity in America. Ages 4–8.

ON JUST MOMS, DADS, AND BABIES

Gutman, A. & Hallensleben A. (2001). *Daddy kisses.* San Francisco: Chronicle Books. This books shows in a special way the way we can celebrate a father's love. Ages 3–6.

Gutman, A. & Hallensleben A. (2001). *Mommy hugs.* San Francisco: Chronicle Books. This books shows in a special way the way to celebrate a mom's love. Ages 3–6.

Meyers, S. (2001). *Everywhere babies*. New York: Red Wagon Books. This book celebrates all the special things *all babies* do. It underscores we are all alike. Ages 3–6.

ON RESILIENCY

Johnson, A. (2004). *Just like Josh Gibson*. New York: Aladdin. This is a story about an African–American grandmother who as a young girl in the forties gets the opportunity to play baseball as the only girl. She was called in like her hero, Josh Gibson. Ages 5–8.

Morrison, T. (1999). *The big box*. New York: Hyperion Books. This is a story about children put in a box by adults and their strong desire to gain personal freedom. Ages 5–10.

Seuss, Dr. (1990). *Oh, the places you'll go*. New York: Random House. Dr. Seuss inspires young and old in this story to succeed in life, despite its ups and downs. Ages 5–adult.

Stepanek, M. (2001). *Heartsongs*. Alexandria, VA: VSP Books. This is a compilation of poems written by a boy expressing hope and optimism for the future. Ages 6 and up.

Stepanek, M. (2001). *Journey through heartsongs*. Alexandria, VA: VSP Books. This is a volume of Mattie's poems stressing peace and faith in mankind. Ages 6 and up.

ON AFFIRMATIONS AND MEDITATIONS

Garth, M. (1991). *Starbright*. New York: HarperCollins Publishing. This is a book of meditations for children, with simple visualizations to help create peaceful images. Ages 7–12.

Payne, L. (1994). *Just because I am*. Minneapolis, MN: Free Spirit Publishing. This is a children's book of affirmations and positive self-talk.

ON EMPOWERMENT

Aboff, M. (1996). *Uncle Willy tickles: A child's right to say NO* (2nd ed.). Washington, DC: Magination Press. This book creates words to use for children to feel they have the right to own their body and say "no" to what doesn't feel good. Ages 5–9.

Browne, A. (1985). *Willy the champ*. New York: Alfred A. Knopf. The story of Willy, a mild-mannered hero who stands up to a bully and shows he is a champion. Ages 5–10.

Kaufman, G., & Raphael, L. (1990). *Stick up for yourself.* Minneapolis, MN: Free Spirit Publishing. This guide for children helps them develop techniques to feel personal power and self-esteem in many life situations. Ages 8–12.

Lalli, J. (1997). *I like being me*. Minneapolis: Free Spirit Publishing. This is a series of poems for children about feeling special. Ages 5–10.

O'Neal. (2003). *When bad things happen: A guide to help kids cope*. St. Meinrad, IN: Abbey Place. This book shares a traumatic event which shapes children's lives. Ages 5–9.

Heegaard, M. (2001). *Drawing together to develop self-control*. Minneapolis, MN: Fairview Press. This is a useful tool to help children develop self-control. Ages 5–10.

ON HOPE AND OPTIMISM

Agee, J. (1985). *Ludlow laughs*. Toronto: A Sunburst Book. Ludlow, a boy who never smiles, learns how laughter can be life changing. Ages 5–10.

Lewis, B. (1992). *Kids with courage*. Minneapolis, MN. Free Spirit Publishing. This book contains stories about young people making a difference by taking a stand. Ages 11 and up.

Piper, W. (1954). *The little engine that could*. New York: Platt & Munk. This story provides children an insight into the value of positive thinking and perseverance. Ages 5–10.

Waber, B. (2002). *Courage*. New York: Houghton Mifflin Co. This is a beautiful book for young children that describes the levels of courage that take place every day. Ages 4–8.

ON BULLYING

Boatwright, B., Mathis, T., & Smith, S. (1998). *Getting equipped to stop bullying: A kid's survival kit for understanding and coping with violence in the schools.* Minneapolis, MN: Educational Media Corporation. This book provides understandings of the dynamics of bullying and empowers children to recognize and deal with bullies. Ages 10 and up.

Bosch, C. (1988). *Bully on the bus.* Seattle, WA: Parenting Press. The book allows the reader to make the choice about how they would resolve a bullying situation. Ages 8–12.

Cohen-Posey, K. (1995). *How to handle bullies, teasers and other meanies.* Highland City, FL: Rainbow Books. This resource helps children with issues of bullying. Ages 8–13.

Johnston, M. (1996). *Dealing with bullying.* New York: Rosen Publishers. A book that defines bullying, explains why bullies act as they do, and ways to change. Ages 4–8.

McCain, R. (2001). *Nobody knew what to do.* Morton Grove, IL: Albert Whitman & Co. This is a true story about bullying that stresses the power of onlookers. Ages 4–8.

Naylor, P. (1991). *King of the playground.* London: Aladdin. Kevin is bullied daily by Sammy. One day he realized Sammy can't actually do all of the things he says he will. Ages 5–9.

Romain, T. (1997). *Bullies are a pain in the brain.* Minneapolis, MN: Free Spirit Publishing. This practical guide helps children cope with bullying problems. Ages 7–11.

Romain, T. (1998). *Cliques, phonies, and other baloney.* Minneapolis, MN: Free Spirit Publishing. This is a story for middle school children that deals directly with issues involving cliques and insincerity. Ages 10 and up.

ON SUICIDE

Cammarata, D. (2000). *Someone I love died by suicide.* Palm Beach Gardens, FL: Grief Guidance, Inc. This is a story for child survivors and caretakers. Ages 5–9.

Garland, S. (1994). *I never knew your name.* New York: Ticknor & Fields. A young boy tells the story of a teenage boy's suicide whose name he did not know. Ages 5–11.

Goldman, L. (1998). *Bart speaks out on suicide.* Los Angeles: WPS Publishers. This is an interactive storybook for children on suicide. It serves as a memory book for their person that died and also gives words for the way they died. Ages 5–10.

Norton, Y. (1993). *Dear Uncle Dave.* Hanover, NH: Shirley Baldwin Waring. This story is by a 4th-grade girl sharing memories of Uncle Dave and his death by suicide. Ages 5–10.

Rubel, B. (1999). *But I didn't say goodbye.* Kendall Park, NJ: Griefwork Center, Inc. This is a practical approach for adults to discuss suicide with children. Ages 9–13.

ON AIDS

Balkwill, F. (1993). *Cell wars.* London: William Collins & Sons. This story for young children explains viruses and good and bad cells. Ages 5–9.

Fassler, D. & McQueen, K. (1990). *The kids' book about AIDS.* Burlington, VT: Waterfront Books. This book approaches the subject of AIDS in a sensitive manner to which young children can relate. Kids can use as a workbook. Ages 4–8.

Girard, L. (1991). *Alex, the kid with AIDS.* Morton Grove, IL: Albert Whitman & Company. This is a story about a boy who has AIDS and the friendships he creates. Ages 6–11.

Hausherr, R. (1989). *Children and the AIDS virus.* New York: Clarion Books. Children tell and show through pictures their experience with the world of AIDS. Ages 5 and up.

McCauslin, M. (1995). *Update: AIDS.* Parsippany, NJ: Crestwood House. This book discussed AIDS in the U.S. and how the disease affects society. Ages 10–14.

McNaught, D. (1993). The *gift of good-bye: A workbook for children who love someone with AIDS.* New York: Dell Publishing. This is an interactive book to help adults and children deal with the painful experience of loving someone with AIDS. Ages 5–10.

Merrifield, M. (1990). *Come sit by me.* Toronto: Women's Press. This is an outstanding resource for adults to educate children on the facts about AIDS. Ages 4–8.

Moutoussamy-Ashe, J. (1993). *Daddy and me.* New York: Alfred A. Knopf. This is a photographic saga of Arthur Ashe and his daughter during their journey with AIDS. Ages 4 and up.

Sanford, D. (1991). *David has AIDS*. Portland, OR: Multnomah Press. David struggles with the disease of AIDS. Ages 7–11.

Verniero, Joan. (1995). *You can call me Willie*. New York: Magination Press. This is a practical story for children about AIDS. Ages 5–10.

Wiener, L. & Pizzo, P. A. (1994). *Be a friend*. Morton Grove, IL: Albert Whitman and Co. This book is written by children with AIDS. Ages 5 through adulthood.

Wolf, Bernard. (1997). *HIV positive*. New York: Dutton Children's Books. This resource for children includes photographs and explanations about AIDS. Ages 8–13.

 # Books for Teens and Young People

ON LGBT ISSUES

Amaechi, J. (2007). *Man in the middle*. Bristol, CT: ESPN Publishing. This is the story of the first openly gay professional basketball player.

Bass, E., & Kaufman, K. (1996). *Free your mind: The book for gay, lesbian, and bisexual youth and their allies*. New York: HarperCollins. This book offers practical information for youth on GLBT issues and for the adults surrounding them.

Bauer, M. D. (Ed.). (1994). *Am I blue? Coming out from the silence*. New York: Harper-Trophy Publishers. This is an excellent resource for LGBT youth and parents.

Benduhn, T. (2003). *Gravel queen*. New York: Simon & Schuster. This story centers on emerging sexual identity of a clique of high school teenagers with same-sex attraction.

Brelin, C. & Tyrkus, M. (Eds.) (1997). *Outstanding lives*. Detroit, MI: Visible Ink Press. This is a profile of lesbian and gay men and their contributions to society.

Chandler, K. (1995). *Passages of pride: Lesbian and gay youth come of age*. New York: Times Books. Six teens tell their stories of coming out.

Chase, C. (1999). *Queer 13: Lesbian and gay writers recall seventh grade.* New York: William Morrow & Co. This book presents 25 stories of experiences of LGBT youth at age 13.

Colapinto, J. (2000). *As nature made him: The boy who was raised as a girl.* New York: Harper Collins. This books takes a deep look at the plight of transgender youth.

Due, L. (1995). *Joining the tribe: Growing up gay and lesbian in the '90s.* Lancaster, PA: Anchor Books. This is a portrayal of the journey of gay youth growing up in the nineties.

Edelman, L. (2004). *NO future: Queer theory and the death drive.* London: Duke University Press. This is a theoretical discussion on the ambiguity of the projected future of the homosexual population today.

Garden, N. (1992). *Annie on my mind.* New York: Farrar Straus & Giroux. This is a story of two 17-year-old girls whose friendship turns into a love relationship.

Hartinger, Brent. (2003). *Geography club.* New York: Harper. Teens realize they are not the only gay and lesbian youth at their high school. They secretly create a support group called the geography club.

Heron, A. (Ed.). (1994). *Two teenagers in twenty: Writings by gay and lesbian youth.* Boston: Alyson. Teens tell their LGBT recognition and disclosure with friends and family.

Huegel, K. (2003). *GLBTQ: The survival guide for queer and questioning teens.* Minneapolis, MN: Free Spirit. This book presents GLBTQ questions, resources, and tips.

Huser, G. (2003). *Stitches.* Toronto: Groundwood. Travis is a sensitive teenage boy, teased and bullied by many at school. There is an undercurrent throughout the story that he is attracted to other boys.

Lehmkuhl, R. (2006). *Here's what we'll say.* New York: Carroll & Graf. This book shares a story of growing up, coming out, and being gay in the U.S. Air Force Academy.

Levithan, D. (2006). *Wide awake.* New York: Knopf. This is an honest account of a gay teenager in an optimistic future filled with the possibility for gay and lesbian young adults of social activism and personal and political goals that can be reached.

Marcus, E. (2000). *What if someone I know was gay?* New York: Penguin Putnam Readers. This is a book that addresses questions about gay and lesbian people.

Moore, L. (Ed.). (1998). *Does your mama know? An anthology of black lesbian coming out stories.* Washington, DC: Redbone Press. This is a series of stories, poems, interviews, and essays for high school students depicting the coming out of African-American youth.

Myracle, L. (2003). *Kissing Kate*. New York: Dutton. Lisa struggles with her strong feelings for her best friend Kate.

Ochs, R. (2000). *Bisexual resource guide*. Boston: Bisexual Resources Center. This resource guide provides essential information relating to bisexuality.

Peters, J. (2003). *Keeping the secret*. New York: Little. Holland, a popular high school senior, realizes she is intensely attracted to another girl at school.

Piassa, Rev. S. (2003). *Queeries: Questions lesbians and gays have for God*. Dallas, TX: Sources of Hope Publishing. This book shares many e-mails youth have sent seeking spiritual connectedness and question for God.

Singer, B. (1994). *Growing up gay/Growing up lesbian: A literary anthology*. New York: New Press. Fifty-one prominent lesbian and gay writers and scholars share coming out stories.

Tuaolo, E. (2006). *Alone in the trenches*. Naperville, IL: Sourcebooks, Inc. The author explains his journey as a gay man in professional football.

Woog. D. (1999). *Friends and Family: True stories of gay America's straight allies*. Boston: Alyson Books. This is a collection of stories about straight allies fighting for LGBT rights that include children and teachers. Ages 12 and up.

ON SUICIDE

Grollman, E., & Malikow, M. (1999). *Living when a young friend commits suicide*. Boston: Beacon Press. This book discusses death by suicide, and how to talk about it.

Harper, J. (1993). *Hurting yourself*. Omaha, NE: Centering Corporation. This is a pamphlet for teens and young adults who have intentionally injured themselves.

Kuklin, S. (1994). *After a suicide: Young people speak up*. New York: G.P. Putnam's Sons. This book addresses young people who are survivors after a parent suicide.

McDaniel, L. (1992). *When happily ever after ends*. New York: Bantam Books. Shannon is a teen who struggles with living with her father's violent death by suicide.

Nelson, R., & Galas, J. (1994). *The power to prevent suicide*. Minneapolis, MN: Free Spirit Publishing. This book is useful in involving teenagers with suicide prevention and practical suggestions and examples about suicide with which teens can identify.

ON AIDS

Kittredge, M. (1991). *Teens with AIDS speak out*. New York: Simon & Schuster. Teenagers with AIDS talk about their experience.

ON LGBT PARENTS

Bechard, M. (1999). *If it doesn't kill you*. New York: Viking Children's Books. This is a book about a middle school boy's struggle to deal with his dad coming out. Ages 12 and up.

Bernstein, R. (2005). *Families of value: Personal profiles of gay and lesbian parents*. New York: Marlowe & Co. This book tells powerful stories of families with gay and lesbian parents who are at the forefront of social change in America. Teens and young adults.

Garden, N. (2000). *Holly's secret*. New York: Farrar, Straus and Giroux, Inc. This is the story of Holly, an adopted daughter of a lesbian couple, who keeps a secret. Ages 12 and up.

Garner, A. (2004). *Families like mine: Children of gay parents tell it like it is*. New York: HarperCollins. This book addresses some of the most challenging issues that arise among gay parents and their families. Teens to young adults.

Gillespie, P. (Ed.). (1999). *Love makes a family: Portraits of lesbian, gay, bisexual, and transgender parents*. Amherst: University of Massachusetts Press. This is a beautifully illustrated book sharing pictures and interviews of (LGBT) families. All ages.

Homes, A. M. (1990). *Jack*. New York: Random House. Fifteen-year-old Jack struggles to redefine "family" when his divorced dad discloses he is gay. Ages 14 and up.

Miller, D. (1993). *Coping when a parent is gay*. New York: Rosen Publishing Group. This is a collection of stories by young people sharing their experience of a gay parent.

Ripslinger, J. (2003). *How I fell in love and learned to shoot free throws*. Brookfield, VT: Roaring Brook. A high school boy falls in love. He discovers his girlfriend has two moms. Teens.

Romero, W. (2000). *Long Way Home*. Port Orchard, WA: Windstorm Creative Limited. Eleven-year-old Veronica is involved in a custody battle between her abusive dad and her mom who has come out as a lesbian. Ages 14 and up.

Salat, C. (1999). *Living in secret*. New York: Bantam. Amelia leaves her custodial dad and goes to live with Mom and her girlfriend. Ages 14 and up.

Snow, J. (2004). *How it feels to have a gay or lesbian parent: A book by kids for kids of all ages*. New York: Harrington Park Press. This book gives a voice to the thoughts, feelings, and experiences of children, adolescents, and young adults with same-sex parents. Ages 12 and up.

Woodsin, J. (1997). *From the notebooks of Melanin Sun*. New York: Scholastic. The journey of a 14-year-old African-American boy after he learns his mother is gay. Teens.

ON EDUCATING ABOUT LGBT HISTORY

Jennings, K. (Ed.). (1994). *Becoming visible: A reader in gay and lesbian history for high school and college students*. Boston: Alyson. This resource covers 2,000 years of history and a diverse range of culture on gay and lesbian issues. Teens and young adults.

 # Resources for Caring Adults

ON LGBT ISSUES

Baker, J. (2002). *How homophobia hurts children*. New York: Harrington Park Press. This book shares the damage homophobia can create for children and teens and encourages the nurturance of diversity at home, at school, and in the community.

Clark, D. (1997). *Loving someone gay*. Berkeley, CA: Celestial Arts Publishing. This book written by a therapist offers practical, compassionate guidance for gay and lesbian youth, their families, loved ones, and counselors.

Crawford, S. (1996). *Beyond dolls and guns*. Portsmouth, NH: Heinemann. This book presents over one hundred ways to help children avoid gender bias.

Pinello, D. (2006). *America's struggle for same-sex marriage*. New York: Cambridge University Press. This book chronicles the struggle for same-sex marriage in the U.S. and examines the political controversies surrounding the civil institution of marriage.

ON PARENTING LGBT CHILDREN

Bernstein, R. (2003). *Straight parents, gay children: Keeping families together*. New York: Thunder's Mouth Press. This is an excellent resource for parents of LGBT children.

DeGeneres, B. (1999). *Love, Ellen*. New York: Rob Weisback Books. This is a mother's story of loving her child and sharing her lesbian daughter's journey after disclosure.

Photograph by Kyna Shilling

Dew, R. (1994). *The family heart: A memoir of when our son came out*. New York: Ballantine Books. This is a compelling story of a parent's journey of learning of their child's homosexuality and depression. Their journey evolved with support and love.

Goodman, E. (2004). *Child of my right hand*. Naperville, IL: Sourcebooks, Inc. This is a novel portraying deep emotions when a son comes out as being gay.

Herdt, G. & Koff, B. (2000). *Something to tell you: The road families travel when a child is gay*. New York: Columbia University Press. The book focuses on average families and the consistency of patterns of change including loss, blame, and guilt followed by acceptance after a child's disclosure of homosexuality.

Jennings, K. (2003). *Always my child*. New York: A Fireside Book. This is an excellent and honestly informative guide for parents in understanding their gay, lesbian, bisexual, transgender, or questioning son or daughter. Kevin explains the world children encounter and the sexual identity issues many deal with.

Wythe, D., Merling, A., Merling, R., & Merling, S. (2000). *The wedding*. New York: Avon Books. This is a wonderful and compelling story of one family's journey in creating, sharing, and loving through the process of joining together for a gay marriage ceremony.

ON ADOLESCENCE

Carnegie Council on Adolescent Development. (1995). *Great transitions: Preparing adolescents for a new century.* New York: Carnegie Corporation. This is a comprehensive and positive report on information about adolescents in today's world.

ON ANGER AND STRESS MANAGEMENT

Toner, P. (1993). *Management and self-esteem activities.* West Nyack, NY: The Center for Applied Research in Education. This is a health curriculum sharing activities to help children fare better under stress.

Whitehouse, E., & Pudney, W. (1996). *A volcano in my tummy.* Gabriola Island, Canada: New Society Publishers. A curriculum for children providing anger management plans.

ON SUICIDE

Aarons, L. (1996). *Prayers for Bobby: A mother's coming to terms with the suicide of her gay son.* San Francisco: Harper. This book presents a mother's struggle to reconcile her son's homosexuality and suicide.

Bolton, I. (1983). *My son . . . My son . . . .* Atlanta, GA: Bolton Press. Iris Bolton's personal story of her son's suicide is deeply moving and revealing.

Gardner, S. (1990). *Teenage suicide.* Englewood Cliffs: NJ. Julian Messner Publisher. This book examines reasons and causes of teenage suicide and offers practical solutions.

MacLean, G. (1990). *Suicide in children and adolescents.* Lewiston, NY: Hogrefe & Huber Publishers. This is a practical and hands-on guide that helps in working with children and young people at risk of killing themselves.

McEvoy, M., & McEvoy, A. (1994). *Preventing youth suicide.* Holmes Beach, FL: Learning Publications, Inc. This is a powerful handbook for educators and human service professionals to help prevent youth suicide.

Rickgarn, R. (1994). *Perspectives on college student suicide.* Amityville, NY: Baywood. This book offers a valuable perspective on working with challenging circumstances involving student suicide ideation.

Rubel, B. (1999). *But I didn't say goodbye.* Kendall Park, NJ: Griefwork Center. This is a book for parents and professionals to help child suicide survivors.

Sandefer, K. (1990). *Mom, I'm all right.* Garretson, SD: Sanders Printing Co. This is a book for parents and caring professionals addressing teen suicide. It's a mother's own story about her child's suicide and advice and helpful warnings.

Stillion, J., & McDowell, E. (1996). *Suicide across the lifespan—Premature exits, Second Edition.* New York: Taylor & Francis. This book is designed for college students to help them examine developmental principles applying to suicide.

ON AIDS

Goldman, L. (2001). *Breaking the silence: A guide to helping children with complicated grief/suicide, homicide, AIDS, violence, and abuse.* 2nd ed. New York: Taylor & Francis. This is a resource on helping children and teens with complicated grief issues such as AIDS.

Lawrence, R. (2000). *Sharing the light.* Las Vegas, NV. Ronald Lawrence Publishers. This is the story of the journey of a friendship through the illness of AIDS.

ON BULLYING

Brohl, K., & Corder, C. (1999). *It couldn't happen here.* Washington, DC: Child Welfare League of America. This book recognizes and discusses the needs of many of today's desperate children.

Fried, S., & Fried, P. (1996). *Bullies and victims.* New York: M. Evans and Co. This book describes the schoolyard as a battlefield with practical solutions to help children.

Goldman, L. (2005). *Raising our children to be resilient: A guide to helping children cope with trauma in today's world.* New York: Taylor & Francis. This book provides a chapter on bullying with practical ideas and resources useful for parents and professionals

Hazler, R. (1996). *Breaking the cycle of violence.* Bristol, PA: Taylor & Francis. This book offers good interventions for bullying and victimization.

Ross, D. (1996). *Bullying and Teasing.* Alexandria, VA: ACA Publishers. A book on childhood bullying and teasing and what educators and parents can do.

Curricula and Resources

ON LGBT ISSUES IN SCHOOLS

Casper. V. (1992). Breaking the silence: Lesbian and gay parents and the schools. *Teachers College Record.* 94(1), 109–37.

Donahue & Satterwaite. (1994). *Breaking the classroom silence: A curriculum about lesbian and gay human rights.* New York: Amnesty International.

Family Pride Coalition. (1999). *Opening doors: Lesbian and gay parents and schools.* This is a very helpful resource for educators and families advocating for children of same-sex families. http://www.familypride.org.

First Amendment Center. (2006). *Public schools and sexual orientation: A First Amendment framework for finding common ground.* Arlington, VA. First Amendment Center.

Gillespie, P., & Kaeser, G. (2003). *In our family: Portraits of all kinds of families.* Amherst, MA: Family Diversity Project. This curriculum works in conjunction with the exhibit of the same name to explore all types of families.

Kim, B. ((with Logan, J.). (2002). *"Let's get real" curriculum guide* (guide to accompany the film "Let's get real"). San Francisco: The Respect For All Project. Women's Educational Media.

Lamme, L., & L. Lamme. (2003). *Welcoming children from sexual minority families into our schools.* Phi Delta Kappa Educational Foundation. Bloomington, IN. This is a booklet written by a lesbian mom and her daughter on how to help LGBT families in the school.

Logan, J. (with Chasnoff, D & Cohen, H.). (2002). *That's a family! Discussion and teaching guide* (viewing guide to accompany film *That's a Family*). San Francisco. The Respect for All Project Women's Education Media.

Mitchell, L. (1999). *Tackling gay issues in school: A resource module.* GLSEN Connecticut and Planned Parenthood of Connecticut.

Wong, D. (1995). *School's out: The impact of gay and lesbian issues on America's schools.* Boston: Alyson Publications.

ON BULLYING

Beane, A. (1999). *The bully-free classroom*. Minneapolis, MN: Free Spirit Publishing. This book contains strategies for teachers.

Bitney, J. (1996). *No-bullying curriculum*. Minneapolis, MN: Johnson Institute. This is a manual for preventing bully-victim violence in schools.

Carlsson-Paige, N., & Levin, D. (1998). *Before push comes to shove*. St. Paul, MN: Redleaf Press. This is a conflict resolution curriculum for teachers to help young children use nonviolent behavior.

Garrity, C., Jens, K., Porter, N., & Short-Camilli, C. (2000). *Bully-proofing your school* (2nd ed.). Longmont, CO: Sopris West. This is a guide for school interventions against bullying.

Star. (1998). *No-bullying curriculum*. Chattanooga, TN: Star. This curriculum gives classroom teachers tools to deal with bullying.

Star. (1998). *No putdowns: Character-building violence prevention curriculum*. Chattanooga, TN: Star. A school-based curriculum for violence prevention.

Photograph by Kyna Shilling

ON SUICIDE

Celotta, B. (1991). *Generic crisis intervention procedures*. Gaithersburg, MD: Celotta. This is a practical manual for youth suicide crisis intervention in the schools.

Goldman, L. (2001). *Breaking the silence: A guide to help children with complicated grief/suicide, homicide, AIDS, violence, and abuse* (2nd ed.). New York: Taylor & Francis. This is a practical resource to help young people with issued of complicated grief.

Leenaars, A., & Wenckstern, S. (1990). *Suicide prevention in schools.* New York: Hemisphere Publishing Corporation. The authors outline suicide prevention in schools.

Smith, J. (1989). *Suicide prevention.* Homes Beach, FL: Learning Publications, Inc. This crisis intervention curriculum provides a school program on teen suicide prevention.

 # Videos for Children and Young People

ON LGBT ISSUES

DePaola, T. (2001). *Oliver button is a star.* Monson, MA: Huntvideo. This story tells of a boy ridiculed by parents and peers because he would rather sing and dance that play sports or engage in *normal* boy activities. It is a lesson on embracing differences.

Epstein, R., & Schmiechen, R. (1984). *The times of Harvey Milk.* San Francisco: Black Sand Productions. This is a dramatically moving film about the first openly gay person elected to political office in California and tragically brutally assassinated.

Hunt, L. (Narrator). (1997). *Out of the past: The struggle for gay and lesbian rights in America.* New York: A-PIX Entertainment. This film explores the first Gay Straight Alliance.

O'Donnell, R. (2006). *All aboard! Rosie's family cruise.* New York: HBO, Inc. This documentary shares Rosie's voyage with many LGBT families and their freedom to express feelings.

ON FAMILY DIVERSITY

Chasnoff, D., & Cohen, H. (2000) *That's a family*. San Francisco. The Respect for All Project. Women's Ed. Media. Features kids talking about their different kinds of family structures, and explaining to their peers what they would like them to know about their familes. www.respectforall.org.

COLAGE. (2000). New York: Sugar Pictures. *Our house: A very real documentary about kids with gay and lesbian parents.*

ON BULLYING AND NAME-CALLING

Chasnoff, D., & Cohen, H. (2003). *Let's get real*. San Francisco. Documentary film for students 6–9. The Respect for All Project. Women's Ed. Media. Middle school students talk about their real experiences with name-calling, bullying and the prejudice that fuels it. www.respectforall.org.

DePaola, T. (2001). *Oliver button is a star*. The Oliver Button Project. This is a story for all families with childhood memories. It shares the life of a little boy who likes to sing and dance rather than play sports or engages in activities "normal" boys enjoy and the teasing he is subjected to.

ON TEEN DEPRESSION

Tee Productions (2003). *Inside I ACHE: A guide for professionals working with teens regarding suicide*. Orange Village, OH: Tee Productions. This excellent video offers insights for professionals and students in dealing with suicide.

In the Mix, PBS Series. New York: Castleworks. This series includes *9/11: Looking Back . . . Moving Forward, Teen Solutions to Racism, Action Against AIDS, Competition and Stress, Teen Immigrants, Gun Violence, Depression on the Edge.* These films for teens and by teens express meaningful information on relevant adolescent issues.

✣ Videos for Adults

ON PARENTING LGBT CHILDREN

Montefiore Medical Center in Association with Thirteen/WNET: New York. Keeping Kids Healthy Episode #: KKH (KPKH 213) (37). *Parenting gay teens: Straight parents should know.* July, 2003.

Seitchik, V. (1994). *Queer son: Family journeys to understanding and love.* Cape May, NJ.

Spadola, M. (2000). *Our house: A very real documentary about kids with gay and lesbian parents.* Available from www.frif.com.

Triangle Video Productions. (1994). *Always my kid: A family guide to understanding homosexuality.* Houston, TX.

Woman Vision Video. (1994). *Straight from the heart: Stories of parents' journeys to a new understanding of their lesbian and gay children.* Dee Mosbacher, producer.

ON AFRICAN-AMERICAN ACCEPTANCE OF LGBT YOUTH

Woman Vision, (1996). *All god's children.* The Gay and Lesbian Task Force, and The Nation al Black Lesbian and Gay Leadership Forum.

ON CHILDREN WITH LGBT PARENTS

COLAGE. (2005). *In my shoes: Stories of youth with LGBT parents.* San Francisco: Frameline Distribution.

Lesbian and Gay Parents Association. (1994). *Both of my moms' names are Judy.*

ON EDUCATION AND LGBT ISSUES

Chasnoff, D., & Cohen, H. (1996). *It's elementary - Talking about gay issues in school.* San Francisco. The Respect for All Project, Women's Education Media. Teachers in public and private (K–8) schools around the country model ways to teach about gay and lesbian topics. http://www.respectforall.org.

Chasnoff, D., & Cohen, H. (2000). *That's a family.* San Francisco. The Respect for All Project. Women's Education Media. Features kids talking about their different kinds of family structures, and explaining to their peers what they would like them to know about their families. http://www.respectforall.org.

Chasnoff, D., & Cohen, H. (2003). *Let's get real.* San Francisco. Documentary film for students 6–9. The Respect for All Project. Women's Education Media. Middle school students talk about their real experiences with name-calling, bullying and the prejudice that fuels it. http://www.respectforall.org.

Chasnoff, D., & Cohen, H. (in press). *Staightlaced.* The Respect for All Project. Women's Education Media. Teenagers talk candidly about the limitations of strict gender roles and make the connection to homophobic attitudes that hurt everyone, regardless of sexual orientation. For high school and college students. http://www.respectforall.org.

Jennings, K. (1994). *Teacher in 10: Gay and lesbian educators tell their stories.* Los Angeles: Alyson Publications.

Public TV Newsmagazine Series. October–November. *In the life: Back to school.*

ON ANTIBIAS

GLSEN. 1998. *I just want to say:* Anti-Gay Bias in Schools.

ON LGBT ISSUES IN THE MEDIA

Brokeback Mountain. (2005). This story is about two gay cowboys and their love relationship during an era of great hostility against homosexuals.

Boys Don't Cry. (1999). The film is based on a hate crime involving homophobia.

The Family Stone. (2005). This movie portrays a family with a genuine inclusion of a gay son and his partner.

In and Out. (1997). This is a film about a beloved teacher who eventually comes out as a gay male. He receives community support and affirmation.

Transamerica. (2005). This controversial film tells of the journey of gender change and the challenges that are faced emotionally and through relationships.

The Truth About Jane. (2001). The story of a teenage girl who reveals to her mom she is a lesbian and their journey into understanding and acceptance. Hearst Entertainment.

 # Exhibits for Schools and Community Organizations

LOVE MAKES A FAMILY: Portraits of lesbian, gay, bisexual, and transgender parents and their families. Family Diversity Project. This exhibit features diverse families with GLBT adults, dads and moms, grandparents, and teens and it contributes to the process of reducing the destructive power of prejudice and homophobia and makes the world safer.

IN OUR FAMILY: Portraits of all kinds of families. Family Diversity Project. This exhibit addresses all kinds of families including multigenerational, immigrant, blended, adoptive, foster, multiracial, lesbian and gay-parented, interfaith, single-parented, or families with members who are physically or mentally challenged. This is a valuable resource and catalyst for antibias education for young people and adults.

These exhibits can be brought to a community, school (K–12), library, workplace, house of worship, or diversity event. Contact information includes Family Diversity Project website at http://www.familydiv.org, e-mail infor@familydiv.org, or phone 413-256-0502.

THAT'S SO GAY. COLAGE. This exhibit is a series of photo and text portraits. It is an educational tool created to raise awareness of the diverse experiences of LGBT families. It is available on CD. Contact information includes e-mail thatssogay@colage.org or phone 415-861-5437. An extensive resource guide is also available.

Current Magazines

Current magazines are often useful in presenting information for the LGBTQ and straight population. Youth find areas of interest including fashion, politics, events, and so on. A review of the material is recommended to assure the content is appropriate for young people.

The Advocate: http://www.advocate.com. This is a crucial magazine for the LGBTQ community, offering interviews, cover stories on celebrities and politics, and special insights into the arts and entertainment media.

OUT: http://www.out.com. *OUT* is a magazine that presents feature stories and reports on fashion, well-known individuals in all walks of life, and reviews of film, music, and so on, and sometimes reports on controversial topics.

DETAILS: http://www.details.com. *DETAILS* is a contemporary magazine that appeals to the gay and straight community. It presents current topics that explore the LGBT world, as well as current articles on fashion, media, celebrities, and present-day issues.

GENRE: http://www.genremagazine.com. This magazine is geared toward gay men.

GIRLFRIENDS: http://www.metrosource.com. *GIRLFRIENDS* is a magazine geared toward the lesbian population.

 # Free Pamplets on LGBT Topics

HUMAN RIGHTS CAMPAIGN FOUNDATION

Resource guide to COMING OUT for gay, lesbian, bisexual, and transgender Americans.

A straight guide to GLBT Americans.

Living openly in your place of worship.

Resource guide to COMING OUT for African Americans.

Guia de recursos Par SALIR Del CLOSET para: GLBT (Spanish).

PFLAG

Be yourself: Questions & answers for gay, lesbian, bisexual & transgender youth.

Faith in our families: Parents, families and friends talk about religion and homosexuality.

Our daughter, our sons: Questions & answers for parents of gay, lesbian & bisexual people.

PFLAG bisexuality resource packet.

Open the straight closet: A guide for understanding issues facing families with gay, lesbian, bisexual or transgender spouses.

Nuestras hijas y nuestros hijos: Preguntas y respuestas para padres de gays, lesbianas y bisexuales (Spanish).

From our HOUSE to the SCHOOLHOUSE: Families and friends partnering for safe schools.

COLAGE

Focus on my family: A Queerspawn anthology.

GLSEN

GLSEN SAFE SPACE: A how-to guide for starting an allies program.

FAMILY PRIDE COALITION

Talking to children about our families.

Lesbian, Gay, Bisexual, and Transgender Organizations: Support for All

PFLAG • GLSEN • COLAGE • GLAAD • LLEGO
HUMAN RIGHTS CAMPAIGN
GAY STRAIGHT ALLIANCE NETWORK
STUDENT PRIDE • THE POINT FOUNDATION
THE FIRST AMENDMENT CENTER
FAMILY PRIDE COALITION
WELCOMING SPIRITUAL AND RELIGIOUS GROUPS

"We can't solve a problem with the level of thinking that created it."

Albert Einstein

Community and national resources are essential to engage and support gay, lesbian, bisexual, and transgender youth and their families and friends to broaden the spectrum of freedom of life for all. Together as individuals and groups, new ways of instilling respect for diversity are continually being created and expanded to enlarge the circumference of the circle of our children's world.

 # For Young People

Advocates for Youth
2000 M St. NW Suite 750
Washington, DC 20003
202 419-3420
http://www.advocatesforyouth.org

City at Peace, Inc.
1328 Florida Ave. NW
Washington, DC 20009-4824
202 319-2200
http://www.cityatpeacedc.org

COLAGE: Children of Lesbians and Gays Everywhere
1550 Bryant St. Suite 830
San Francisco, California 94103
415 861-5437
415 861-KIDS
http://www.colage.org

Gay–Straight Alliance Network
1550 Bryant St. Suite 800
San Francisco, CA 94103
415 552-4229
http://www.gsanetwork.org

Hetrick-Martin Institute for Lesbian and Gay Youth
2 Astor Place
New York, NY 10003
212 647-2400
http://www.hmi.org

Matthew Shepard Foundation
301 Thelma Drive #512
Casper, WY 82609
307 237-6167
http://www.MatthewShepard.org

National Youth Advocacy Coalition (NYAC)
1638 R St. NW #300
Washington, DC 20009
202 319-7596
http://www.nyacyouth.org

Sexual Minority Youth Assistance League (SMYAL)
410 7th Street SE
Washington, DC 20003-2707
202 546-5940
http://www.smyal.org

Student Pride USA
121 West 27th Street, #804
New York, NY 10001
212 727-0135
http://www.studentprideUSA.org

The Point Foundation: The National LGBT Scholarship Fund
PO Box 11210
Chicago, IL 60611
1 866 33 POINT
http://www.thepointfoundation.org

For Community

Equality Maryland, Inc.
8121 Georgia Avenue, Suite 501
Silver Spring, MD 20910
1 888 440-9944
http://www.EqualityMarlyand.org

Gay Asian Pacific Support Network (GAPSN)
PO Box 461104
Los Angeles, CA 90046
213 368-6488
http://www.gapsn.org

Gay and Lesbian Medical Association (GLMA)
459 Fulton St., Ste. 107
San Francisco, CA 94102
415 255-4547
http://www.glma.org

GLAAD (Gay and Lesbian Alliance Against Defamation)
150 West 26th St., #503
New York, NY 10001
800 GAY-MEDIA
http://www.glaad.org

Human Rights Campaign (HRC)
919 18th St. NW #800
Washington, DC 20006
800 777-4723
http://www.hrc.org

Lambda Legal Defense and Education Fund
120 Wall St., #1500
New York, NY 10005-3904
212 809-8585
http://www.lambdalegal.org

Mautner Project for Lesbians with Cancer
1707 L St. NW, Ste. 230
Washington, DC 20036
202 332-5536
http://www.mautnerproject.org

National Association of People with AIDS
8401 Colesville Rd. Suite 750
Silver Spring, MD 20910
240 247-1023
http://napwa.org

National Black Lesbian and Gay Leadership Forum
1714 Franklin St., Suite 100-140
Oakland, CA 94612
510 302-0930
http://www.nblglf.org

National Gay and Lesbian Task Force (NGLTF)
1700 Kalorama Rd. NW
Washington, DC 20009-2624
202 824-0450
http://www.ngltf.org

LLEGO-National Latina/o Lesbian, Gay, Bisexual & Transgender Organization
1420 K St. NW, Suite 200
Washington, DC 20005
202 408-5380
http://www.llego.org

Servicemembers Legal Defense Network
PO Box 65301
Washington, DC 20035-3244
202 328-3244
http://www.sldn.org

The First Amendment Center
1101 Wilson Blvd.
Arlington, VA 22209
703 528-0800
http://www.firstamendmentcenter.org

Teaching Tolerance
400 Washington Ave.
Montgomery, AL 36104
334 956-8200
http://www.tolerance.org

 # For Families and Friends

Family Acceptance Project: Cesar E. Chavez Institute
San Francisco State University
3004 16th St. #301
San Francisco, CA 94103
415 522-5558
http://www.familyproject.sfsu.edu

Family Diversity Projects, Inc.
PO Box 1246
Amherst, MA 01004-1246
413 256-0502
http://www.lovemakesafamily.org

Family Pride Coalition
P.O. Box 65327
Washington, DC 20035-5327
202 331-5015
http://www.familypride.org

Food & Friends
219 Riggs Road, NE
Washington, DC 20011
202 269-2277
http://www.foodandfriends.org

Gay and Lesbian Parents
Coalition International
PO Box 50360
Washington, DC 20091
202 583-8029
http://www.GLPCI.org

Photograph by Kyna Shilling

L.A. Gay and Lesbian Center
McDonald/Wright Building
1625 N. Schrader Boulevard
Los Angeles, CA 90028-6213
323 993-7400
http://www.lagaycenter.org

PFLAG
Parents, Families and Friends of Lesbians and Gays
1726 M St. NW, Suite 400
Washington, DC 20036
202 467-8180
http://www.pflag.org

For Educators

GLSEN: Gay, Lesbian and Straight Education Network
90 Broad Street
New York, NY 10004
212 727-0135
http://www.glsen.org

Sexuality Information and Education Council of the United States
130 W. 42nd St. Suite 350
New York, NY 10036-7802
212 819-9770
http://www.siecus.org

Women's Educational Media
2180 Bryant Street Suite 203
San Francisco, CA 94110
415 641-4616
http://www.womedia.org

For Welcoming Religious and Spiritual Groups

Affirmation (Mormon)
Box 46022
Los Angeles, California 90046
213 255-7251
http://www.affirmation.org

Affirmation (United Methodist)
PO Box 1021
Evanston, IL 60204
http://www.umaffirm.org

Al-Fatiha Foundation (Muslim)
PO Box 33015
Washington, DC 20033
Email: info@al-fatiha.org
http://www.al-fatiha.org

American Baptists Concerned/Massachusetts
PO Box 368
Newton Center, MA 021159
978 745-8259
http://www.rainbowbaptists.org

Association of Welcoming and Affirming Baptists
PO Box 259257
Madison, WI 53725
608 255-2155
http://www.wabaptists.org

Axios—Eastern & Orthodox Christian Gay Men & Women
328 West 17th Street, #4F
New York, NY 10011
212 989-6211
http://www.qrd.org/qrd/www/orgs/axios

Brethren/Mennonite Council for Lesbian & Gay Concerns
2720 East 22nd St. Suite 209
Minneapolis, MN 55406
612 343-2060
http://www.webcom.com/bmc

Buddhist Association of the Gay and Lesbian Community
Box 1974
Bloomfield, NJ 07003

Casa de Cristo Evangelical Church
1029 E. Turney
Phoenix, AZ 85013
602 265-2931
http://www.casadecristo.org

Christian Lesbians Out Together
PO Box 436
Planaterium Station, NY 10024
617-267-9001

Conference for Catholic Lesbians
PO Box 853
Greenport, NY 11944
http://www.cclonline.org

Dignity, Inc. (Roman Catholic)
15500 Massachusetts Avenue NW
Suite 11
Washington, DC 20005
202 861-0017
http://www.dignity.org

Emergence International (Christian Scientist)
Box 581
Kentfield, CA 04014-0581
415 548-1818
http://www.emergenceinternation-al.org

Evangelicals Concerned
311 East 72nd Street
Suite 1-G
New York, NY 10021
212 517-3171
http://www.ecwr.org

Friends for Lesbian, Gay, Bisexual, and Transgender Concerns (Quaker)
143 Campbell Ave
Ithaca, NY 14850
607 272-1024
http://www.flgbtgc.quaker.org

Gay American Indians
1347 Divisadero St. #312
San Francisco, CA 94115
415 621-3485

Gay Buddhist Fellowship
2215-R Market St. PMB456
San Francisco, CA 94114
415 974-9878
http://www.gaybuddhist.org

Gay, Lesbians and Affirming Disciples Alliance (Disciples of Christ)
Box 19223
Indianapolis, IN 46219-0223
319 324-6231
http://www.gladalliance.org

Honesty (Southern Baptist Convention)
603 Quail's Run Road #C-1
Louisville, KY 40207
502 261-0338
http://www.gaychurch.org

Integrity, Inc. (Episcopal)
1718 M St PM Box 148
Washington, DC 20036
202 462-9193
http://www.integrityusa.org

Interfaith Working Group
Box 11706
Philadelphia, PA 19101
215 235-3050
iwg@libertynet.org

Lifeline, Inc (Baptists)
8150 Lakecrest Drive
Box 619
Greenbelt, MD 20770-1461
http://www.gaychurch.org

Lutherans Concerned
Box 10461
Fort Dearborn Station
Chicago, IL 60610
651 665-0863
http://www.lcna.org

More Light Presbyterians
Box 38
New Brunswick, NJ 08903-0038
908 932-7501
http://www.mlp.org

National Gay Pentecostal Alliance
Box 1391
Schenectady, NY 12301-1391
518 372-6001
http://www.gaychurch.org

New Ways Ministry (Roman Catholic)
4012 29th Street
Mt. Rainier, MD 20712
301 277-5674
http://www.gaychurch.org

Nichiren Association (Buddhist)
Box 1935
Los Angeles, CA 90078

Reconciling Congregation Program
(RCP)
3801 N. Keeler Ave.
Chicago, IL 60641
773 736-5526
http://www.rcp.org

Photograph by Kyna Shilling

Reformed Church in America Gay Caucus
Box 8174
Philadelphia, PA 19101-8174

Religious Science International
PO Box 2152
Spokane, WA 99210
1 800 662 1348
http://www.rsintl.org

Seventh-Day Adventist Kinship International
Box 3840
Los Angeles, CA 90078-3849
West 213 876-2076 East 617 436-5950
http://www.sdakinship.org

Sovereignty (Jehovah's Witnesses)
Box 27242
Santa, CA 92799

Unitarian Universalist Association's Office of Bisexual, Gay, Lesbian and
Transgender Concerns
25 Beacon St.
Boston, MA 02108
617 948-6475
obgltc@uua.org

Unitarian Universalist Office for Lesbian and Gay Concerns
167 Milk St.
Boston, MA 02115
617 742 2100
http://www.uua.org/obgitc/

United Church Coalition for Lesbian/Gay Concerns
18 College Street
Athens, OH 45701
614 593-7301
http://www.ucccoalition.org

United Lesbian and Gay Christian Scientists
Box 2171
Beverly Hills, CA 90213-2171

Unity Fellowship Church Movement (African American)
5148 West Jefferson Blvd.
Los Angeles, CA 90016
323 938-8322
www.unityfellowshipchurch.org

Universal Fellowship of Metropolitan Community Churches
5300 Santa Monica Boulevard
Suite 304
Los Angeles, CA 90029
213 464-5100
http://www.ufmcc.com

Welcoming and Affirming Baptists/San Francisco Bay Area
PO Box 3183
Walnut Creek, CA 94598
925 459-9053
http://rainbowbaptists.org

World Congress of Gay and Lesbian Jewish Organizations
PO Box 23379
Washington, DC 20036
202 452-7424
http://www.wcgljo.org

Wingspan, St. Paul Reformation Lutheran Church
100 North Oxford Street
Saint Paul, MN 55104
612 224-3371
http://www.wingspan.org

 # For Bisexual Youth

BiNetUSA
4201 Wilson Blvd., #110-311
Arlington, VA 22203
1 800 585-9368
http://www.binetusa.org

Bisexual Resource Center
PO Box 1026
Boston, MA 02117
617 424-9595
http://www.biresource.org

Bi without Borders
PO Box 581307
Minneapolis, MN 55458
Email: biwithoutborders@coolmail.com
http://bisexual.org/g/biwithoutborders/

 # For Transgender Youth

The American Boyz
212A South Bridge Street, Suite 131
Elkton, MD 21921
410 620-2161
http://www.amboyz.org

FTM International (FTM)
1360 Mission Street, Suite 200
San Francisco, CA 94103
415 553-5987
http://www.ftm-intl.org

Gender Education and Advocacy (GEA)
PO Box 65
Kensington, MD 20895
301 949-3822
http://www.gender.org

The International Foundation for Gender Education (IFGE)
PO Box 229
Waltham, MA 02254-0229
781 899-2212
http://www.ifge.org

The Renaissance Transgender Association
987 Old Eagle School Rd., Suite 719
Wayne, PA 19087
610 975-9119
http://www.ren.org

For Suicide Information

American Association of Suicidology
4201 Connecticut Ave. Suite 310
Washington, DC 20008
202 237-2280
http://www.suicidology.org

SPEAK (Suicide Prevention Education Awareness for Kids)
423 Dumbarton Road
Baltimore, MD 21212
410 377 4004
http://www.speakforthem.org

Suicide Awareness/Voice of Education SA/VE
PO Box 24507
Minneapolis, MN 55424-0507
612 946-7998
http://www.save.org

The Jason Foundation
A Promise for Tomorrow
P.O. Box 616
Hendersonville, TN 37077
1 888 881-2323
http://www.jasonfoundation.com

The Yellow Ribbon Program
Light for Life Foundation of America
P.O. Box 644
Westminster CO 80030-0644
303 429-3530
http://www.yellowribbon.com

Youth Suicide National Center
120 Wall St, 22nd floor
New York, NY 10005
888 333-AFSP
http://www.afsp.org

❦ For AIDS Information

AIDS Atlanta
1132 W. Peachtree Street, NW
Suite 102
Atlanta, GA 30309
800 342-2437
http://www.aidatlanta.org

AIDS Action Committee
131 Clarendon St.
Boston, MA 02116
617 536-7733 (Hotline)
617 437-6200
http://www.aac.org

American Academy of Child and Adolescent Psychiatry
Committee on HIV Issues
3615 Wisconsin Avenue, NW
Washington, DC 20016
202 966-7300
http://www.aacap.org

American Academy of Pediatrics
Committee on School Health
141 NW Point Boulevard
PO Box 297
Elk Grove Village, IL 60009-0927
800 433-9016
http://www.aap.org

American Foundation for AIDS Research
1515 Broadway, Suite 3601
New York, NY 10032
212 719-0033
http://www.amfar.org

American Red Cross
AIDS Education Office
1709 New York Avenue NW
Washington, DC 20006
202 434-4074
http://www.redcross.org

National AIDS Information Clearinghouse
PO Box 6003
Rockville, MD 20850
800 458-5231
http://www.cdcnpin.org

Pan American Health Organization/WHO
AIDS Program
525 23rd Street, NW
Washington, DC 20037
202 861-4346
http://www.paho.org

Pediatric AIDS Network
Children's Hospital of Los Angeles
4650 Sunset Boulevard, Box 55
Los Angeles, CA 90027
213 669-5616
http://www.childrenshospitalla.org

San Francisco AIDS Foundation
PO Box 6182
San Francisco, CA 94101
415 861-3397
http://www.sfaf.org

The AIDS Health Project
Box 0884
San Francisco, CA 94143
415 476-6430
http://www.ucsf-ahp.org

❦ Hotlines

Counseling, Information, Referrals
888 THE-GLNH (888 843-4564)
http://www.glnh.org

Friends for Survival, Inc.
Suicide Loss Hotline
1 800 646-7322
http://www.friendsforsurvival.org

Gay and Lesbian National Hotline
1 888 643-GLNH
http://www.glnh.org

Lyric Youth Talkline
800 96-YOUTH
http://www.lyric.org

National AIDS Hotline
1 800 342-AIDS
1 800 344-7432 (Spanish)
1 800 243-7889 (TTY)
http://www.aidshotline.org

National Gay and Lesbian Youth Hotline
1 800 347-TEEN
http://www.odysseyyouth.org

National Mental Health Association Crisis Line
1 800 969-NMHA
STD Information Line

Sexually Transmitted Diseases
800 227-8922
http://www.nmha.org

Suicide Hotline
1 800 SUICIDE (24 hours/7 days a week)

The Trevor Hotline
http://www.thetrevorproject.org

Crisis Intervention for Lesbian, Gay, Bisexual, and Transgender Youth
1 800 850-8078
http://www.glsen.org

❧ References

Ahrens, F. (2007, April 7). Disney's theme weddings come true for gay couples. *The Washington Post,* pp. A1, A6.

Alford, S. (2003). *Adolescents-at risk for sexually transmitted infections.* Advocates for Youth. Retrieved April 8, 2006 from http://www.advocatesforyouth.org/publications/factsheet/fssti.htm

Angelo, M. (2006, February 15). *Larry King Live* [Television broadcast]. Atlanta: CNN.

Associated Press. (2007). *Don't ask, don't tell revisited.* Retrieved March 1, 2007 from http://www.military.com

Bernstein, R. A., (2003). *Straight parents, gay children.* New York: Thunder's Mouth Press.

Bluegrass Fairness. (2006). *Talking points about pedophilia.* Retrieved December 5, 2006 from http://www.bluegrassfairness.org/pages/TP-pedophilia.asp pp. 1–2.

BostonEdge. (2007, February 28). *First service member wounded in Iraq comes out.* Retrieved March 1, 2007 from http://www.edgeboston.com/index.php?ci=108&ch=news&sc=glbt&sc2=news&sc3=&id=1 pp. 1–2.

Brelin, C., & Tyrkus, M. (Eds.). (1997). *Outstanding lives: Profiles of lesbians and gay men.* Detroit, MI: Visible Ink.

Bright, C. (2004). Deconstructing reparative therapy: An examination of the processes involved when attempting to change sexual orientation. *Clinical Social Work Journal, 32*(4), 471–481.

Brown, P. (2006, December 2). Supporting boys or girls when the line isn't clear. *The New York Times.* Retrieved December 3, 2006 from http://www.nytimes.com/2006/12/02/us/02child.html?-r&hp&ex=1165122000&en=4ba... pp. 1–3.

Burn, S. M. (2000). Heterosexuals' use of "fag" and "queer" to deride one another: A contributor to heterosexism and stigma. *Journal of Homosexuality, 40*(2).

Carlson, P. (2007, February 6). Liz Taylor's candle blowout. *Washington Post Style Section,* pp. C1, C7.

CBS Video. (2006, March 12). Gay or straight? *60 Minutes* [Television broadcast]. New York: CBS News.

CNN News, (2006, October 6). Stockwell, A., editor of the Advocate, CNN NEWS [Television broadcast]. 10/10/06. Atlanta: CNN.

Chasnoff, D., & Cohen, H. (1996). *It's elementary: Talking about gay issues in school.* San Francisco. The Respect for All Project, Women's Educational Media.

Cloud, J. (2005, October 10). The battle over gay teens. *Time,* 42–51.

Cohn, D. (2001, June 20). Census shows big increase in gay households, *The Washington Post,* p. A01. Retrieved June 5, 2007 from http://www.fedglobe.org/news.htm#census.

Cooperman, A. (2006, December 7). Conservative rabbis allow ordained gays, same-sex unions. *The Washington Post,* pp. A1, A17.

Cooperman, A., & Whoriskey, P. (2006, November 15). Christian groups move to condemn gay sex. *The Washington Post,* pp. A1, A10.

D'Augelli, A., Grossman, A., Salter, N., Vasey, J., Starks, M., & Sinclair, K. (2005). Predicting the suicide attempts of lesbian, gay, and bisexual youth. *Suicide and Life-Threatening Behavior. 35*(6), 12/05. The American Association of Suicidology. pp. 646–659.

DeGeneres, B. (1999). *Love, Ellen.* New York: Rob Weisback Books.

Dell'Orto, G. (2007, February 17). Gay pastor loses ruling, but not his flock—yet. *The Washington Post,* pp. B8, B9.

Dvorak, P. (2006, April 18). One soggy day, a cluster of rainbows. *The Washington Post,* pp. B1, B9.

Earls, M. (2005). Advocates for youth: The facts: GLBTQ youth. Retrieved October 14, 2006 from http://advocatesforyouth.org/publications/factsheet/fsglbt.htm.

Earls, M. (2005a). Advocates for youth citing United States Conference of Mayors. (1996). HIV prevention programs targeting gay/bisexual men of color (2nd ed.). [HIV Education Case Studies] Washington, DC: The Conference. Retrieved June 31, 2007 from http://www.advocatesforyouth.org/publications/factsheet/fsglbt.htm

Elias, M. (2007, February 7). Gay teens coming out earlier to peers and family. *USA Today,* Retrieved March 7, 2007 from http:/www.usatoday.com/news/nation/2007–02–07-gay-teens-cover_x.htm, pp. 1–5.

Ellis, L., & Ames, M. A. (1987). Neurohormonal functioning and sex orientation: A theory of homosexuality-heterosexuality. *Psychological Bulletin, 101,* 233–258.

Fan, M. (2007, February 23). For gays in China, "Fake marriage" eases pressure. *The Washington Post,* p. A12.

Farhi, P. (2007, February 7). Mars scraps Snickers ad after complaints. *The Washington Post,* pp. C1, C7.

Feller, B. (2006, March 11). Christian, gay groups unite on settling school conflicts. *Santa Barbara News Press,* p. B2.

Ferro, U. (2005). *Tanny's meow.* West Tisbury, MA: Marti Books.

Ferro, U. (2006). *Wishing for kittens.* West Tisbury, MA: Marti Books.

Ferro, U. (2007). *Mother's day on Martha's Vineyard.* West Tisbury, MA: Marti Books.

First Amendment Center and BridgeBuilders. (2006). Public schools and sexual orientation. *First Amendment Center,* pp. 1–3.

Floyd, F., Stein, T., Harter, K., Allison, A., & Nye, C. (1999). Gay, lesbian, and bisexual youth: Separation-individuation, parental attitudes, identity consolidation, and well-being. *Journal of Youth and Adolescence, 28*(6), 409–420.

Gillespie, P. (Ed.). (1999). *Love makes a family: Portraits of lesbian, gay, bisexual and transgender parents and their families.* Amherst: University of Massachusetts Press.

GLSEN. (2001, October 10). *National school climate survey.* Retrieved August 8, 2007 from http://www.glsen.org/cgi-bin/iowa/all/news/record/827.html

GLSEN. (2002). Creating an inclusive school prom. Retrieved May 15, 2002 from http://www.glsen.org/cgi-bin/iowa/all/news/record/547.html

GLSEN. (2003). *GLSEN safe space: A how-to guide for starting an allies program.* Retrieved August 1, 2007 from http://www.glsen.org/binary-data/GLSEN-ATTACHMENTS/file/294-2.PDF pp. 1–35.

GLSEN Pittsburgh. (2005, March 31). *First annual making proms safe for all* report. Retrieved May 12, 2006 from http://www.glsenpgh.org.

GLSEN. (2005, September 15). Students across the country take "pledge" to be allies. Retrieved May 11, 2006 from http://www.glsen.org/cgi-bin/iowa/student/library/record/1851.html, pp. 1–3.

GLSEN. (2005, September 18–25). *Ally week.* Retrieved May 11, 2006 from http://dayofsilence.org/ally/

GLSEN. (2006a, March 30). GLSEN's 10th national day of silence expected to be largest to date. Riley Norton contact. Retrieved April 3, 2006 from http://www.glsen.org/cgi-bin/iowa/all/news/record/1916.html

GLSEN. (2006b, January 23). No Name-Calling Week. Retrieved March 28, 2006 from http://www.nonamecallingweek.org/cgi-bin/iowa/all/news/record/52.html.

Griffith, K. (2005, July 19). Gay parenting 2005: Escape from the red states. *The Advocate*. pp. 42–46.

Grove, L. (2005, February 17) For RuPaul, Diller a thriller. *New York Daily News*. Retrieved May 7, 2007 from http://www.nydailynews.com/gossip/2005/02/17/2005-02-17_for_rupaul_diller_a_thriller_print.html.

Haynes, C. (2006, March 9). A moral battleground, a civil discourse. *USA Today: OP/ED*. Retrieved September 13, 2006 from http://www.usatoday.com/news/opinion/editorials/2006-03-19-faith-edit_x.htm, pp. 1–4.

Haynes, C. (2006, July 9). In debates over homosexuality, schools should be both safe and free. First Amendment Topics. Retrieved April 11, 2007 from http://www.firstamendmentcenter.org/commentary.aspx?id=17118, p. 3.

Healy, P. (2001, February 28). Massachusetts study shows high suicide rate for gay students. *Boston Globe,* p. 4.

Herek, G. (2004). Beyond "homophobia": Thinking about sexual prejudice and stigma in the twenty-first century. *Journal of NSRC (National Sexuality Resource Center), 1*(2), 6–24.

Herek, G. (2006a). Facts about homosexuality and child molestation. Retrieved December 3, 2006 from http://psychology.ucdavis.edu/rainbow/htlm/facts_molestaton.html. 1–16.

Herek, G. (2006b). Legal recognition of same-sex relationships in the United States: A social science perspective. *American Psychologist, 61*(6), 607–621.

Herek, G., Chopp, R., & Strohl, D. (2007). Sexual stigma: Putting sexual minority health issues in context. In I. Meyer & M. Northridge (Eds.), *The health of sexual minorities: Public health perspectives on lesbian, gay, bisexual, and transgender populations,* New York: Springer.

Holmes, W., Slap, G. (1998). Sexual abuse of boys. *JAMA, 280*(21), 1855–1860.

Huckaby, J. (2006). A message from PFLAG's exexutive director, Jody Huckaby. Egg rolling. *PFLAG Newsletter.* jnavetta@pflag.org

Human Rights Campaign. Out in scripture: Preaching resource. Retrieved June 5, 2007 from http://www.hrc.org/scripture

Hunter, S. (2006, February 2). Lost horizon: A picture of the mountain between two Americas. *The Washington Post.* pp. C1, C5.

Johnson, C., & Johnson, K. (2000). High-risk behavior among gay adolescents: Implication for treatment and support. *Adolescence, 35*(140), 619–637.

Johnson, D., & Piore, A. (2004, October 18). At home in two worlds. *Newsweek,* pp. 52–54.

Johnson, K. (2001, April 11). *Gay teen suicide: On the rise*. Retrieved April 10, 2006 from http://www.emglish.iup.edu/liberalstudies/gay_teen_suicide.htm

Joyce, A. (2006, September 24). For gays, some doors open wider. *The Washington Post,* pp. F1, F6.

Katz, P. A. (1986). Modification of gender-stereotyped behavior: General issues and research considerations. *Sex Roles, 14,* 591–602.

Kaufman, M. (2007, February 15). Hardaway makes anti-gay comments on radio. *MiamiHerald.com*. Retrieved February 15, 2007 from http://www.miami.com/mld/miamiherald/news/16700045.htm

Keeping Kids Healthy. (2003) Parenting gay teens: What straight parents should know. Episode KKH 311. New York: Thirteen WNET. Aired September 5/6 2003.

Kelly, M. (2006, February 17). Open dialogue is key for parents of gay son. *The Washington Post*, p. C08.

Kennedy, Sarah. (2006, May 23). The importance of prom. *The Advocate,* p. 24.

Kim, B. with Logan, J., Chasnoff, D. (Director) & Cohen, H. (Exec. Producer). (2004). *"Let's Get Real" Curriculum Guide*. San Francisco: The Respect for All Project Women's Educational Media.

Kitts, R. (2005). Gay adolescents and suicide: Understanding the association. *Adolescence*, Fall 2005, 40, 159, *Research Library Core*, pp. 621–628.

Kort, J. (2006, October 12). Homosexuality and pedophilia: The false link. *Between the Lines News,* 1441 Retrieved December 12, 2006 from http://pridesource.com/article.shtml?article=20520

Landolt, M., Bartholomew, K., Saffrey, C., Oram, D., & Perlman, D. (2004). Gender nonconformity, childhood rejection, and adult attachment: A study of gay men. *Archives of Sexual Behavior, 33*(2), 117–128.

Laudadio, M. (2006, August 7). Lance Bass: I feel like myself. I'm not hiding anything. *People Magazine,* pp. 86–90.

Lee, F. (2006, April 3). On HBO, Rosie O'Donnell's cruise for gay families. *The New York Times*, pp. 1–3. Retrieved April 4, 2006 from http://www.nytimes.com/2006/04/03arts/telelvision/03rosi.html?ex=1301716800&en=573

Lee, G. (2007, January 24). Gay stays in Virginia. *The Washington Post,* p. C2.

Lehmkuhl, R. (2006). *Here's what we'll say: Growing up, coming out, and the U. S. Air Force Academy*. Editorial Review: Book Description. Retrieved February 16, 2007 from http://www.amazon.com/Heres-What-Well-Say-Growing/dp/0786717823/ref=pd_sim_b_3

Lehoczky, E. (2005, August 19). Rough going overseas. *The Advocate,* pp. 47–48.

LeLand, J. (2006, November 8). A spirit of belonging, inside and out. *New York Times,* Section 9, pp. 1, 6.

LeVay, S. (1993). *The sexual brain.* Bradford, MA: Bradford Books.

Lindley, L., & Reininger, B. (2001). Support for instruction about homosexuality in South Carolina public schools. *The Journal of School Health, 71*(1), 17–22.

Lithwick, D. (2006, March 12). Why courts are adopting gay parenting. *The Washington Post,* p. B2.

Logan, J. with Chasnoff, D. & Cohen, H. (2002). *That's a Family! Discussion and Teaching Guide.* (Viewing Guide). The Respect for All Project. San Francisco: Women's Education Media.

Mallon, G. P. (Ed.). (1999). *Social services with transgendered youth.* Binghamton, NY: Harrington Park Press.

Mallon, G. & Woronoff, R. (2006). Busting out of the child welfare closet: Lesbian, gay, bisexual, and transgender-affirming approaches to child welfare. *Child Welfare*: Mar/Apr 2006; *85*(2); Research Library Core. pp. 115–122.

Martin, A., & Heetrick, E. (1988). The stigmatization of the gay and lesbian adolescent. *Journal of Homosexuality, 15,* 163–183.

McConaghy, N. (1998). Paedophilia: A review of the evidence. *Australian and New Zealand Journal of Psychiatry, 32*(2), 252–265.

McFarland, W. P. (1998). Gay, lesbian, and bisexual student suicide. *Professional School Counseling, 1*(3), 26–29.

Merriam-Webster Online Dictionary. (2006). Heterosexism. Retrieved June 4, 2007 from http://www.m-w.com/dictionary/heterosexism

Mastoon, A. (1997). *The Shared Heart: Portraits and stories celebrating lesbian, gay, and bisexual young people.* New York: HarperCollins Publishers.

Mufioz-Plaza, C., Quinn, S., & Rounds, K. (2002). Lesbian, gay, bisexual and transgender students: Perceived social support in the high school environment. *The High School Journal, 85*(4), 52–63.

Mustanski, B. Chivers, M., & Bailey, J. (2002). A critical review of resent biological research on human sexual orientation. *Annual Review of Sex Research.* Society of the Scientific Study of Sex, Mount Vernon, NY: *13,* p. 89.

Myers, D. (2005). *Exploring psychology: Sixth edition in modules.* New York: Worth Publishers.

National Youth Advocacy Coalition. (2003, March/April). A blueprint for justice, NYAC Visions Brochure. Washington, DC: *Poverty and Race Research and Action Council Journal* (PRRAC). Retrieved May 4, 2007 from http://www.nyacyouth.org/Final-Blueprint.pdf

Nullis, C. (2006, November 15). Gay marriage endorsed in S. Africa. *The Washington Post,* p. A15.

Ocamb, K. (2001). Anderson, Newton-John help raise $124,000 for GLBT teen suicide hotline. *Lesbian News, 26*(6), p. 13.

OUT. (2005). Serving GLBTQ Youth. *OUT Workshop,* p. 30.

OutProud. (2007). *HIV/AIDS. Facts, figures, information & statistics.* Retrieved August 3, 2007 from http://outproud.org/facts.html.

O'Donnell, R. (2006, April 6 aired). All aboard! Rosie's family cruise. New York: Home Box Office (HBO), Inc.

Pawelski, J., Perrin, E., Foy, J., Allen, C., Crawford, J., Del Monte, M., Kaufman, M., Klein, J., Smith, K., Springer, S., Tanner, J., & Vickers, D. (2006). The effects of marriage, civil union, and domestic partnership laws on the health and well-being of children. *Pediatrics, 118*(1), 349–364.

PFLAG. Update SC, (1994). Gay and lesbian stats, Retrieved March 25, 2006 from http:www.pflagstatesc.org/statistics.htm

PFLAG. (1997). From our house to the schoolhouse.

PFLAG. (2002). *Be yourself: Questions & answers for gay, lesbian, bisexual & transgender youth.* Washington, DC: PFLAG.

PFLAG. (2005). *Is homosexuality a sin?* Washington, DC: PFLAG.

PFLAG, Metro DC. (2005a). *Answers to youths' questions brochure.* Washington, DC: PFLAG.

PFLAG, Metro DC. (2005b). *Is homosexuality a sin?* 2nd ed. Washington, DC: PFLAG.

PFLAG, Metro DC. (2005c). *Safe schools brochure.* Washington, DC: PFLAG.

PFLAG. (2006). Ex-gay ministries and reparative therapy. Retrieved April 8, 2006 from http://www.pflag.org/index.php/id=280

PFLAG. (2006). *Our daughters & sons: Questions & answers for parents of gay, lesbian, and bisexual people.* Washington, DC: PFLAG.

PFLAG. (2006a). Faces and names: PGLAG news and notes. *PFLAGPOLE,* p. 11.

PFLAG. (2006b). *IBM: A true PFLAG hero. PFLAGPOLE,* p. 8.

PFLAG *Phoenix (2007, June 6 last update) today's gay youth:* The ugly, frightening statistics, Retrieved June 11, 2007 from http://www.pflagphoenix.org/education/youth-stats.html.

Ploderl, M., & Fartacek, R. (2005). Suicidality and associated risk factors among lesbian, gay, and bisexuals compared to heterosexual Austrian adults. *Suicide and Life-Threatening Behavior, 35*(6), 661–670.

Project 10: A brief history. Retrieved June 04, 2007 from http://www.project10.org/index.html

Public Use Microdata Sample (PUMS). (2000). Census. United States Census Bureau. Retrieved March 25, 2006 from http://www.gaydemographics.org/USA/PUMS/nationalintto.htm

Romero, P. (1999). Impact of racism, homophobia and poverty on suicidal ideation among Latino gay men. *Berkley McNair Research Journal, 7,* 115–128.

Rutter, P., & Soucar, E. (2002). Youth suicide risk and sexual orientation. *Adolescence, 37*(147), 289–299.

Saltzburg, S. (2004). Learning that an adolescent child is gay or lesbian: The parent experience. *Social Work, 49*(1), 109–118.

Savage, T., Harley, D., & Nowak, T. (2005). Applying social empowerment strategies as tools for self-advocacy in counseling lesbian and gay male clients. *Journal of Counseling and Development, 83,* 131–137.

Savin-Williams, R. (2005). *The new gay teen.* London: Harvard University Press.

Shalikashvili, J. (2007, January 2). OP-ED: Second thoughts on gays in the military. *New York Times.* Retrieved January 30, 2007 from http://www.nytimes.com/2007/01/02/opinion/02shalikashvili.html?ex=1325394000&en=9

Sheridan, C. (2007, February 9). Amaechi becomes first NBA player to come out. ESPN.COM. Retrieved February 15, 2007 from http://sports.espn.go.com/nba/news/story/?id=2757105

Smolinsky, T. (2001, December 14). What do we really think: A group exercise to increase heterosexual ally behavior. GLSEN, Retrieved May 11, 2006 from http://www.glsen.org.cgi-bin/iowa/educator/library/record/888.html

Stahl, L. (2006, March 12). The science of sexual orientation. *60 Minutes* [Television broadcast]. New York: CBS News.

Stepp, L. (2001, June 19). A lesson in cruelty: Anti-gay slurs common in school. *The Washington Post,* pp. A1, A7.

Stone, C. (November/December, 2004). Counselors and courts: Bully prevention for gay, lesbian, and bisexual youth. *ASCA School Counselor*. American School Counseling Association.

Tuaolo, E. (2006). *Alone in the trenches*. Naperville, IL: Sourcebooks.

Ueno, K. (2005). Sexual orientation and psychological distress in adolescence: Examining interpersonal stressors and social support process. *Social Psychology Quarterly, 68*(3), 258–277.

Van Leeuwen, J., Boyle, S., Salomonsen-Sautel, S., & Baker, D. (2006). Lesbian, gay, and bisexual homeless youth: An eight-city public health perspective. *Child Welfare, 85*(2), 151–171.

Van Wormer, K., & McKinney, R. (2003). What schools can do to help gay/lesbian/ bisexual youth: A harm reduction approach. *Adolescence, 38*(151), 409–420.

Vargas, J. (2007, February 28). Defending his country, but not its "don't ask, don't tell" policy. *The Washington Post*, pp. C1, C8.

Wester, S., Vogel, D., Wei, M., & McLain, R. (2006). African American men, gender role conflict, and psychological distress: The role of racial identity. *Journal of Counseling & Development, 84,* 419–429.

Whitbeck, L., Chen, S., Hoyt, D., Tyler, K., & Johnson, K. (2004). Mental disorder, subsistence strategies, and victimization among gay, lesbian, and bisexual homeless and runaway adolescents. *The Journal of Sex Research, 41*(4), 329–342.

Wides-Munoz, L. (2006, March 4). Report: Gay preventon programs harm teens. Associated Press. National Gay and Lesbian Task Force. DC. Retrieved May 30, 2007 from http://www.release.ctm?releaseID=923

Wikipedia.com (2007). Same-sex marriage in the United States. Retrieved July 17, 2007 from http://en.wikipedia.org/wiki/Same-Sex_Marriage_in_the_United_States.

Winerip, M. (2007, April 1). Accepting gay identity, and gaining strength. *New York Times*. Retrieved August 1, 2007 from http://www.nytimes.com/2007/04/01/nyregion/nyregionspecial2/01RParenting.html?ex=1333080000&en=06bf5f17 9f51c5a4&ei=5088&partner=rssnyt&emc=rss.

Wythe, D., Merling, A., Merling, R., & Merling S. (2000). *The wedding*. New York: Avon Books.

Zara, J. (2006, March 31). A Peace of the spotlight: Local teens take on topical issues, including gay crushes, in a new stage production. *The Washington Blade,* pp. 1–3. http://www.washblade.com/2006/3-31/locallife/feature/lft.cfm.

❧ About the Author

Linda Goldman has a Fellow in Thanantology: Death, Dying, and Bereavement (FT) with an MS degree in counseling and Master's Equivalency in early childhood education. Linda is a Licensed Clinical Professional Counselor (LCPC) and a National Board Certified Counselor (NBCC) provider. She worked as a teacher and counselor in the school system for almost 20 years. Currently, she has a private grief therapy practice in Chevy Chase, Maryland. She works with children, teenagers, families with prenatal loss, and grieving adults. Linda shares workshops, courses, and training on children and grief and currently teaches as adjunct faculty in  the Graduate Program of Counseling at Johns Hopkins University. She has also taught as adjunct faculty at the University of Maryland School of Social Work/Advanced Certification Program for Children and Adolescents and has lectured at many other universities including Penn State University, the University of North Carolina, and the National Changhua University of Education in Taiwan, as well as in numerous school systems throughout the country. She has taught "Working with LGBT Youth" (2006–2007) at the University of Maryland School of Social Work. Linda has written many articles, including Healing Magazine's *Creating Safe Havens for Gay Youth in Schools* (2006).

Linda has worked as a consultant for the National Head Start Program, National Geographic, and was a panelist in the National Teleconference: *When a Parent Dies: How to Help the Child.* She has appeared on the Diane Rehm Show to discuss children and grief. She was named by *The Washingtonian Magazine* as one of the top therapists in the Maryland, Virginia, and DC area (1998) and again named by *The Washingtonian Magazine* as a therapist to go to after the terrorist attacks in 2001. She has served on the board of ADEC (The Association for Death Education and Counseling), and is presently on the advisory board of SPEAK, Suicide Prevention Education Awareness for Kids, RAINBOWS for Our Children, and the advisory board of TAPS (the Tragedy Assistance Program for [Military] Survivors) as their Children's Bereavement Advisor. Linda is the recipient of the ADEC Clinical Practice Award 2003.

Linda Goldman is the author of *Life and Loss: A Guide to Help Grieving Children* (1st ed., 1994/2nd ed., 2000). Her second book is *Breaking the Silence: A Guide to Help Children with Complicated Grief* (1st ed., 1996/2nd ed., 2002). Her other books include *Bart Speaks Out: An Interactive Storybook for Young Children on Suicide* (1998), a Phi Delta Kappan International fastback, *Helping the Grieving Child in the School* (2000), and a Chinese edition of *Breaking the Silence* (2001), the Japanese edition of *Life and Loss* (2005), and *Raising Our Children to be Resilient: A Guide for Helping Children Cope with Trauma in Today's World* (2005) and a children's book *Children Also Grieve: Talking about Death and Healing* (2005) and a Chinese translation of *Children Also Grieve* (2007). Linda also created a CD-ROM *A Look at Children's Grief* (2001). Her op/ed "Cut Out Guns, Bullying" appeared in the *Baltimore Sun* in March 2001. She was an important part of the *Washington Post* article "How to Talk to Kids About Suicide."

Linda contributed in many ways after 9/11. She authored the chapter about children, "Talking to Children about Terrorism" in *Living With Grief: Coping With Public Tragedy* (2003). She contributed to *The Journal for Mental Health Counselors* in their special grief issue in the article "Grief Counseling with Children in Contemporary Society" 2004. She was a strong part of the TAPS (Tragedy Assistance Program for Survivors) response team at the Pentagon Family Assistance Center, conducted a workshop about children and grief at the 2002/2004/2005/2006 TAPS National Military Survivor Seminar, and authored articles including "Helping Children with Grief and Trauma" (2002/2003) and "Fostering Resilience in Children: How to Help Kids Cope with Adversity" (2005).

Linda participated on the PBS Program *Keeping Kids Healthy: Children and Grief,* which aired in October 2006. She is the recipient of *The Tenth Global Concern of Human Life Award 2007* given by Taiwan's Chou, Ta-Kuan Cultural & Education Foundation.

Index

on family diversity, 293
mission statement, 262
poster, 176
College dormitories, 50–51
Coming out
Internet as vehicle, 75–76
issues of, 247, 264
national project, 263
professional assistance for, 163
resource guide, 263, 297, 298
risks, 69–72
family rejection, 70–72
homelessness, 70–72
school, 69–70
youth speaks about, 72–73
Community Counseling Center, 124
Corporate partnerships, 259–260
Counseling
based on repairing, 128
essential piece of program for, 131
faith-based religious, 129
finding the right counselor, 123–127
foundation, 114
goals, 91–92
incorporating interventions with,
114–132
information, 318
interventions for, 123
techniques, 132–133
Creative arts, 126, 140–148, 218
Cultural diversity, 105–113

D

Davis v. Monroe County Board of Education,
166
Day of Silence, 121–122, 261
Definitions, 25–27
DeGeneres, Betty, 200. 287, 322
DeGeneres, Ellen, 56, 179, 287
Depression, 78, 104, 114, 204
finding a partner and, 96
rejection and, 97, 116
resources on, 293
risk for, 99, 129

seeking help for, 78
silent rage projected inwardly as, 94
suicide ideation and, 104
video on, 293
Discrimination, 59, 62, 132
complaints of, 52
elimination of, 21
employment, 251, 260
of homosexual youth, 101–102
outlawing, 122, 170, 231, 256
prohibition of, 122, 231
racial, 277
standing up against, 156, 228, 256, 264
Double jeopardy, 110
Drescher, Jack, 47

E

Early childhood education, 10, 241
inclusion concepts for, 169
project for, 177
sexual orientation in, 20
Educator(s), 102, 160
Christian, 51, 167
core inclusion concepts for, 169–170
negative messages from, 160
professional training for, 163
questionnaire regarding LGBT students,
188–189
support for, 307
support of, 101, 161, 164
tips for, 52
Encouragement, 79–80, 91, 223

F

Facebook.com, 47
Faith in Action Award, 258
Families of Color Network, 253
Family pride coalition, 298
Family support, 55, 253. *See also* PFLAG
lack of, 100–101
Federal Marriage Amendment, 256
Focus on the Family, 47
Frank, Barney, 60

speaks out about being gay, 72–73
support for (*See also* Support)
    categories for, 162–163
    group, 152, 301
    peer, 45, 92, 95, 150–151
    school, 82, 101, 160, 161, 164, 307
    social, 160
LGBTQ, 26
Lifelong partnership, 61
Lipstick Lesbian, 35
Love Makes a Family, 107, 109, 113

M

Magazines, 297
Marlboro Man, 35
Marriage, 220–222
Media portrayal, 54–55, 295
Metrosexuality, 26
Middle school education, 169
Military Readiness Enhancement Act, 63
Military service, 53–54, 61, 63–64, 127
Music, 144–146

N

National Coming Out, 82, 263
National outreach program, 24
Native Americans, 108–109
Navratilova, Martina, 62
New Gay Teenager, 47
No Name-Calling Week, 179
    creative expression contest, 180

O

O'Donnell, Rosie, 60, 236
Organizations, 299–318
Out in Scripture, 60
Outspoken, 68
Outstanding Lives, 60

P

Parent(s), 214

alienation from, 198
educator questionnaire regarding, 188
encouragement of, 223
gay, 118
interventions, 209, 217, 2115
LGBT, 236, 285, 294
of LGBT, 214, 224, 287, 294
questionnaire, 206
reaction to coming out, 81–82
responses, 197–200
role in safe environment, 208
support groups, 207
tips for, 52
Parents, Families, and Friends of Lesbians and
    Gays (PFLAG). *See* PFLAG
Pedophilia, 42–43
PFLAG, 298
    Asian members, 207
    bisexual resource packet, 298
    civil rights initiatives, 254, 258
    Faith in Action award, 258
    history of, 248
    lobbying, 256
    marriage amendment and, 256–257
    as model for LGBT activism, 247
    parade, 216
    priorities, 252
    scholarship program, 253
    school safety agenda, 252
    state-by-state organizing of, 251
    website, 306
Poetry, 146–148
Prejudice, activities for combating, 170–174
Prom policies, 48
Public Schools and Sexual Orientation Guide,
    51, 52

Q

Queer, 19
    defined, 26
Queer as Folk, 56
Queer Eye for the Straight Guy, 54, 55
Queering the mainstream, xxvii, 30–31
Questionnaire, 140–142